"Parents, teachers, and administrators all start out with the child's best interests at heart when designing an IEP, but all too often, they fall short of that goal. *Navigating Special Education* is a practical guide to frontloading the process by putting relationships and communication first. The premise is unique because the authors have used their vast experience to gain insight into a winning mindset: Clear communication leads to trust. In a trusting partnership, creativity can thrive, and children can receive a first-class education directly suited to their individual needs."

—*Enia Noonan, parent, general education teacher, special education teacher*

"I found *Navigating Special Education* to be very thorough in explaining every aspect of the IEP process. The case studies/example stories presented were especially helpful as lead-ins to some chapters and sections. The book is clearly written by authors who are experts in their field. They are knowledgeable about every step of the process and give good advice for parents on how to do everything from beginning the IEP procedure to revising it, as well as tactics on how to suggest changes or disagree with a school district's recommendations."

—*Marisa Starr, parent of a child with an IEP*

"As a parent who has attended years of IEP sessions, I have a tremendous appreciation for Peggy and Tamara's expertise that they share in their book. It is an excellent, comprehensive resource loaded with relatable case studies, step-by-step guidance, examples, and a full glossary. Their 5-C Model is a practical approach to the complicated IEP world. I highly recommend *Navigating Special Education* to both parents and administrators."

—*Mary Abbazia, parent and managing director of Impact Planning Group*

"Whether you are new to the special education process or have years of experience, there is always room for productive and positive conversations. *Navigating Special Education* provides the pathway to fruitful partnerships through connection, mutual respect, and communication. The relationships between members of the IEP team are built on trust and openness, with one clear goal steering the ship: the success of the student. For parents and educators alike, *Navigating Special Education* offers concrete examples of how to work together so that the entire team can approach their meetings without unnecessary anxiety and stress, leading to the best possible outcomes for the students."

—*Kristen R. Massimo, MAEdL, school principal and special education consultant*

D0218139

"As a coach and college professor, I have looked for years for a resource that supports educators in developing a consistent, nonadversarial approach to the IEP development and implementation. This must-read book highlights the importance of communication in building a strong partnership between parents and educators with the goal of creating an actionable plan everyone can support. Peggy and Tamara's methodologies can help all stakeholders in navigating the intricacies of collaboration, consensus building, and agreement on required service delivery."

—*Lauri Susi, retired professor, University of North Carolina–Greensboro, education coach, professional development trainer*

"*Navigating Special Education* by Peggy S. Bud and Tamara L. Jacobson targets parents of children with special needs who are new to the process of working with educators in developing appropriate interventions to meet their child's educational needs. It also aims to increase those educators' sensitivities to the importance of collaborative communication when partnering with parents.

The authors' thesis is that good communication skills, outlined in their 5-C Model of Communication, along with listening, perspective-taking, and data collection, are required in building positive home–school partnerships. The authors' public school careers in speech-language pathology, teaching, administration, and supervision and their experiences as a parent of a child with special needs make them well-qualified to tackle the subject matter presented in the book.

The book is written in a positive tone and an organized manner. The book's strength comes from its focus on the role communication plays in either derailing or assisting successful outcomes in the special educational process in public school settings. Both parents and educators will likely find, as I did, that the many case vignettes included in the book are instructive and bring clarity to the authors' point of view. I particularly recommend it to parents new to the special education process."

—*Sherrill Werblood, PhD, licensed clinical psychologist, assistant clinical professor of psychology, Yale Child Study Center*

"*Navigating Special Education* is a very useful resource for parents trying to obtain educational support for their children. Encouraging positive communication and using a data-driven approach, it helps promote a win-win situation for parents and educators. This book provides helpful historical context and constructive advice illustrated with real-life examples to handle what can be an overwhelming and tense process. I wish I had read this book earlier and have already applied the practical learnings to build a positive partnership and successfully support my son's educational experience. I am a better parent because of it."

—*Hilary Kinney, parent and author of* Project Management for Parents

Navigating Special Education

The Power of Building Positive Parent–Educator Partnerships

Navigating Special Education

Education

The Power of Building Positive Parent–Educator Partnerships

PEGGY S. BUD

TAMARA L. JACOBSON

Senior Vice President: Tony Schiavo
Vice President, Editorial: Jennifer Kilpatrick
Vice President, Marketing: Mary Sasso
Director of Editorial Operations: Jennifer Cahill
Cover: Michael Bud

SLACK Incorporated
6900 Grove Road
Thorofare, NJ 08086 USA
856-848-1000 Fax: 856-848-6091
www.slackbooks.com
ISBN: 978-1-63822-090-9
© 2023 by SLACK Incorporated

Authors' Note: We consider the ideas, strategies, and suggestions laid out in this book to be recommendations that support best practices. Special education services differ from state to state. Therefore, the process and procedures outlined in our book follow the intent of the Individuals with Disabilities Education Act (IDEA), which may differ state to state based on how your state interprets the law.

Peggy S. Bud and *Tamara L. Jacobson* reported no financial or proprietary interest in the materials presented herein.

The procedures and practices described in this publication should be implemented in a manner consistent with the professional standards set for the circumstances that apply in each specific situation. Every effort has been made to confirm the accuracy of the information presented and to correctly relate generally accepted practices. The authors, editors, and publisher cannot accept responsibility for errors or exclusions or for the outcome of the material presented herein. There is no expressed or implied warranty of this book or information imparted by it. Care has been taken to ensure that drug selection and dosages are in accordance with currently accepted/recommended practice. Off-label uses of drugs may be discussed. Due to continuing research, changes in government policy and regulations, and various effects of drug reactions and interactions, it is recommended that the reader carefully review all materials and literature provided for each drug, especially those that are new or not frequently used. Some drugs or devices in this publication have clearance for use in a restricted research setting by the Food and Drug and Administration or FDA. Each professional should determine the FDA status of any drug or device prior to use in their practice.

Any review or mention of specific companies or products is not intended as an endorsement by the author or publisher.

SLACK Incorporated uses a review process to evaluate submitted material. Prior to publication, educators or clinicians provide important feedback on the content that we publish. We welcome feedback on this work.

Library of Congress Control Number: 2023930590

For permission to reprint material in another publication, contact SLACK Incorporated. Authorization to photocopy items for internal, personal, or academic use is granted by SLACK Incorporated provided that the appropriate fee is paid directly to Copyright Clearance Center. Prior to photocopying items, please contact the Copyright Clearance Center at 222 Rosewood Drive, Danvers, MA 01923 USA; phone: 978-750-8400; website: www.copyright.com; email: info@copyright.com

Printed in the United States of America.

Last digit is print number: 10 9 8 7 6 5 4 3 2 1

DEDICATION

We dedicate *Navigating Special Education: The Power of Building Positive Parent–Educator Partnerships* to our husbands, Matt and Alan, our children, and grandchildren.

We appreciate the patience and support of our families and friends.

We cherish the partnership and friendship we have forged that has allowed us to create a shared vision on how to build *positive partnerships between home and school.*

We value all of the amazing educators and parents who have tried to formulate a shared vision when addressing the needs of their special education students.

—Peggy S. Bud and Tamara L. Jacobson

TABLE OF CONTENTS

Dedication..*vii*
Acknowledgments..*xi*
About the Authors..*xiii*
Preface...*xv*
Principles and Best Practices of Special Education.......................*xvii*
Yesterday's Dream...*xix*
Preliminary Parent–Educator Self-Reflection Questionnaire............*xxi*

Part I   **The IEP Process, Communication, and Teamwork**............ 1
Chapter 1   Communication and Special Education 3
Chapter 2   5-C Model of Communication: 13
        Conversation, Collaboration, Cooperation,
        Compromise, and Consensus
Chapter 3   Sections of the IEP 33
Chapter 4   Active Versus Passive Listening 51
Chapter 5   Setting the Tone of a Meeting 59
Chapter 6   How to Respectfully Disagree 67
Chapter 7   Partnerships Build Trust....................................77
Chapter 8   The Importance of Teamwork 95

Part II   **Analysis of an IEP**... **103**
        I Do Not Like These IEPs...................................105
Chapter 9   IEPs Versus 504 Plans......................................107
Chapter 10   Fair Access..117
Chapter 11   The What and Why of S.M.A.R.T. Goals.............143

Part III   **Data and Correspondence** **149**
Chapter 12   Data Collection...151
Chapter 13   Written Correspondence...................................169

Part IV   **Strategies for Resolving Conflicts** **181**
Chapter 14   Hiring an Educational Consultant 183
Chapter 15   Conflict Leads to Creative Solutions 195
Chapter 16   Facilitated IEP Meetings, Mediation, and Due Process...........199
Chapter 17   Negotiation and Compromise.............................203

Epilogue 207
Concluding Parent–Educator Self-Reflection Questionnaire 210
References 211
Glossary 215
Appendix 225
Index 267

ACKNOWLEDGMENTS

Alone we can do so little; together we can do so much.

—*Helen Keller*

The words of Helen Keller were the driving force in writing our book. We could not have written it without the love and support of our families, friends, colleagues, and, of course, our students. We have used their stories to highlight and support the principles we teach and the practices we recommend, changing the names to provide for anonymity.

We want to thank Michael Bud of SquareSquared for his professional expertise. He worked with us to create the perfect images to engage all audiences and to establish our brand. His creative insights helped us achieve an aesthetically pleasing balance between text and visuals.

Our book would not have been possible without the help and guidance provided to us by the SLACK team: Tony Schiavo, who believed in our message and took our book through the peer review process and is always there to listen; Jenn Cahill, who has worked diligently to edit the book so that the layout is perfect; Mary Sasso and Saige Avery, who are creating all the marketing materials; and the rest of the SLACK team who have worked to get our book to publication. Without you, our vision would not be published today!

We want to thank Julia Masch, Sofia Barbosa, and Gabriella Snyder who worked tirelessly to edit our book for grammar and punctuation errors, checked accuracy of quotes and citations, and held us to task by making sure what we wrote was easily understood by nonprofessionals.

Finally, we would like to thank our colleagues, supervisors, and the attorneys who directly or indirectly taught us the ins and outs of special education and the importance of best practice when addressing the needs of students. This book could not have been written if those bright and talented professionals were not willing to "teach" and mentor us.

ABOUT THE AUTHORS

Peggy S. Bud is a licensed speech-language pathologist and school administrator with more than 30 years of experience in public education. She founded Speaking Skillfully to provide consultation services to families of children with disabilities and to help business professionals bridge the communication gap. As a communication coach, educator, speaker, and author, she utilizes her background in cognitive neuroscience and language to teach effective communication strategies.

Peggy serves as a vital voice for families and facilitates collaborative special education teams, putting her extensive knowledge from her time as a special education administrator to use as she assists both sides of the IEP team. She advises families on how to successfully advocate for their child by having data-driven conversations and building strong home and school partnerships. Additionally, she provides professional development opportunities to educators, teaching them how to effectively communicate with parents, write strong educational plans, and differentiate their instruction to address the needs of all students.

Peggy teaches her clients how to "up their executive presence" across all platforms, strengthen their nonverbal and verbal skills, and understand the power of active listening. She provides customized training to organizations and their leadership, teaching them how bias impacts communication, decision-making, and relationships. It also directly links to recruitment, hiring, promotions, and employee retention.

Her clients come from many fields including medical, legal, financial, marketing, insurance, engineering, and education. She brings her expertise to organizations by giving customized talks and group training sessions. She has spoken at national conferences, women's summits, rotary clubs, libraries, and more.

In addition to her private consulting practice, Peggy is the Community Outreach Director of Kids Are Talking, Director of Recruitment for The Financial Executives Consulting Group, a member of the Leadership Team of The Financial Executives Networking Group, serves on the Board of Directors of Bridge Academy (a charter school in Bridgeport, Connecticut), and Earthplace, a non-profit organization where science, conservation, and education meet. She holds a Bachelor of Science from Indiana University, as well as a Master's of Science and sixth-year Certificate in Educational Leadership from Southern Connecticut State University. Her motto is: *It's more than what you say, it's how you say it.* Visit her website: www.PeggyBud.com. Follow her on linkedin.com/in/peggy-bud-8404b524 or on Facebook at Speaking Skillfully.

Tamara L. Jacobson has more than 30 years of experience advocating for children throughout the United States.

Tamara previously taught English as a second language (ESL), theater arts, history, public speaking, and language arts for more than 18 years. She served as the head of curriculum and instruction for 5 years and as supervisor, then as assistant principal for 4 years. She holds lifetime and praxis certificates in administration and supervision K-12, ESL/bilingual education/dual language K-12, history K-12, communication arts (public speaking, debate, forensics) K-12, early childhood education PreK-3, and elementary education K-6.

Tamara worked as an educational consultant for Total Training Solutions, Ask the Educators, and East Coast Special Needs Advocacy and is currently the executive director of East Coast Educational Consulting LLC. She has conducted hundreds of workshops for teachers, teacher-aides, therapists, administrators, boards of directors, parent associations, and private community organizations.

Tamara is the mother of three daughters, one of whom lives with severe significant physical and cognitive developmental delays. Her daughter inspires her daily to make a difference in the educational landscape of practice.

Combining her interests in education and theater, Tamara has an acting and theater arts MFA in Directing. She has owned and directed Stars Theater and Dance Academy for many years. In 2011, she was profiled in Cambridge's Who's Who as a successful businesswoman.

Tamara holds a post-graduate certificate in Administration & Supervision with a concentration in Urban Studies. Currently, she is a doctoral candidate in Learning & Organizational Change at Baylor University. She is expected to graduate in May 2023.

In 2012, Tamara graduated from the "Partners in Policymaking in the State of NJ" program, a nonpartisan advocacy group that looks at legislation affecting marginalized communities. She is affiliated with the following organizations and conferences: American Education Research Association, Council for Exceptional Children, Academy for Educational Studies Critical Questions in Education Symposium, Carnegie Project on Special Education Doctorate, Southeastern Universities Graduate Research Symposium, and Baylor Education Research Conference.

Tamara has authored four published pieces: *Navigating Special Education, A Different Kind of Wonderful, Understanding the Andragogical Learning Experiences of High School Students With Severe Autism Spectrum Disorder (ASD) During the COVID-19 Pandemic,* and *Sofia Makes Her Mark.*

PREFACE

It's been 10 years since we met in a special education chatroom on LinkedIn. We were engaged in a discussion about current educational issues and quickly discovered we had similar core beliefs related to teamwork and collaboration. They differed dramatically from the other educators. This was the beginning of our relationship as it relates to our approaches to general education, special education, therapeutic services, and programming, which has been built on the tenet of communication.

We both believe in the importance of forming collegial bonds between parents and school districts to avoid adversarial relationships. We highly value the importance of data collection, negotiation, and compromise in the development of an Individualized Education Plan (IEP). It didn't take us long after meeting to decide to collaborate on a book. Sadly, the project had many stops and starts due to logistics; we live 100 miles apart.

However, when COVID-19 hit and technology for working remotely expanded, we seized the opportunity to complete our book, sharing what we believe are best practices and developing the 5-C Model of Communication framework: conversation, collaboration, cooperation, compromise, and consensus.

When working with our clients, we practice what we preach in the book and use a coordinated approach to creating the best possible educational outcomes. *Navigating Special Education: The Power of Building Positive Parent–Educator Partnerships* tells engaging, true stories presented as case studies and uses meaningful quotes and targeted language to help parents and educators understand what it takes to create a successful special education program. We provide easy-to-use strategies on how to build vital partnerships to bridge the home–school communication gap.

Our book will serve as a resource for parents and educators on how to work collaboratively to address their students' needs. We increase parents' core understanding of the special education process and the specialized language used at IEP meetings and expand educators' knowledge of the importance of communication, collaboration, and perspective-taking. Parents and educators can build strong partnerships using the skills presented in our book. Everyone will be better prepared to participate in all meetings actively and with the proper knowledge.

Navigating Special Education was written to raise awareness of the role communication plays in the IEP process. We teach parents and educators that how they interact with each other is key to the team's success. We intend to provide tools on how to build partnerships that ensure everyone's voice is heard, understood, and considered. However, to us it is more than understanding the process; it is about incorporating the 5-C Model of Communication, listening, and perspective-taking. We believe using all these skills and strategies will forge a meaningful, trusting relationship.

One of the essential tools outlined in our book is data collection. We believe gathering and sharing clear evidence to support concerns is the best way to demonstrate transparency and to have honest conversations. Data is the cement that binds the bricks of a parent-school partnership. Our book provides extensive data collection guidelines, including templates and tables that parents and educators can use. Evidence-based conversations between all IEP team members (parents, educators, and administrators) are the most meaningful way to address a student's academic, social-emotional, and behavioral needs.

When conversations ask open-ended questions, the results will lead to sustainable relationships between home and school. When everyone works together, stress and anxiety are significantly reduced, and meetings are more productive. Being equal participants in the process allows everyone to work together actively and successfully on the student's behalf. Our goal is to help parents and educators learn how to listen and understand each other's perspectives so they can have authentic and meaningful conversations and develop effective programming.

We wrote this book to create a resource manual for parents and educators by using our insights and knowledge from more than 60 years of combined experience. We have broken down the process into easy-to-understood parts. Each school or school district has its own unique culture. We highlight the core similarities to help parents be active members of the IEP team and educators become more tuned to the value of collaboration.

After reading our book, we believe parents and educators can implement our tips and strategies, communicate more effectively with one another, and build positive partnerships. That will mean that everyone will be an active member of the child's educational team and play a vital role in the development of the IEP. Our vision is that the ideas presented in *Navigating Special Education* will lead parents and educators to work collaboratively to advocate for their child rather than feel the special education process "hijacked" them.

PRINCIPLES AND BEST PRACTICES OF SPECIAL EDUCATION

Navigating Special Education: The Power of Building Positive Parent–Educator Partnerships helps parents and educators build positive partnerships.

How?

- Becoming knowledgeable about the special education process
- Developing a shared vision
- Effectively communicating using the 5-C Model of Communication
- Working as a team to advocate for the student's needs

The information in *Navigating Special Education* uses six principles found in the Individuals with Disabilities Education Act (IDEA), which was passed in order to protect the rights of all students with disabilities.

The principles of this ground-breaking and very important federal law include:

1. Parents are provided a copy of their procedural safeguards
2. Students are provided a Free Appropriate Public Education (FAPE)
3. Students must have an appropriate comprehensive evaluation to determine eligibility and educational needs
4. Parents and educators will work together to develop an appropriate IEP
5. Parents and students (when appropriate) must be included in the decision-making process (IEP team)
6. All educational services must be delivered in the Least Restrictive Environment (LRE)

To meet the needs of students with disabilities, every state is required to follow the standards outlined in IDEA. Each state has the right to interpret the rules and pass laws on how these principles will be delivered. State laws cannot contradict IDEA or provide a student less support, services, or protection than the federal law requires, but can provide more.

Yesterday's Dream

Dr. Seuss said, "Oh, the places we'll go …"

Some of these places will be fun and exciting, some will be difficult to navigate, and others will be places we'd rather not go, but life doesn't always give us choices. So instead of focusing on what you didn't get, celebrate what you got. Make lemonade out of lemons and enjoy drinking it down to the very last drop.

As soon as a family knows they are going to have a baby, they begin to formulate the hopes and dreams for their soon-to-be-born child and themselves. They make plans, decorate the child's room, even decide where the child will go to college. Many parents envision all momentous occasions: birthdays, bar mitzvahs, sweet 16 parties, proms, weddings, and even the birth of their first grandchild. Some families decide the child's career: doctor, lawyer, teacher. Others assume their child will take over their family's business or follow in their footsteps. Many parents are lucky enough to have children who will fulfill their hopes and dreams, while others will have to change "yesterday's dream." When either at birth, early childhood, or even during their teenage years, a child is medically identified as having a disability, parents are likely left devastated. Their child's disability, whether mild or profound, will change the trajectory of their life and their family's path. Some students develop illnesses as children, while others develop their disabilities over time. In all cases, the child and family's journey changes because of these diagnoses. "Yesterday's dream" is no longer possible!

What does this all mean? It means that the parents' original plans for momentous occasions and career choices will be different. When parents are faced with an unexpected diagnosis at any time throughout their child's life, there is a feeling of disappointment and a loss of what could have been. This is normal. It takes a paradigm shift on the part of the whole family to embrace a new vision.

There are many resources and opportunities to help families. From the moment parents, students, and educators join the child's journey called "special education," they find some things challenging and many others simple and beautiful. There will be ups and downs as the family travels on their child's new path from childhood to adulthood. Embracing a new "shared vision" requires perseverance, with a little grit. The result is then a positive journey, filled with new hope and success. The entire family and the exceptional child will be the best that they can be.

—*Peggy S. Bud and Tamara L. Jacobson*

PRELIMINARY PARENT–EDUCATOR SELF-REFLECTION QUESTIONNAIRE

Purpose: To identify your role in the special education community and where you see yourself. Do your attitudes and perceptions come from previous experiences? Are you open to working with the team as partners? As you answer the questions below, please reflect honestly. This questionnaire will help to identify a baseline related to your prior knowledge of the special education process. At the end of the book, you will have another opportunity to reflect and to see if your mindset has changed.

What is your attitude regarding the IEP process?
- ☐ Comfortable   ☐ Intimidated   ☐ Other

What is your knowledge regarding the IEP process?
- ☐ Excellent   ☐ Fair   ☐ Poor

Why do you believe the student requires special education services?
- ☐ Academic   ☐ Social   ☐ Behavioral/
- ☐ Speech   ☐ All   Emotional

What are your perceptions regarding how others view special education teachers?
- ☐ Positive   ☐ Negative   ☐ No Opinion

What are your perceptions regarding how others view parents of children with disabilities?
- ☐ Positive   ☐ Negative   ☐ No Opinion

What are your perceptions regarding how others view a child with disabilities?
- ☐ Positive   ☐ Negative   ☐ No Opinion

What are your perceptions regarding students leaving the classroom for support?
- ☐ Positive   ☐ Negative   ☐ No Opinion

Do you use criteria/data to discuss concerns about the student in the IEP meeting?
- ☐ Yes   ☐ No

What are your perceptions regarding how others measure or label a student?
- ☐ Respectfully   ☐ Intelligently   ☐ Uneducatedly

How do you view the special education services in your district?
- ☐ Positive   ☐ Negative   ☐ No Opinion

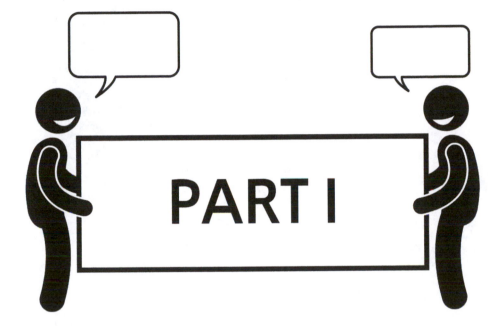

PART I

THE IEP PROCESS, COMMUNICATION, AND TEAMWORK

1

Communication and Special Education

The single biggest problem with communication is the illusion that it has taken place.

—George Bernard Shaw

> Special education is the practice of providing specially designed instruction, modifications, and accommodations to meet a student's unique needs and ensure they are able to access the general education curriculum of their school district.

Bud, P. S., & Jacobson, T. L.
Navigating Special Education: The Power of Building
Positive Parent–Educator Partnerships (pp. 3-12).
© 2023 SLACK Incorporated.

The Individualized Education Plan is commonly referred to as the IEP. We are going to begin this book by providing an overview of the special education process, also referred to as the IEP process, and will highlight the importance of communication at every step of the way.

The Individuals with Disabilities Education Act (IDEA) is the federal law that outlines the guiding principles that drive services and procedures related to all of special education. We have listed seven of the aspects of the IEP process as a way to introduce important steps and begin to develop a common language between parents, educators, and administrators (U.S. Department of Education, 2000). Our purpose is to ensure everyone is coming from the same place and speaking the same language as they *navigate special education* and learn *how* to build positive parent–educator partnerships. We know it is easier to communicate when everyone uses the same terminology.

PRE-REFERRAL

Before a student is referred to an IEP team, alternative procedures and programs in general education must be explored and, where appropriate, implemented into the general education classroom instruction.

REFERRAL

If parents suspect their child may have a disability that requires specialized instruction and/or related services, they need to send a written request for an evaluation to the school administrator. If educators suspect a child may have a disability that requires specialized instruction and/or related services, they will invite parents to an IEP meeting to discuss the concerns and recommend an evaluation. In both cases, parents must sign permission before an assessment can be done.

EVALUATION AND RE-EVALUATION

Evaluations are the objective tools used to determine eligibility. These assessments use standardized tests and anecdotal records to identify the student's specific learning needs. A multidisciplinary team, which includes a school psychologist and special education teacher, conducts the assessments. Sometimes assessments are also done by a speech-language pathologist, occupational therapist, or physical therapist. Students must be re-evaluated at least once every 3 years (triennial review) to determine if they continue to have a disability that requires special education and related services.

IDENTIFICATION OF A DISABILITY

A student must have one of these disabilities in order to be eligible for special education services. Federal law IDEA (2004) identifies the following categories: (1) Autism Spectrum Disorder, (2) Deaf-Blindness, (3) Developmental Delay (3- to 5-year-olds only), (4) Emotional Disturbance, (5) Hearing Impairment (deaf or hard of hearing), (6) Intellectual Disability, (7) Multiple Disabilities, (8) Orthopedic Impairment, (9) Other Health Impairment (includes attention-deficit/hyperactivity disorder [ADD/ADHD]), (10) Specific Learning Disability, (11) Speech or Language Impairment, (12) Traumatic Brain Injury, and (13) Vision Impairment.

ELIGIBILITY

To receive a special education classification and services, the assessments are presented to the IEP team at an IEP meeting. The team, which includes parents, teachers, and administrators, reviews the results of the testing and determines eligibility based on:

1. Student has a documented disability as outlined in IDEA
2. Disability adversely affects the student's academic, social-emotional, and/or behavioral performance
3. Student requires specialized instruction

If the team agrees the student meets the three criteria, they will determine eligibility for special education services and design an IEP to address the student's unique educational needs.

THE INDIVIDUALIZED EDUCATION PLAN

The IEP is a legal document. It drives all aspects of the student's special education support and services, which includes type of program (instruction model), placement, goals, and objectives. An IEP must be reviewed and revised at least yearly. At the annual IEP meeting, the school district and/or parents may request additional support, removal of specific supports and services, and/or a program change. We recommend that any type of change be based on data (U.S. Department of Education, 2000).

IMPLEMENTATION OF THE
INDIVIDUALIZED EDUCATION PLAN

Special education teachers and related services professionals are required to deliver, with efficacy, the program exactly as outlined in the student's IEP.

HOW DID IT ALL BEGIN?

We think everyone would agree parents are their child's first teacher and play a primary role in their child's education. From the moment their child is born, parents guide and teach their children—how to eat, walk, talk, and survive. Beyond these basic survival skills, initially parents taught their children how to read and write. Education has always been interdependent on the culture, religion, race, knowledge, and experiences of the family.

Education began in the home and then expanded to churches and single-room schoolhouses. Today public education is available to all students from age 5, and in some cases age 3, through high school graduation or even age 22. At the beginning, education was individualized because there were children of varying ages and abilities all going to school in the same classroom together. Heterogeneous, not homogeneous, education was the norm. Teachers were responsible for teaching all children, taking them from where they were and moving them forward (Kober, 2020, pp. 1-2).

Initially, school availability and accessibility were limited and school attendance was not compulsory. It was not compulsory until 1852, when Massachusetts became the first state to establish a law for compulsory (required) education. Sadly, it took almost 70 years for every state to make school attendance mandatory for all children (Kober, 2020, pp. 3-4).

In 1922 when all children were required to attend school (compulsory education), states were still allowed to expel students for a variety of reasons, including poor academic performance. This meant that the educational needs of children with disabilities were not taken into consideration. Often, children's cognitive abilities or IQ determined whether they were able to attend school (Esteves & Rao, 2008). Until the 1960s, terms like *learning disabilities* and *ADD/ADHD* were not factored into the equation regarding the student's ability to successfully learn and participate in public education.

Section 504 of the Rehabilitation Act of 1973 and the Education for All Handicapped Children Act of 1975 were considered groundbreaking when they were first legislated. Prior to these laws, teachers and administrators educated students using the tools and strategies available to them: bibles, ink written novels, chalk boards, and slates. The quality of education and special education varied from state to state. The passage of IDEA introduced novel federal procedures and mandates for public schools requiring them to address the educational needs of students with disabilities (Esteves & Rao, 2008). These include the six principles, along with the steps that we listed at the beginning of this chapter.

In every chapter of this book, we will expand on the details and implications of IDEA, Free Appropriate Public Education (FAPE), Americans with Disabilities Act (ADA), Rehabilitation Act of 1973, and other important special needs laws. These laws drive the special education support and services children in the public schools receive today. Although these laws have been revised several times, their basic tenets remain the same. It is important for parents and educators to understand that even though federal law drives the special education process, states are allowed to interpret the laws. Our founding fathers made education a "state's" right.

Since each state interprets IDEA differently, administrators, educators, and parents may find procedures reflected in the book do not follow what currently occurs in their state or district. We believe our suggestions are best practice, even though some of the concepts, information, and ideas may be new to some readers. In all cases, they follow the core principles of the law. We strongly believe any novel changes described are positive and can lead to transparency, better home–school communication, and positive educator–parent partnerships.

In summary, IDEA outlined the procedures that must be followed when identifying a child with a disability, as well as the guidelines on how to develop an appropriate IEP (American Psychological Association, 2017). We suggest that parents and educators understand the implications of the law, as it will help them work together to address the needs of the student.

> *Special education law: Ensures all children with disabilities are given the same opportunity to receive FAPE as their typically developing peers.*

Forming positive home–school partnerships is the best way to ensure the student is appropriately educated. When Congress wrote IDEA, the law identified five crucial people who were required to be on the IEP team and were responsible for making decisions related to the child's education. We want to point out that the law listed parents first. This suggests that the lawmakers understood the importance of parents participating in designing their child's special education plan. The other four required team members are a general education teacher, a special education teacher, a school administrator or their designee, and a person who can interpret evaluation results (IDEA, 2004, §1414). Although the law does not require the person who interprets the evaluation to be a psychologist, we believe it is best practice to have a psychologist at every meeting.

We want to highlight the importance of both parents and educators understanding their roles and responsibilities at all stages of the IEP process: designing a comprehensive evaluation, reviewing the assessments, identifying the child's disability, and reviewing the specific concerns that require specialized instruction along with developing the most appropriate program to address the student's special education needs. In addition to the five core members of the IEP team, other professionals that might be included on the team and have input into the development of the IEP are a speech pathologist, occupational therapist, physical therapist, behaviorist, and school nurse. All team members are important to the process and have an equal voice on the team. Parents should be aware that they can invite any professional (consultant, advocate, attorney), friend, or family member to the IEP meeting.

We believe it is crucial for parents and educators to work together, as partners, at all stages of the IEP process. From our perspective, this begins the moment a parent, educator, or administrator suspects the student might have a disability that is significantly impacting their education. IDEA states that the team must work on behalf of the student until they graduate from high school and/or are dismissed from special education. Only when everyone speaks the same language, understands one another's perspectives, and values each other's voices can the team truly form a partnership.

Communication is an integral part of any partnership and essential when it comes to *navigating the special education process*. Our hope is for parents and educators to understand that how they communicate with each other directly affects the team's success, which translates into the student's success! This book will provide everyone with tools and strategies on how to build a positive partnership so all voices are heard, understood, and considered.

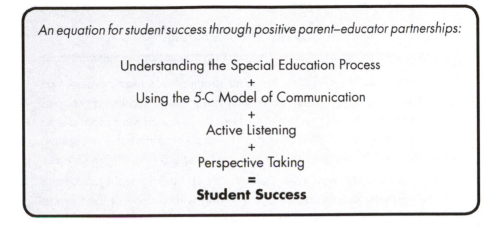

An equation for student success through positive parent–educator partnerships:

Understanding the Special Education Process
+
Using the 5-C Model of Communication
+
Active Listening
+
Perspective Taking
=
Student Success

THE INDIVIDUALIZED EDUCATION PLAN TEAM

IDEA identified the people who were required to be members of the child's IEP team and who would be the decision makers (American Psychological Association, 2017). However, the law did not specifically delineate how the team members should work together to achieve their common goal: the child's education. In order for the IEP team to successfully address a child's educational needs, we recommend the team forms a partnership. Partnerships are built upon a shared vision, cooperation, and joint rights and responsibilities. The partnership welcomes deep conversations and is built on valuing the strengths and expertise of all team members. When teachers and families work together as partners, they are able to collaborate on all educational decisions because their voices are heard and respected.

Communication, from our perspective, is what drives the success of any meeting or relationship. When parents and educators embrace effective communication practices (which we are calling the 5-C Model of Communication), they have the tools and strategies needed to build strong, positive relationships. The foundation of a partnership is based on the importance of having productive conversations, which encourage everyone to collaborate and cooperate, be open to compromise, and, in the end, reach consensus. Everyone's voice is heard, understood, and taken into consideration. Using these strategies helps to reduce communication breakdowns.

The case study *How Is My Child Reading?* is a good way to begin to discuss the positive parent–educator partnership journey. It highlights the role communication plays in the IEP process and how easily messages can be misunderstood and misinterpreted. Our goal is to help teachers and parents see themselves as partners in the development of the child's educational program. We hope that this case study will bring to life the IEP process and demonstrate how transparency builds trust.

How Is My Child Reading?

According to Mr. and Mrs. Pleasant, Sammy was reading about six levels below his peers. They felt he was not making academic progress and requested a meeting with his teacher. They wanted the school district to evaluate their son. What they didn't realize was that "by requesting an evaluation," they were actually starting the special education process.

The assistant principal, Miss Demetri, set up an IEP meeting. Sammy's parents received an official invitation, along with a copy of their Procedural Safeguards. The purpose of the document was to explain all the important policies and laws related to special education and how they protected the family. However, the legal jargon was intimidating and confusing. Sammy's parents felt stressed and anxious. All they had done was to request a meeting because they believed Sammy needed some extra help.

The night before the meeting, both parents had a restless night. They arrived at the meeting feeling worried and apprehensive. *Would they be able to explain their concerns to Sammy's teacher? Would she be willing to provide Sammy with the extra help?*

When Mr. and Mrs. Pleasant arrived at school the next morning, they were escorted into a conference room by the administrative assistant, Mrs. Harper. There were many educational professionals sitting around the table. Nobody looked at them as they entered the room, except for Sammy's teacher, Mrs. Lopez, who smiled and nodded her head in acknowledgment.

Miss Demetri began the meeting by asking each person to introduce themselves and explain their role. Miss Demetri then stated that the purpose of the meeting was "parent request," meaning that Sammy's parents had been the ones to suggest that he should be evaluated for special education. Mr. and Mrs. Pleasant felt like Miss Demetri was blaming them for calling this meeting.

Miss Demetri asked Sammy's teacher to go first. Mrs. Lopez began by saying Sammy was a cute, happy, third grader who enjoyed chatting with his friends and running around the playground. She went on to describe his performance in school, which in IEP lingo is referred to

continued on next page

as the student's Present Level of Academic Achievement and Functional Performance (PLAAFP). While explaining his progress in reading, writing, and math, she specifically mentioned that he was an average student and making progress in multiple areas such as social studies and gym.

Mrs. Lopez's report was completely subjective and lacked concrete evidence to support her claims. She did not show a video of Sammy reading or share any of his writing samples or journal reflections. Without presenting any evidence or data, she concluded her report by saying, "I have no concerns about Sammy's academic progress and I do not believe he requires special education."

Mr. and Mrs. Pleasant were surprised by the teacher's comments. It sounded as if she was describing a completely different child from the little boy they saw at home. They were living with a child who was clearly struggling academically and was demonstrating anger and frustration at home. They took a deep breath before responding.

The anger Mr. and Mrs. Pleasant felt clearly permeated the room. Their volume rose and their bodies tensed up. Mrs. Pleasant began by say that Sammy has been reading the same book to them every night for the past 6 months. Mr. Pleasant added that their evenings were filled with fighting over homework. Unless one of them sat down with Sammy, read him the directions, and helped him every step of the way, he was unable to complete any of his homework. Mrs. Pleasant added that when an assignment required Sammy to write more than a simple sentence, he had a complete melt-down.

Mr. and Mrs. Pleasant reiterated that they believed Sammy was not making appropriate academic progress, which is why they had requested an evaluation. They acknowledged that they too thought he was smart and capable. As Sammy's parents spoke, the educators were looking down at their papers or phones. Many were staring at them, arms folded and expressionless.

We cannot emphasize enough that communication plays an important role in the IEP process and the building of home–school partnerships. Many of the communication breakdowns in *How Is My Child Reading?* could have easily been avoided. Both *what you say* and *how you say it* contribute to miscommunication and misunderstandings. We believe that when parents and educators work collaboratively, the tone and trajectory of the meeting changes.

We know that stress, anxiety, and confusion can be easily reduced when parents understand the school's procedures and protocols related to all aspects of their child's education. It is also important for teachers and administrators to listen to the parents' perspective. We want to remind you that hearing someone's perspective does not mean you agree with it. However, when all team members value the perspectives of others, they are open to listening and having open and honest conversations. Effective communication between home and school becomes the foundation on which to build a successful partnership.

2

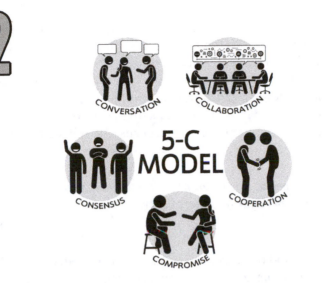

5-C Model of Communication

Conversation, Collaboration, Cooperation, Compromise, and Consensus

By using the 5-C Model of Communication (conversation, collaboration, cooperation, compromise, and consensus) at every step of the Individualized Education Plan (IEP) process, parents and educators will be able to build partnerships that lead to student success.

THE 5-C MODEL OF COMMUNICATION

Communication plays a critical role in the IEP process. We have created the 5-C Model of Communication as an exemplary tool that parents and

Bud, P. S., & Jacobson, T. L.
Navigating Special Education: The Power of Building Positive Parent–Educator Partnerships (pp. 13-32).
© 2023 SLACK Incorporated.

educators can use to help them successfully work together. This original model, if followed step-by-step, will allow the team to work with transparency, develop trust, and reach the end game—which is creating a shared vision regarding the student's education plan. The 5-Cs are an easy-to-use strategy that can help parents, educators, and administrators avoid communication breakdowns. By embracing the importance of having deep conversations, collaboration, cooperation, compromise, and consensus, the IEP team will be able to form a partnership.

Remember teamwork begins by building trust, and the only way to do that is to overcome our need for invulnerability.

—Patrick Lencioni

Stress, anxiety, and misunderstandings are greatly reduced if parents and educators are open to engaging in meaningful, authentic conversations.

CONVERSATION

When two or more people talk, share ideas, feelings, and/or opinions, they are having a conversation. It is how they get to know each other and develop more intimate relationships. The quality of their conversation is what drives their relationships. Judith Glaser, author of *Conversational Intelligence* (2016), believed we all have this core ability. She outlined different levels of conversation, which are used for different purposes and with different people.

Conversations usually begin as tell/ask exchanges. There is very little trust at this level, since this type of conversation is only about providing and/or taking in information. We can easily have this type of dialogue with a total stranger since we are sharing nothing personal. As people get to know each other and begin to trust each other, their conversations become more dynamic. They move along the conversation continuum and feel comfortable advocating and inquiring. It is only when conversations lead to people openly sharing and discovering things about the other person that trust has been established and conversations become productive. It is at this level that we feel comfortable being both honest and transparent, which allows us to learn from one another.

Every good conversation starts with accurate listening, which includes hearing and processing what the other person is saying and leads to deep conversations. IEP teams start to work as partners when they are able to have open and honest dialogues. The knowledge everyone gains from meaningful conversations can be used to develop the most appropriate program for the student. When each team member shares what they believe the child needs to be successful, then their truthful and candid exchanges can be used to create a shared vision.

We realize that sometimes parents are reluctant to contribute to the conversation because they do not think what they have to say is relevant or will be viewed by the educators as important. Yet, parents, just like teachers, have valuable information to share. Only when everyone's voice is heard, and both the home and school perspective are understood, can the IEP team partner in the development of the child's educational program.

Don't be afraid to have an honest conversation.

COLLABORATION

If everyone is moving forward together, then success takes care of itself.
—Henry Ford

Collaboration is the act of working with others to create something. Successful collaboration requires mutual respect. We cannot stress enough the importance of parents feeling welcomed into the school culture. It is what allows them to build alliances with school board members, administrators, and teachers. It is important that parents, educators, and administrators believe everyone brings value to the meeting, that their opinions and expertise contribute to the conversation. It is crucial that educators and parents verbally recognize and acknowledge how others are contributing.

Through open and honest conversations, which require effective communication skills, the IEP team is on a path to collaboration. It is also important for teams to be mindful of obstacles and to work cooperatively to address them. When teams embrace everyone's input, they are better able to improve programming and develop more effective ways to address students' needs. Without collaboration, this probably would not be possible.

Collaboration forms the foundation on which parents and educators can develop a shared vision for how to best meet the student's academic, social-emotional, and behavioral needs. Lewis and O'Neill, authors of *Where's the Office,* argue that a shared vision should go beyond yourself. We believe that in order to develop a program to address the child's needs, you have to create a "shared vision (which) enables you to take the concept, created in your mind, and project it into the heart of another" (Lewis & O'Neill, 2021, p. 45). This is the true meaning of collaboration: IEP teams forming partnerships by developing a shared vision, rather than remaining focused on the specifics of the current program or IEP. Going from team to partners may seem like a giant leap, yet it is possible and will make a big difference in the effectiveness of the IEP process.

COOPERATION

Teamwork is the ability to work together toward a common vision.
—Andrew Carnegie

Shared Vision

Coupled with the IEP team collaborating to develop new opportunities or new programs for a student is the act of cooperation. This core skill is essential across all aspects of our life. Very young children learn the importance of taking turns and working together to accomplish a goal. An important part of cooperation is learning how to balance our own needs with those of others.

The IEP team members should work cooperatively to accomplish their goal. Collaborative thinking is what helps teams to create a shared vision of clarity of purpose, hope, and the ability to co-create the most appropriate program for the child. With cooperation and teamwork comes mutual support. Since we accomplish more together than alone, when teams work cooperatively they are able to create and complete paths of future possibilities. When teams work cooperatively and collaboratively, everyone wins!

It is our hope that educators and parents see the value of cooperation, which is key to teams working together and accomplishing a mutual goal. Often when the IEP team works cooperatively, they discover innovative ways to ensure student success. Cooperation may actually lead to the development of a dynamic program, one that the team had not previously considered. The reason is that now everyone is looking at the student's educational needs and progress through a variety of lenses.

We believe the ability to collaborate and cooperate is linked to parents and teachers understanding and respecting each person's role in the IEP process. We want to remind all team members that each person brings a different set of experiences and knowledge to the meeting. This gives the team the ability to look at the situation from different angles. Let's celebrate the team's diversity, as it is the key to new possibilities and innovative solutions. The cooperative efforts of families and educators result in strong programs and vital partnerships—everyone working to co-create a unique program that specifically identifies, addresses, and targets the student's needs.

Shared Vision: Getting What Is Needed

In the last few months, Mr. and Mrs. Franklin had attended several IEP meetings to discuss their daughter Joanna's educational needs. Joanna is 6 years old and attends first grade at the local elementary school. She was having major meltdowns over the course of her academic day, which required removal from her classroom. It was unclear what triggered these outbursts. Academically, Joanna was performing on grade level.

Before identifying Joanna as a special education student, the district had completed a comprehensive academic and behavioral assessment that included a review of the report from Dr. Butler, a highly respected child and adolescent psychiatrist and Joanna's family therapist. Dr. Butler diagnosed Joanna with both a bipolar disorder and a personality disorder. Based on the diagnosis and her behavior, the team identified Joanna as a student with a social-emotional disability and developed an IEP that included special education instruction, counseling, and a one-on-one paraprofessional.

continued on next page

Mr. and Mrs. Franklin felt it was unacceptable that Joanna was spending most of her school day in the hall with her paraprofessional, Miss Leader. That was the reason they had requested today's IEP meeting. They knew that within 30 minutes of each day, their daughter had a major meltdown that required removal from the classroom. Joanna was then expected to complete her schoolwork in the hall. With support from Miss Leader, she would calm down and return to the classroom. However, within about 30 minutes, something would trigger an outburst and she would again be removed from her classroom.

Mr. and Mrs. Franklin came to the IEP meeting with a vision. They wanted the school district to place Joanna in an out-of-district setting that had the resources to address both her academic and emotional needs. They didn't want her being constantly isolated from her peers.

The district did not share their vision. Mr. Brown, the elementary special education supervisor, stated that the school-based team believed the district could provide Joanna a safe program that addressed her academic and emotional needs with the help of the one-on-one paraprofessional recommended by the IEP team. He said an out-of-district program did not represent the Least Restrictive Environment (LRE), which was the district's obligation under the Individuals with Disabilities Education Act.

The parents had invited Dr. Butler to today's IEP meeting. It was their hope that she could further explain their vision—why it was important to place Joanna in an out-of-district setting where her social-emotional outbursts could be more effectively addressed. Dr. Butler reiterated that cognitively, Joanna was performing at the top of her class in spite of spending a large portion of each day in the hall. She was able to decode and comprehend at a first-grade reading level, and her math skills were at grade level. However, social-emotionally, Joanna has limited filters, which she needs to be successful in her first-grade classroom. Dr. Butler reported that Joanna was on medication, but it did not seem to be reducing the number of meltdowns she had at school each day.

Mrs. Robertson, the special education teacher, reported on Joanna's academic progress, agreeing she was performing on grade level even though she completed most assignments in the hall. Mrs. Robertson explained that a behavior chart/reward system was being used to track the length and duration of her outbursts and what triggered them. The data

continued on next page

indicated that Joanna spent more than half of her day in the hall. It suggested that the most effective strategy was having Joanna work in a quiet, dimly lit setting with an adult sitting next to her.

Mrs. Robertson and the rest of the school-based team did not share the parents' vision; they thought attending the district school was the most appropriate placement. Joanna's classroom teacher, Mrs. Smith, said her classmates were safe, and unless she was having an outburst, she actively participated in class discussions and activities. Mrs. Franklin acknowledged that several children in her class lived in the neighborhood and played with Joanna after school. Joanna considered them to be her friends, however, recently these children were refusing to play with her. Their parents said it was due to her school meltdowns.

Mr. and Mrs. Franklin continued to feel adamantly about outplacement. However, they agreed to the school team's request to collect information so they could create a program that would allow Joanna to remain in her current classroom. Everyone agreed that she was young, had friends at school, and it was in her best interest to attend the district school. The parents agreed to reconvening the meeting in 30 days, since they too wanted Joanna to attend school with her friends, if possible. Dr. Butler stated she would try a different medication.

The goal was for the team to develop a shared vision regarding the best program for Joanna.

In less than 2 weeks following the IEP meeting, Joanna had a major unexplained outburst. She started throwing things and yelling. She hit the teacher, the paraprofessional, and injured one of the students. The parents were called in for an emergency IEP meeting. This time the school-based team and the parents had a shared vision on how best to address Joanna's educational needs. Everyone agreed the school district could not provide Joanna with an appropriate program.

A private, special education school in the next town that had the resources to address Joanna's emotional and academic needs appeared to be the most appropriate program. The classrooms were small, three to five students, and there were limited distractions. If Joanna had a meltdown, she could be pulled aside without leaving the classroom. After visiting the program, Mr. and Mrs. Franklin agreed to the placement. Consensus was reached because everyone now had the same vision regarding what was educationally best for Joanna.

COMPROMISE

The most successfully designed IEPs are the result of teams listening to each other and having deep conversations. Differences of opinion regarding the best way to meet the student's needs reveal the *what* and *why*, as well as the *values* of parents and educators. This information becomes the foundation of the *cooperative* and *collaborative* conversations needed to reach a compromise.

When everyone takes into consideration the student's needs, concerns of parents, and the school district, the conversation moves to a place where, with some give and take, compromises can and will emerge. These compromises are often what lead to innovative thinking and the development of great programs, ones that would not have been created without collaboration and compromise. Unless everyone is open to compromise, conversations may turn adversarial.

Deep conversations are more likely to occur when everyone knows the end goal and has a shared vision related to providing the student an appropriate program and services. Working together on the student's behalf means having data-driven conversations, which can include embracing the use of the 5-C Model of Communication. Through the use of effective communication skills and strategies, the IEP team is able to address their disagreements and reach a consensus.

From our perspective, most effective programs are not developed in a vacuum but rather in partnership. Sometimes parents disagree with educators because the parents believe what they are advocating is best for their child. Teachers also believe what they are proposing is in the child's best interest. Having respectful conversations about their disagreements is okay because they lead to perspective-taking.

We recommend parents and educators use this strategy as a way to organize their thoughts so they can effectively share their perspective with the team. Prior to a meeting or just before speaking, organize your thoughts. Write down your opinion, concerns, feelings, or recommendations. Use no more than three bullet points and include data or evidence to back up your thinking. Tell what you think is best for the student and why.

Using this strategy removes some of the emotion from the conversation. The speaker is able to clearly and succinctly deliver their message. This helps others listen to what is being said, how it is being said, and hopefully understand the speaker's perspective. Only when everyone is able to ask questions, discuss recommendations, and share opinions can the team reach a solution. These conversations can also provide insight into what is negotiable and what might not be, helping the team identify compromises that will result in reaching consensus. All the while, keep in mind having a shared vision is likely to be the best way to appropriately address the student's needs.

We have all sat in meetings and felt that reaching a consensus seemed impossible because there didn't seem to be a common ground for a compromise. If this happens at an IEP meeting, it might put the student's educational program in jeopardy. If parents and educators come to a stalemate, we suggest parents or the school district hire a neutral, nonbiased person to facilitate the conversation. This person can help both sides reach a compromise and/or consensus.

Because an educational consultant has a strong knowledge of the special education process, along with the ability to listen and understand the perspective of the parents and the district, they can help the IEP team reach a compromise. We suggest consultants initially meet with the family outside of the formal IEP meeting and help them understand the special education process, the educational terminology being used, and the legal responsibilities of the school district. If possible, we also recommend they meet with the educators as a way to understand their perspective. They will then be in a better place to successfully facilitate the conversation and help the team (parents and educators) to reach a consensus.

How to Organize Your Thoughts

Strategy for parents and educators to effectively share their perspective with the team.

- Using no more than three bullet points, list your opinion, concerns, feelings, or recommendations.
- Include data/evidence to tell what you think is best for the student and why.

Consensus

Consensus demands communication.

—John Dewey

When the team accepts the IEP or an action plan, they have reached consensus or an agreement on how to best address the child's needs. This is the last step in the 5-C Model of Communication. In the words of John Dewey (1916), one of the founding fathers of education, *consensus demands communication!* We want to remind everyone that without meaningful conversations, the IEP team is not going to reach an agreement. Even with deep conversations, the team will probably need to agree to some compromises along the way.

Like compromise, building consensus is a process that requires perspective-taking, candid conversations, and being able to visualize the end result. It is the parents' and educators' willingness to *compromise that allows the team to reach consensus.* Through perspective-taking and listening, everyone becomes more open to making adjustments to their recommendations and their vision. They are ready and able to find new and creative alternatives.

Sometimes it seems difficult to know where to start when trying to reach consensus. However, when teams use the 5-C Model of Communication and active listening, they are better able to ask questions and discuss possible ways to compromise. Their relationship is also more likely to move from team to partner as they work together to reach consensus on how to best address the child's needs.

Throughout the book we will present case studies and text to provide additional insights into how and why the 5-C Model of Communication can assist parents, educators, and administrators in building positive, trusting, and transparent relationships.

Let's Begin With How Is My Child Reading?

The IEP meeting in Chapter 1 was scheduled because Sammy's parents requested an academic evaluation. Mr. and Mrs. Pleasant were not aware of the implications of their request. They made the request because they believed that was the correct protocol. We believe if an administrator or case manager had followed up their request with an informal meeting, the communication breakdowns might have been averted. Often parents don't know what they don't know.

Sammy's parents wanted to find a way to get him extra help. A conversation about the process would have helped the family feel their concerns were valued and their input welcomed. In most cases, all parents want is to have an open and honest conversation with their child's teacher. It is important for educators and administrators to keep in mind that parents aren't always familiar with school procedures and protocols.

WAYS USING THE 5-C MODEL COULD CHANGE MEETING TRAJECTORIES

Introductory Meeting

Conversations avert problems. We suggest that best practice would be to have a "coffee and conversation" meeting between parents and a key member of the IEP school-based team prior to the initial IEP meeting. This could prove to be an important first step in building a successful partnership. The purpose of this short meeting (no more than 30 minutes) would be to give the parents a brief overview of the special education process and to explain the Procedural Safeguards document. *(Most districts send the Procedural Safeguards with the IEP invitation and parents feel overwhelmed when they read all of the legalese.)*

Having a brief, informal conversation can reduce the parents' stress and make them feel welcome as members of their child's educational team. It also provides an opportunity for parents to ask questions before the formal meeting. If the administrator or case manager speaks to parents one-on-one prior to the IEP meeting, think of it as a golden opportunity for them to begin to form a relationship with the family. Remember, relationships build partnerships.

Greeted by an Administrator

When parents are greeted by the administrator vs. an administrative assistant, it creates a positive tone. Since parents usually arrive at the meeting feeling nervous and overwhelmed, this simple act can make them feel they are part of a team. Key members of the child's education greet and welcome the parents.

In *How Is My Child Reading?*, Miss Demetri stated that the parents were *important* members of the IEP team, setting a positive tone to the meeting. However, then she stated that "the parents called the meeting" without explaining the process. This changed the tone of the meeting, because Sammy's parents interpreted her statement incorrectly. They felt they were being blamed for requesting an IEP meeting. We know this was not the administrator's intent; however, what she said was a scripted response that unintentionally had that effect.

There were many communication breakdowns that occurred because the parents did not understand the special education process. In addition, the nonverbal language of staff (no verbal hello or eye contact) as they entered the room exacerbated their uneasiness and added to their feeling unwelcome. We recommend parents and educators smile, nod, and greet each other as they enter the room. A simple "hello" and welcoming body language helps to reduce everyone's anxiety.

Introductions

We suggest that at the beginning of all meetings, the administrator or case manager asks everyone to introduce themselves, as occurred in the case study. The introductions can act as a meeting icebreaker and clearly identify each team member's role. They are also important because there may be new school-based team members attending the meeting. Staff changes from year to year and grade level to grade level.

Agenda

We believe it is best practice that all meetings have an agenda, which can help parents be prepared to actively participate in the conversation. When the administrator presents an overview of the meeting verbally along with a written agenda, it helps to ensure everyone is on the same page. In addition, an agenda is an easy way to provide a brief explanation of each step, which helps to familiarize parents with the order of the meeting. We consider an IEP meeting to be a conversation and think of an agenda as a tool that clarifies what is discussed and why.

Effective Communication

Everyone needs to hone their effective communication skills: verbally, vocally, and nonverbally. Words matter, which is why we suggest parents and educators use data to drive the IEP conversations. It is hard to argue with evidence. Effective communication also includes active listening and perspective-taking. All aspects of communication work together to help team members build strong positive home–school partnerships.

Did you know it takes less than 7 seconds to make a good first impression? Think of a warm greeting from the administrator as a positive first impression. Think of the school-based staff not welcoming the parents verbally or nonverbal as a negative first impression. We can make a great second impression, it just takes a lot more work to change a person's first impression.

Of course, words matter. Did you know that your nonverbal message speaks louder than words and is usually remembered before or instead of the words? When we reflect on a conversation, our first thoughts are usually what the person said nonverbally, either through gestures or vocal attributes, such as rate, volume, or tone. Eye contact and a smile are important parts of any conversation and help others feel welcome. Looking directly at a person when they are speaking sends the message that you are listening and care about what they are saying, although it doesn't necessarily mean you agree with it.

Trust

Trust happens when the listener feels what the speaker is saying is both accurate and truthful. To build a positive partnership, parents must build trust with a welcoming administration and IEP team. In this chapter, we have already indicated our position that best practice for building trust during the IEP process would be for the administrative team to invite the child's parents to a preconference. Meeting in advance of the IEP annual review will make the parents feel like welcome members of the IEP team. The aim of the preconference is to diffuse parents of any existing anxieties, uncertainties, or irritation when given the opportunity to bring questions to the IEP team in a more comfortable general setting. At the commencement of the official meeting, all parties will have already developed some form of goodwill toward one another. We believe that this strategy will work toward building the trust vital to achieve the best outcome for the student.

Further, having and sharing evidence is the best way to establish credibility and build trust. In the scenario *How Is My Child Reading?* neither parents nor educators presented any documentation to support their statements regarding Sammy's performance.

If either Sammy's parents or his teacher had shown a 30- to 60-second video clip of Sammy reading, along with a copy of the book, they would have provided evidence that demonstrated his reading ability. In the case of Sammy's parents, the video would have provided data that highlighted their concerns. If, in addition to the video, Sammy's teacher had provided other data, such as test scores, reading journals, math homework, etc., she too would have been providing the parents with concrete evidence to support her perspective. It is hard to argue with data!

The Power of Deep Conversations

Mr. Rodriguez called Ms. Jackson to tell her that Justin had failed his last two tests: the science unit test and a weekly math quiz. Ms. Jackson was surprised, since Justin had not shared that information with her.

The purpose of the phone call between Mr. Rodriguez and Justin's mom was to discuss how together they could unpack the problem—why he was suddenly struggling at school. Up until this point, Justin was a solid B student.

Ms. Jackson said that Justin had studied for the tests and had even asked her to quiz him on the science terms. She said he seemed to know the subject matter, so she was surprised that he failed the test. Math had always been his favorite subject. His computation skills had also been strong, which made her wonder why he would fail the weekly computation review.

Mr. Rodriguez asked Ms. Jackson how things were going at home. Was Justin sleeping? Were there any changes to his normal routine? She said she didn't know why Justin was struggling. Nothing had changed.

Initially, Ms. Jackson felt Justin's teacher was holding her responsible for his failed exams. Then, Mr. Rodriguez commented that lately Justin seemed sad and was isolating himself from his friends. She realized that his teacher was genuinely trying to find out why Justin was suddenly having difficulty.

At that moment, Ms. Jackson felt she could open up and share what was happening in the family. Both her personality and her culture made it hard for her to share personal information with a non-family member. Then she decided that telling Mr. Rodriguez about her mother's illness might help Justin. She explained that her mother was very ill and might die. Although she lived in Mexico, Justin was very close to his grandmother and spent 6 weeks with her every summer.

Now that they were having a conversation, Ms. Jackson asked Mr. Rodriguez if he thought Justin's grandmother's illness might be affecting his ability to concentrate. This led to an even deeper conversation. By sharing private information, which was outside her comfort zone, Ms. Jackson began to build a partnership with Justin's teacher. She realized

continued on next page

that together they could help Justin. Mr. Rodriguez agreed to let Justin know that he understood he was worried about losing his grandmother. He would also let him retake the science test orally to reduce his stress, since based on his class participation Justin knew the material.

Mr. Rodriguez offered to speak to the social worker, who periodically came into the class to lead discussions about topics affecting the students' mental well-being. He would ask her how to best have a group conversation without personalizing it and making Justin feel uncomfortable.

Forming a parent–teacher partnership put Justin on the path to success.

There are many reasons why parents are reluctant to have open and honest conversations with their child's teachers. In some cultures, this is taboo. Other times, parents worry that sharing a problem reveals a weakness or suggests that they are not being an effective parent. Sometimes they are honestly not aware that the family situation will have a direct impact on the child's school success. In *The Power of Deep Conversations,* Ms. Jackson's reluctance to share that Justin's grandmother was deathly ill interfered with his school success. Once she shared the problem, Mom and Mr. Rodriguez were able to form a partnership to address the problem.

When situations such as illness, loss of a job, or death arise, we recommend that parents share this information with their child's teacher as soon as possible. This is part of honesty and transparency, which builds trust. These conversations will allow parents and educators to work together to address the situation, which may avert academic, social-emotional, or behavioral problems occurring related to the home crisis.

Understanding the Process and the Terminology

In order to have positive parent–educator partnerships, it is crucial that everyone understands the special education process. Parents are often unfamiliar with the law, the process, and school, district, and state procedures related to how a child will be provided with special education support. Although general education teachers are familiar with the educational terminology, they are not as well-versed in the details of special education law or procedures as the special education staff. When everyone is on the same page regarding their understanding and expectations, there will be less stress and anxiety, which will lead to a more cohesive team.

Everyone's voice on the team should be considered equally important! However, we realize that when people voice their opinions, it can create communication breakdowns. That is why we encourage everyone to keep in mind that *both* **what** *is said* and **how** *it is said* are crucial to having a successful conversation. It is our belief that the 5-C Model of Communication provides structure when building positive parent–school partnerships. It is also central to creating productive dialogues to ensure students get what they need, rather than what the district might have to offer or what the parents want.

> *There are many ways to listen, talk, have a good conversation, and build a meaningful relationship. A conversation creates new cards; it doesn't merely reshuffle the old ones.*

Every good conversation starts with good listening. Ms. Jackson listened to Justin's teacher, and his teacher responded with empathy and concrete suggestions related to what was happening in the family. Thus, the role of empathy in facilitating meaningful, deep conversations becomes abundantly clear.

How does one show empathy toward others? Every member of the IEP team at the table, just as in any organization, desires to feel validated in two important ways: they want to be seen and they want to be heard. The ability to not just understand all parties present but convey a shared sense of understanding is critical in a situation where the adversarial parent vs. school district dynamic can play out. The facilitation of a sense of mutual empathy for the entire group is best generated when members feel seen and heard. A comprehensive, deep conversation is most beneficial when there is a sense of mutual empathy among each member in attendance.

Only through deep conversations can parents, teachers, and administrators learn about each other—their needs, hopes, dreams, and challenges. Having open and honest dialogues provides the platform for gaining knowledge and building relationships. When the conversations are honest and transparent, it is easier to address a child's school challenges.

It is not surprising that when deep conversations occur at an IEP meeting, all team members gain a clearer understanding of the perspectives of others. We encourage these same types of conversations to happen outside of IEP meetings. For example, through parent–teacher mini-meetings, in a neutral space such as the library or cafeteria or via phone, FaceTime, or Zoom, parents and the child's teacher can become better prepared to participate in the formal IEP meeting. These meetings help parents see themselves as a part of the IEP team and how, together with the teacher, they can work collaboratively to ensure that their child gets what they need.

In Justin's story, the solution to the problem was not testing or special education services, it was about trust and transparency. Although testing and data are an integral part of education, they do not compare to relationship building when it comes to productivity and being an active and integral team member. It is important that everyone is able to objectively identify and express their concerns. It was through truthful and authentic conversational exchanges that the cause of Justin's current school challenges was identified and could now be addressed.

COMMUNICATION ATTRIBUTES

It is important to understand the attributes of effective communication. In some cases, words only make up a small percentage of your message. According to Albert Mehrabian, unless the same message is sent verbally and nonverbally, the listener will more likely remember your nonverbal message. This is referred to as the 7.33.58 Rule: 7% of a message is words; 33% tone, volume, rate, and clarity; and nonverbal gestures and body language are 58% (Mehrabian, 1971).

> *A conversation is a meeting of minds*
> *where each person has a chance to share.*

Let's make the most out of our conversations! We suggest everyone keep in mind that *at the end of the day, parents and educators want the same thing: to provide the child with the most appropriate program that will meet their educational needs.* New and innovative solutions are usually the result of open and honest conversations. They allow everyone to think outside of the box. When two or more people have two-way dialogues, their conversations become the springboard to finding the *best,* and often innovative, ways to address the child's needs.

Unquestionably, each IEP team member has a different perspective regarding how to best address the child's learning, including academic, social-emotional, and behavioral needs. The accumulation of information comes from conversations that can be used to assist team members in making appropriate recommendations. Data, evidence, and concerns must be articulated clearly. It is okay when someone gets emotional; it shows they are passionate about the child. However, it is never okay to yell, scream, or intimidate anyone on the team.

Small talk is best at the beginning of any conversation because it tends to ease tension and sets the tone for building relationships. *Examples:* Are you doing anything for vacation? Do you have any other children? What did you do this weekend? Have you seen any good movies or read any good books? These types of questions can reduce the awkward moments, even when they are scripted icebreakers. They help everyone become ready to share their concerns, ask questions, and listen to the other person's perspective. The depth and breadth of the questions are what contribute to the quality of the conversation. Asking *what, why, when, where,* and *how* questions allow everyone to identify and understand the concerns around the table.

Conversations come in many forms. According to David W. Angel (2016), they can be categorized into four types: discourse, dialogue, diatribe, and debate (Figure 2-1). In general, conversations tend to be either competitive or cooperative. Of course, the goal is to have conversations at an IEP meeting that are both supportive and cooperative, dialogues or discourse. Competitive or argumentative conversations, debates and diatribes, or rants tend to lead to less productive outcomes.

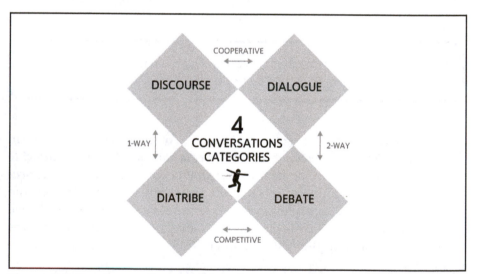

Figure 2-1. Four types of conversation: discourse, dialogue, diatribe, and debate. (Adapted from Angel, D. W. [2016, December 28]. *The four types of conversations: Debate, dialogue, discourse, and diatribe.* https://medium.com/@DavidWAngel/the-four-types-of-conversations-debate-dialogue-discourse-and-diatribe-898d19eccc0a)

Cooperative conversations tend to produce more valuable results. Sometimes, when a teacher or family member wishes to share their expertise or opinion, they can temporarily skew the conversation into being more one-sided. It can be helpful to the team members when someone introduces their expertise into the conversation because it diversifies the opinions of the room. This type of conversation, referred to as discourse, has its place at an IEP meeting.

In our opinion, the best type of conversations at IEP meetings are dialogues that encourage team building and trust. In pivoting to a dialogue, conversations become proactive rather than reactive. Think of a dialogue as a back-and-forth, positive conversation that allows participants to generate constructive comments and positive feedback. A dialogue also promotes brainstorming and problem solving.

One-way conversations can often be counterproductive, whereas two-way conversations allow the process to move forward by giving everyone the opportunity to learn from one another. Two-way conversations support active listening, encourage speaking, and promote the asking of questions. We recommend that parents and educators navigating the special education process focus on having meaningful and constructive dialogues because they are more likely to lead to collaboration and cooperation. We understand, however, that this takes patience and practice.

FOUR CATEGORIES OF CONVERSATIONS

The four categories of conversation (discourse, dialogue, diatribe, debate) provide a framework for looking at how we communicate. It also shows the type of conversation depending on the quadrant (cooperative, one-way, two-way, or competitive). The visual also lets the reader see how they could change the type of conversation.

It is crucial that all members of the IEP team focus the conversation on the development of a shared vision as it relates to the life goals of the student. The school district and the student's family must move cooperatively and demonstrate their support of each other's positions. Nonetheless, throughout the process of communication cultivated by deep conversation, parents, teachers, and administrators may lose sight of the bigger picture. We believe that this process should avoid becoming solely about the positions of the parents or the school district; the student must be at the center of the conversation.

In some cases, the student could be present during the IEP meeting if they wish to speak for themselves and are of appropriate age and ability. Directly including the student will remind the IEP team of the genuine presence of the student in this process, as well as the implications for the student's future.

If the student cannot be present at the IEP meeting, we believe it would be beneficial to include the student in other ways. Providing the student's photo, biography, writing sample, and other informative materials at the meeting incorporates the very person the entire process revolves around.

The IEP team's decisions directly impact the present and future of the student's life. Successful educational outcomes that better the life of the student are at the heart of our inspiration and practice. We believe that a sense of mutual empathy among members of the IEP team—an empathy that facilitates openness, transparency, and reflective opinion—will enable consensus to be reached more quickly. Naturally, the winner of this process becomes the student and their family.

Communication between parents, teachers, and educators is continually changing and evolving. Initially, most parent–teacher interactions were face to face. Over time, educators and parents expanded how they spoke to each other through phone calls and handwritten notes. Today most people have access to email and texting, making home–school communication more electronic.

With COVID-19, technology had a great impact on home–school communication. Virtual communication became the preferred way for parents, educators, and students to communicate, using such platforms as FaceTime, Zoom, Skype, and Google Meets. The United States was able to revolutionize communication across all sectors of society and regions of the country. All families—rich and poor, urban and suburban—were now communicating electronically. State mandates ensured families had access to electronic tools such as Chrome books, iPads, or laptops. Internet providers across the country offered free access to families and educators to support online learning (Gouëdard et al., 2020). In mid-2020, communication was predominantly virtual, which included online learning, virtual meetings, and texts. Of course, phone and email remained a part of everyone's repertoire. By 2022, schools and parents resumed some in-person meetings and conversations; however, much of home–school communication continues to be virtual or electronic communication.

New ways of communicating were both limited and expanded through computer interactions. They created new challenges related to the IEP process, which literally changed overnight. Meetings were now virtual, which made it more difficult to understand nonverbal cues and changed the tone and protocols of a conversation. When participating virtually, interrupting or adding to a conversation is more difficult and requires more intentionality on the part of the meeting facilitator.

Of course, there was an upside to virtual communication. It allowed more flexibility when it came to parents and even students attending meetings. Educational staff could log on between lessons or log on more easily and frequently. There also seemed to be a decrease in fear, anxiety, and emotions when meetings were held on the computer vs. attending meetings in the school. We believe this was because meetings on the computer were considered to be on neutral ground. When parents went into the school, they sometimes viewed it as a meeting on the school's turf, which they found intimidating.

Sections of the IEP

As we begin to review the sections of the Individualized Education Plan (IEP), it is important to keep in mind that the development of the student's IEP is a team process, as outlined in the Individuals with Disabilities Education Act (IDEA). In addition to understanding the process, we encourage parents and educators to embrace our 5-C Model of Communication. Using it every step of the way will help move parents and educators from merely being a member of the child's IEP team to forming a positive home–school partnership.

Too often we focus on our own perspective and do not think of the perspective of others. We suggest that each of us step outside of ourselves in order to work collaboratively with all IEP team members in the development of the

Bud, P. S., & Jacobson, T. L.
*Navigating Special Education: The Power of Building
Positive Parent–Educator Partnerships* (pp. 33-49).
© 2023 SLACK Incorporated.

most appropriate educational plan. We acknowledge that sometimes parents feel their voices are not heard, valued, or considered when speaking to educational professionals. That is why we remind parents that IDEA considers them to be an important member of the IEP team. IDEA identifies five people who must attend IEP meetings. Interestingly, parents are listed first, which means that the list is not in alphabetical order. The other members are an administrator, general education teacher, special education teacher, and a person knowledgeable in interpreting evaluations and testing—often the school psychologist (IDEA, 2004).

The IEP team is representative of all perspectives. Although parents are not educational experts, they are experts when it comes to their child. Parents are best qualified to report on what happens outside of the school day and at home. On the other hand, teachers and other school professionals are educational experts. They have a deep knowledge of the curriculum, the special education process, and the programs available within their district. By including parents as required members of the child's education team, IDEA makes it very clear that everyone's voice is crucial to the development of the IEP.

The more parents and educators learn about the child through the lens of each team member and understand the special education process, the better able everyone is to collaboratively develop a plan that best meets the child's educational needs. *We want to applaud U.S. Congressional lawmakers because they understood the value of having both parents and educators on the IEP team* (IDEA, 2004).

Experienced teachers and special education administrators are usually fluent in the intent of the law and the inner workings of special education. Parents and some general education staff are often less knowledgeable. The only way an IEP team can work collaboratively to develop the student's program is when everyone—including the parents—fully understands the process and is able to effectively communicate with all team members. Only then can the IEP team work collaboratively to develop the student's educational program, which from our perspective is the team's universal goal.

KEY SECTIONS OF THE
INDIVIDUALIZED EDUCATION PLAN

Present Level of Academic Achievement and Functional Performance

This section of the IEP describes how the student is currently performing in all areas of their school day. Prior to the IEP meeting, educators who are members of the school-based team gather data and record it under "strength, concerns, and how concerns are impacting educational performance." At the meeting, teachers and support staff report on the student's performance in the following areas: language arts, math, science, and social studies; communication, behavior, and social-emotional ability; and general health, mental health, vocational skills, fine and gross motor skills, and activities of daily living.

In many cases, the teachers will indicate that the student's performance is age-appropriate; they mark it N/A for "not applicable." When there are concerns, best practice suggests educators use data, such as test scores, grades, and anecdotal information, to describe the student's strengths, areas of concern, and how those concerns are directly impacting the student's ability to successfully access the curriculum. Whenever a teacher identifies an area of concern and indicates how it is impacting the student's ability to access the curriculum, it is incumbent upon the team to develop goals and objectives to address the concerns. When there are no concerns, there is no need for any type of specialized instruction.

Parent–Student Input

Adjacent to the Present Level of Academic Achievement and Functional Performance (PLAAFP) section is an area labeled Parent–Student Input. Either before or after the educators' report on the student's PLAAFP, the parents (and the student when they attend the meeting) will be asked to share their comments and concerns. (If this does not occur, we recommend parents ask for the opportunity to share their concerns.) What parents (and the student) say needs to be recorded in this section during the meeting. We encourage the team to discuss and consider the parents' input and how to address any of their areas of concern, unless they are already being addressed in the IEP.

There is no legal order for when the parents share their input regarding what they see as their child's strengths or challenges outside of the school day. When (during the meeting) parents are given the opportunity to share their insights varies from district to district and meeting to meeting. We suggest that parents are given an opportunity to share their concerns at the beginning of the meeting. However, the only legal requirement is that concerns are recorded, thoroughly and accurately, on the IEP. In addition to providing input for this section, we encourage parents to make comments and ask questions throughout the meeting.

Conversation Starters

These statements and questions are provided to help parents organize their thoughts prior to an IEP meeting and to help educators when gathering anecdotal information.

1. Describe how you see your child performing at home.
2. How would you describe your child's strengths?
3. Share something your child does at home that demonstrates their strengths.
4. Tell some fears you have regarding your child's ability to learn or be successful in school.
5. What barriers do you think are preventing your child from learning and being successful?
6. What are your hopes and dreams for your child?
7. How do you think your child learns best?
8. What are some of your child's favorite activities outside of the school day?
9. How could your child's interests be incorporated into their school day to build success?
10. Do you have any suggestions regarding IEP changes that would help to more effectively address your child's academic, social-emotional, or behavioral deficits?

The Parent–Student Input statement provides important information to the team. We recommend parents write out their comments and practice reading them prior to the meeting. Doing so can reduce anxiety and build confidence. Sometimes parents report similar concerns to what the school-based team sees; other times, their perspective may differ from the educators. We strongly suggest parents bring data or work examples to the meeting to support their statements and back up their concerns. In the story *How Is My Child Reading,* if the parents had brought data or a video of Sammy reading it would have impacted the conversation. We encourage students 12 years old and above to attend the IEP meetings, write out a brief statement, and read it to the team. Then the team hears the parents' voices and the student's voice; both are very powerful and can help in the decision-making process.

All of the information recorded in the PLAAFP section needs to be considered when developing goals and objectives. We realize parents may feel uncomfortable speaking up at the meeting because they believe their input is not important. We want to reiterate that the information they bring to the meeting is vital to the development of the child's IEP. We discourage parents from merely saying *"I agree with the team"* when asked to share their thoughts and input. We highly recommend that they voice their true feelings and concerns so that their child's needs are addressed.

We remind parents that the school-based team wants to know what is occurring outside of the school day. The parents' perspective is an important part of the process. Sometimes they introduce new concerns or challenges that teachers do not know, such as behavioral issues or struggles related to homework. If parents merely agree with what the educators have said, nothing is accomplished. Parental input also provides valuable information about how/if the student is able to carry over the skills and strategies being taught at school.

Goals and Objectives

Goals and objectives drive the student's entire special education program. These are developed based on the areas of concern as identified in the PLAAFP. The law requires all goals and objectives are written with the intent of being mastered within 1 year (IDEA, 2004). In most cases, we recommended that mastery criteria be at least 80%.

It is best practice to write goals and objectives using a S.M.A.R.T. goal format: specific, measurable, attainable, realistic, and timely (although the specific evaluation procedures and criteria vary from goal to goal). (A more detailed explanation can be found in the S.M.A.R.T. goals chapter.) Part of the development of the goals and objectives include how they will be evaluated and the performance criteria that will be used to measure progress.

There is a direct link between goals and objectives and the type of program the student requires. (A detailed explanation of all program models will be discussed later in this chapter.) Goals and objectives also drive the amount and type of special education instruction and related services, if the student needs paraprofessional support, consultative services, and/or modifications or accommodations.

Delivery of Service

This section of the IEP specifically details all aspects of the student's special education program, placement, and related services. IDEA outlines the educational framework with special education instruction providing the student with academic support and related services providing tools to help the child benefit from special education instruction (2004). Related services include speech-language therapy, occupational therapy, physical therapy, and rehabilitation counseling. Although speech and language support is generally considered to be a related service, when a student's primary disability is language and/or communication, speech may be considered to be part of the instructional services the child requires (IDEA, 2004).

Types and Amount of Services

As stated previously, the type of services and the amount of service hours are linked to the goals and objectives. Each service, whether instructional or related services, has specific goals and objectives. The team decides the frequency of the support required to ensure the student makes meaningful progress on the goals and objectives. The amount of time required is equal to the teaching hours required for the student to benefit from special education and related services instruction and master the goals and objectives. This section also identifies the professional responsible for monitoring the goals and the staff who will implement the instruction. Other services discussed in this section include assistive technology, vocational education, adaptive physical education, individualized health needs, and transportation services.

PARAPROFESSIONAL SUPPORT

The IEP team also determines if the student requires a paraprofessional to assist educators in delivering instruction. The reason the team suggests a paraprofessional varies from student to student. The term *paraprofessional* (sometimes referred to as a teacher aide, paraeducator, instructional aide, or educational assistant) may or may not be a licensed teacher. They are assigned to assist certified staff or a specific student within the classroom, a special education program, or during related services. Their duties vary from teacher to teacher, grade level to grade level, and student to student. However, in all cases, their job is to support and enrich the student's experience at school.

When a school district recommends paraprofessional support, it is to ensure the student is able to successfully access the curriculum so the IEP can be implemented effectively. Sometimes the student requires a dedicated one-on-one paraprofessional; other times they recommend paraprofessional support in a specific classroom or during specific instructional time. Paraprofessionals provide assistance to the student so they can participate in activities with nondisabled peers, such as gym or lunch. This extra support allows them to engage to the maximum extent appropriate in the Least Restrictive Environment (LRE).

Paraprofessionals may provide an extra set of hands for the teacher during group lessons and collaborate with the teacher to provide personalized assistance to the student. There may be a worry that with paraprofessional support the student will become dependent on the adult. Actually, when the paraprofessional is properly trained, they know when to push forward with support and when to step back and fade into the class, allowing for the student's growth and development of their independent skills.

Overview of Paraprofessional's Roles and Responsibilities

- Helping the child with peer partnering across settings.
- Encouraging peer relationships by modeling interactions with other students.
- Checking on and addressing bullying concerns.
- Building inclusivity, especially during lunch and recess.
- Practicing communication skills across all school settings.
- Providing check-ins at the beginning and end of the school day.

Some students require a paraprofessional as a safety aide who is directly responsible for their safety and well-being. They become an extra set of hands and eyes for the child and may facilitate "turn-key communication" between the child, school, and home when they are responsible for feeding, toileting, and ensuring the child does not run out of the building or get injured. In this case, they may be asked to attend home instruction and clinical sessions outside of the school and/or the school day and act as the liaison between the therapist and the classroom teacher.

INDIVIDUAL HEALTH AND TRANSPORTATION PLAN

An Individual Health and Transportation Plan (IHTP) is created to address the specialized needs of students with specific health concerns. The plan outlines how to accommodate the student within their school facilities and during school-related transportation. It is developed to address different types of medical conditions and outlines the specific accommodations and how they will be provided. A copy of the IHTP is on file in the school nurse's office.

Some examples of when an IHTP is developed are:

- Student requires a nurse to ride on the bus and/or attend class with them due to specific medical needs, such as a feeding tube.
- Student has severe allergies and requires a monitored safe eating environment.
- Student has medically caused incontinence and requires customized bathroom privileges, beyond what neurotypical students require.
- Student is medically fragile and requires individual transportation, including an aide, for long field trips or bus trips.

EXTENDED SCHOOL DAY AND EXTENDED SCHOOL YEAR

The team determines if the student requires an extended school day (ESD) and/or an extended school year (ESY). Data are the driving force behind recommending that a student requires these services. The team monitors regression and recoupment during and following weekends, winter break, and spring break. Although the number one reason the team recommends ESY services is for recoupment and regression, the decision must be reviewed on a case-by-case basis.

Related services and academic support can be offered as part of the ESY or ESD recommendation. This includes, but is not limited to, speech and language therapy, occupational therapy, physical therapy, social skills camps, reading, literacy, and math support. When either or both services are recommended, the appropriate boxes are checked off on the IEP. Many times, the final decision for ESY is made at a meeting closer to the end of the school year, especially if the student's annual review occurred earlier in the school year. If that is the case, the district will convene an IEP meeting for the sole purpose of discussing ESY.

IEP teams may recommend ESY as a way to close the academic gap. Regression and "gaps in students' learning" occur in the summer months and over long breaks is related to "Wrightslaw." The decision is based on a review of the student's progress on goals and objectives and considers what is needed to ensure they are educated in the LRE. Wrightslaw states that ESY is a full team decision. It does not have to be limited to the summer months but can also include long breaks in the school calendar and breaks students have to take for medical reasons.

ESY or ESD services can be provided for any reason the IEP team deems necessary, such as due to a student's severe disability that may cause them to take longer to attain critical skills or self-sufficiency goals. If these services are provided beyond the school day or over a vacation, they are considered to be part of ESD services. ESD services can include special tutoring programs and therapies offered to the students, at no cost to their parents, outside of the student's academic day. These programs can also be provided before and/or after school, on holidays, and during winter and spring breaks in the school, home, or at a clinic.

INDIVIDUALIZED EDUCATION PLAN PROGRAM MODELS

The IEP team is required to discuss and consider the different educational models that could be used to deliver the special education to the student, which includes instructional services and related services. It is incumbent upon the team to determine which one is most appropriate based on goals and objectives and types of support services required. If the school-based team makes this decision outside of the IEP meeting and without parent input, the meeting can quickly become adversarial and the district is out of compliance. We reiterate that all programming and planning that drives the student's education must be discussed with the entire team because all decisions have to be team decisions.

The service delivery models are on a continuum from least restrictive to most restrictive. IDEA states all students must spend the maximum time appropriate with typically developing peers in the LRE (U.S. Department of Education, 2022). We encourage school staff to explain why they are recommending a specific type of program and how it provides the most appropriate program in the LRE. If the team is recommending that the student spend a significant amount of their day away from typically developing peers, then they are required to complete the *Least Restrictive Environment Checklist.*

Inclusive Education Model

The student receives their special education support in the general education classroom. This allows the student to participate with general education students to the best of their ability, including riding on the school bus and having lunch with their typically developing peers. In some cases, a one-on-one aide is assigned to accompany them to all general education classrooms to ensure this model meets the student's academic needs.

Pull-Out Versus Push-In Model

The pull-out model requires students to leave their general education classroom and attend part or all of their school days in a resource room or alternative classroom. The special education teacher is responsible for addressing the student's unique educational needs in most or all curricular areas, including reading and math. The pull-out model is often used to deliver individual or group speech, occupational therapy, or physical therapy. The student will receive this instruction in the therapist's room. "In addition, when deemed necessary and appropriate, a student may be pulled out of a general education setting for assistance with completing an exam, benchmark exams, progress monitoring probes, and other assignments" (Professional Learning Board, n.d.).

The push-in model is used when a special education teacher or related services teacher (i.e., speech pathologist, occupational therapist, and/or physical therapist) delivers their IEP services in the general classroom setting. This is also known as an inclusive classroom setting (Morin, 2021). "Services can be provided through IEPs, Response to Intervention (RTI), informal supports, and other instructional interventions" (Morin, 2021). It is best practice that all special education services address the IEP goals by aligning instruction with the curriculum being taught in the classroom.

Co-Teaching Model

The co-teaching model assigns two teachers, a general education teacher and a special education teacher, to a general education classroom. Both teachers educate alongside each other. The special education teachers are responsible for adapting and modifying the material for the students with disabilities in the classroom to ensure all students' learning needs are being met (Cassel, 2019).

Self-Contained Classroom

Some students with more significant disabilities may learn best in a self-contained classroom away from their typically developing peers. Multidiscipline teachers come into the room to address the academic, behavioral, and social-emotional needs of a small group of students. Students on the autistic spectrum, who require one-to-one, applied behavioral analysis therapy (ABA), or other types of specialized instruction, may also be in some type of self-contained classroom. In this educational model, special education teachers are responsible for breaking down all assignments and working with the students one-on-one for the academic portion of their day (Murphy & Beam, 2021).

Resource Room

The intent of special education law is to have students educated with nondisabled peers as much as possible. Some students are able to spend the majority of their academic day with their nondisabled peers. However, they might require some specialized instruction, taught by a special education teacher, during specific periods such as reading, writing, language arts, or math. This instruction is delivered to the students in a different room, often referred to as the resource room (Office of P-12 Education, 2013).

Consultation Model

Consultation is considered to be an indirect service, since it is not provided directly to the student. Instead, special education teachers and/or any related services teachers (e.g., speech, occupational therapy, physical therapy, behaviorist, social worker, psychologists) provide this education to the general education teacher. The frequency and duration of consultative services are identified in the IEP in the portion that says "Additional Supports and Services Required to Implement the IEP" (Office of P-12 Education, 2013).

Examples of Consultation Services

- Conversations between general education and special education staff related to adjusting the learning environment and/or modifying instruction to ensure the student's needs are addressed in the general education classroom.
- Special education teacher and/or related service staff work directly with the classroom teacher to modify the curriculum or the environment.
- Special education teacher and/or related service staff observe the child in the inclusive classroom setting to facilitate carryover of skills.
- Special education teacher and/or related service staff monitor equipment or technology.
- Special education teacher and/or related service staff monitor specific progress related to IEP goals and objectives.

Out-of-District Placement

The most restrictive placement is an out-of-district placement. This program is considered when the student's local school district cannot meet the student's programming needs. The placement can be at a neighboring public school, a regional school, or a private special education accredited school. The type of programs available and considered to be outplacements differ from state to state. However, it is always necessary that the IEP team reaches consensus regarding where the student's outplacement will be and agree that the placement is the most appropriate educational program in the LRE.

Most school districts require that students, if outplaced, attend a state-certified special education program. If a child is placed out of the district, the district is responsible for funding the program and transportation. If for some reason the district does not provide the transportation, the parents are eligible for a transportation stipend, which averages to about $3000 a year nationally (Garvey, 2022).

Modifications and Accommodations

In addition to the specialized instruction outlined in the IEP, the team identifies the types of modifications and accommodations the student requires, including assistive technology. The purpose of these supports is to assist learning in the general education environment and to support the implementation of the IEP. Specifically, modifications and/or accommodations serve three distinct purposes: (1) to ensure the student makes meaningful progress on goals and objectives in the general education curriculum, (2) to enable to the student to participate in extracurricular and nonacademic activities, and (3) to allow the student to be educated and participate with children with and without disabilities.

Accommodations are the adjustments or alterations to the environment, instruction, materials, or equipment that help the student access the curriculum and demonstrate learning. They ensure the student can access the content or complete assigned tasks. An accommodation does not change or alter what is being taught. Instead, it helps the student be more independent by removing barriers. Modifications are changes to what the student is expected to learn based on their abilities.

Both accommodations and modifications appear in the IEP in the form of a checklist. The list should not be viewed as a "pick and choose menu," but instead should be tailored to meet the unique needs of each student. We recommend the team decide which specific accommodations and modifications are required, why, and under what circumstances. Many of the items listed are either strategies or suggestions that are a part of "good instruction." Most students would benefit from some of these strategies some of the time. However, when an accommodation or modification is recommended, it must be used 100% of the time under the circumstances outlined. This means that the student requires the specific accommodation and/or modification in order to successfully access the curriculum.

Examples of Modifications

- Leveled text
- Modification of worksheets, tests, written material
- Reduction of homework and/or class assignments

- Word bank with choices for tests questions
- Keywords and phrases are highlighted for student
- Paraprofessional support provides hand-over-hand

Examples of Accommodations

- Material read out loud or audiobooks
- Chunking information
- Provide visual aids and manipulatives
- Braille
- FM system
- Enlarged text/enlarged fonts
- Reduced amount of text on page
- Note-taking buddy/note-taking support
- Extra time on test or assignments

Transition Planning

There are many types of transition planning. The transition plan specifically outlined in the IEP is designed to help students successfully transition from special education upon high school graduation (U.S. Department of Education, 2000). This is a formal part of the IEP process and is supposed to begin when a student turns 15 years old; although some districts choose to start the process when the student turns 14 years old.

The transition planning conversation, which is outlined in this section of the IEP, is usually built into the student's annual review following their 15th birthday. This may be the first time a student attends an IEP meeting. The purpose of all transition plans is to address three specific areas: education/training, employment, and independent living. Based on the conversation, the team determines how to best prepare the student for their high school graduation based on what their post high school experience might look like. This information, if possible, is student driven.

Transition planning includes the development of specific IEP goals. We suggest that when developing these goals, the team takes into consideration the student's disability, household income, and racial, ethnic, and cultural background. The goals will then reflect the student's needs, how those needs will be met, and how progress will be measured. Examples of questions the team might ask the student: *Do you plan to attend a postsecondary program? What type of employment/job do you want following graduation from high school? Where do you plan to live after graduation?*

The Right Question Makes All the Difference

As is best practice, the district scheduled a follow-up IEP transition meeting to review Maria's current job placement. While the team was waiting for Maria to arrive from class, her parents, Mr. and Mrs. Sanchez, were engaged in some small talk with the team. Then Mr. Jones, Maria's case manager, asked Mr. and Mrs. Sanchez if Maria was still working at Subway. The parents answered "yes."

Mr. Jones and the other school staff felt a sense of relief. They interpreted the parents' response to mean that Maria was successfully working at Subway. The purpose of the IEP meeting was to determine if Maria's current transition goals were appropriate.

The school-based team, based on the parents' "yes," thought that it meant Maria was fulfilling her responsibilities as outlined in the transition plan. They said that there did not appear any reason to recommend changes to her current plan. Mr. and Mrs. Sanchez found this perplexing.

Although Maria was still working at Subway, she was on the verge of losing her job because she was unable to perform most of the tasks required. The only reason she had not been let go was that her supervisor at Subway had not yet found a replacement. Maria's parents knew it was only a matter of time before Maria would be asked to leave her job.

Mr. and Mrs. Sanchez did not know if it was their responsibility to tell the team that Maria was about to lose her job. Instead, they answered the question that they were asked: "Was Maria still working at Subway?"

Maria's parents were whispering to each other, trying to decide how to tell the team about Maria's difficulties at work. At that moment, Maria entered the room. Everyone greeted her. Mr. Jones said that he was happy to hear things were going well at work.

Maria looked at her parents and then started ranting. She didn't understand why Mr. Jones would say that. Everything was not going well at work! As she spoke, she seemed to be holding back tears. Maria said the only thing she was able to do was clear and wash the tables and the counters. She couldn't slice the bread, make sandwiches, or even keep track of the number of loaves being made and how many were needed. At that point she started to cry.

continued on next page

Mr. Jones was speechless. It took him a moment to realize that he had asked Maria's parents a "yes/no" question: "Is Maria still working?" Mr. and Mrs. Sanchez answered the question truthfully, but did not expand on their answer.

Oftentimes parents can be intimidated by the professionals sitting around the table and they do not want to ruffle feathers. In addition, there can be cultural differences. Mr. and Mrs. Sanchez felt it was their responsibility to show respect to people of authority.

If Mr. Jones had asked an open-ended question such as "Tell me how Maria is doing at work," the parents' response would have been very different.

In addition, if the expectations at IEP meetings were for parents to share their concerns and provide input regarding their child's progress, then Mr. and Mrs. Sanchez would have been prepared to do so openly and honestly.

Once Mr. Jones realized that there was a problem, the team, including the parents, began to discuss how to best provide Maria the support she needed to be successful at her job. Mr. Jones suggested assigning Maria a job coach. The parents welcomed this suggestion. Then the team discussed how to amend the goals and objectives to reflect the skills Maria needed to be successful at her job.

Depending on the student's disability, sometimes it is the parents who provide the input. Questions that parents would answer: *Is postsecondary education needed and/or appropriate? Does the student require a one-on-one aide or a service dog? Where will the child live, and what state or federal services are they eligible for?*

The total transition process can take months or years to fully develop and is part of the conversation at every IEP meeting beginning when the child turns 15. Like everything else related to the IEP process, transition planning varies from state to state. However, in all cases recommendations depend on the student's strengths, weaknesses, and IEP goals. In addition to parents, it is important to have the student actively involved in their own transition planning whenever possible. Other important voices are the school counselor and, if applicable, the student's job coach. Both professionals may have valuable insights that they can share with the team and can be instrumental in the development of the transition plan.

It is important to note that the term *transition planning* refers to any time a student is changing placements: moving from grade to grade, to different schools within their district, and to or from an outplacement. Change can be difficult and may present new challenges, which is why it is important to discuss how to best ensure the student's success during any and all transitions. We suggest having an IEP meeting and creating a thoughtful transition plan prior to all transitions. We also believe it is best practice to have an IEP meeting within 30 to 45 days following any change to the student's program or placement. The purpose of this meeting is to assess if the student has successfully adjusted to the change or if there is a need to make modifications or changes to the IEP.

Although transition planning is important, it may be confusing and emotionally stressful to parents and to students, no matter their socioeconomic status or racial or ethnic background. Multigenerational and cultural differences may impact how and if parents speak up at a meeting or ask questions. We recommend educators encourage parents to be an active voice in the process and to ask questions. It is important for parents to understand that by asking questions they will gain valuable knowledge related to appropriately planning for their child. We remind parents and educators that asking open-ended questions drives better conversations.

In Maria's case study, she was able to immediately state the problem to the team. However, many students are not able to articulate the problem or are reluctant to admit that there is a problem. When yes/no questions drive a conversation, it can quickly go off in the wrong direction. Educators should be aware that in many cultures parents feel they should only answer the question they are asked. Thankfully, Maria was able to be her own advocate. We have found that a student's voice can be very powerful. Educators and administrators are usually very open to listening to the student and taking their voice into consideration.

Let's go back to the purpose of the transition IEP meeting, which is for the team to develop goals more specific than "student will be employed." The team discussion should include options such as a job coach or specific objectives to directly target what the student is required to do. When appropriate, provide ongoing feedback to the student regarding how to help them successfully transition beyond high school.

Some children with disabilities are not prepared to graduate high school at 18 and/or may require post high school transition services. Students with disabilities are eligible for services through the age of 21. Due to the COVID-19 pandemic, some states have added a compensatory year for missed instruction. In those states, students will graduate at age 22. The law states that once a student turns 18, they have the legal authority to make decisions for themselves related to school, health care, finances, and all other life decisions. Therefore, if a child is not cognitively or emotionally able to assume this responsibility, parents must ask the court to grant them legal guardianship. This happens when the court determines a child's disability prevents them from being capable of making their own decisions.

MEETING MINUTES AND SUMMARY

An administrator or the case manager takes minutes at the IEP meeting, which is similar to what occurs at any board or organizational meeting. The person taking notes creates a summary of the discussion, which is then recorded on the IEP document. The minutes include concerns voiced during the meeting by the parents and educators, progress reported by educators, and a general summary of the overall discussion, including areas of agreement, compromise, and disagreement.

Meetings are conversations—which means that there is often disagreement. We consider the power of disagreement as a springboard for deeper and more productive conversations. However, we recognize that disagreements sometimes cause the development of the IEP to temporarily come to a standstill. If this happens, a suggested strategy is to *end the meeting and agree to have an informal meeting outside of the formal IEP process.* The minutes need to reflect that the meeting ended before the IEP could be completed and indicate when it will be reconvened. It is at this point the importance of compromise, active listening, and perspective will play a crucial role in the development of the child's education plan. These strategies will help the team accomplish their goal, which is to move beyond the standstill and come to consensus regarding the development of the student's IEP.

> *If disagreements cause a meeting to come to a standstill,*
> *end the meeting, have an informal meeting with the administrator,*
> *and then reconvene the IEP meeting within the next 7 days.*

Active Versus Passive Listening

LISTENING VERSUS HEARING

Effective communication is a dialogue—a back and forth conversation. An important part of having a dialogue involves listening. When one person is speaking, it is important for the other person to actively listen. We realize that many people find it difficult to listen during a conversation because they are busy waiting for the speaker to pause so they can respond. Sadly then, what is occurring isn't a conversation.

During a conversation or an argument, people may ask, "Did you hear me?" because they do not think you were listening. What they really should

Bud, P. S., & Jacobson, T. L.
Navigating Special Education: The Power of Building
Positive Parent–Educator Partnerships (pp. 51-58).
© 2023 SLACK Incorporated.

ask is "Did you process what I said?" or "Do you understand what I am telling you?" The listener probably heard the sounds, but did not necessarily understand the meaning. This is the difference between "listening" and "hearing."

The terms *listening* and *hearing* are often used interchangeably. Hearing is an involuntary act, whereas listening is voluntary. We hear sounds: they travel through the air, enter your ear canal, bombard your eardrum, and then your brain perceives them. Listening, on the other hand, means we not only hear the words but we are also focused and paying attention to what is being said. We are listening for meaning.

However, even if we are listening, we are not always *actively* listening. Being an active listener means you are engaged in the conversation and fully concentrating on what another person is saying. You are both participating in the conversation and open to understanding the other person's perspective. As an active listener, you focus on the meaning of the words, rather than merely hearing the words themselves. The best active listeners ask for clarification, repeat what they hear, and ask follow-up questions. Active listeners tend to have positive facial expressions, such as a smile and eye contact. They nod and/or show they understand what is being said and often lean toward the speaker.

Sadly, much of what we hear we do not remember, even though many of us think we do. Research studies suggest most people do not actively listen, which results in remembering only about 50% of what they hear (Dale, 1947). This happens because the listener isn't focusing on what is being said, but rather waiting for a pause in the conversation so they can speak. Instead of paying attention to the speaker, they are more likely to be thinking about what they want to say. Whereas an active listener builds on what the other person is saying, demonstrating that they are fully engaged in the conversation.

Words Shut Down the Conversation

Lily's parents, Mr. and Mrs. Cashman, were attending an IEP meeting because their daughter appeared to be having difficulty participating in her general education classroom, even with the help of a one-on-one aide. Lily's parents believed the aide, Miss Green, was only intervening when their daughter had a meltdown, started to scream, or refused to do her work. Then Miss Green would take Lily into the hall until she calmed down. Otherwise, they believed Lily's aide was not particularly attuned to her needs.

continued on next page

Before Lily's parents could ask questions or make suggestions, the special education team suggested the possibility of a self-contained classroom where students spend most of the day in the same classroom with the same students. As soon as the words were said, the principal, Dr. Shapiro, noticed Lily's parents stopped listening. Instead, they reverted their focus to their phones.

Dr. Shapiro asked Mr. and Mrs. Cashman to share their thoughts. Mrs. Cashman became very emotional and said putting her daughter in a self-contained classroom would encourage her to have more outbursts because she wouldn't have good role models. Mr. Cashman, who noted that Miss Green was a sweet lady who seemed to like their daughter, accused her of not doing anything to address the triggers causing her to have meltdowns. These open and honest comments reshaped the conversation.

The psychologist, Mrs. Russo, then offered to perform a Functional Behavioral Assessment (FBA). She explained that it meant she would observe Lily in a variety of settings and identify the measurable and observable behaviors surrounding her meltdowns, which included what events happened just prior to the behaviors and any consequences resulting from the behaviors. This assessment could give the team a better understanding of what triggered her meltdowns, how best to address them, and interventions to try. This would all be laid out in what the psychologist described as a Behavior Intervention Plan.

The special education teacher, Mrs. Garcia, noted that Lily seemed to be overwhelmed in math class. She suggested pre-teaching the math concepts that would be introduced in the next day's lesson to decrease her math anxiety. She would also work with Lily's aide to develop coping strategies instead of immediately removing her from the classroom.

This productive conversation was able to address the reasons why the teacher had recommended a self-contained classroom in the first place. It also explained why Lily's parents had felt it was not an appropriate placement. The meeting helped parents and educators understand the others' perspective and the importance of trying strategies before immediately changing a program or placement.

Because the team engaged in a conversation that included sharing information and asking questions, Lily was able to remain in her general

continued on next page

education classroom. Through constructive dialogue and the help of the FBA, Lily's IEP was revised. These changes ensured that she was more successful social-emotionally, academically, and behaviorally. Her parents realized not being open to the IEP team's suggestions had initially shut down the conversation. It was only when they asked "why" the special education teacher recommended a self-contained classroom was the conversation steered in the right direction.

Many people only half listen, becoming distracted either by their own thoughts or by other events in the environment. Poor listening interferes with our ability to remember what we have heard and to actively participate in the conversation. Not understanding what is being said or not agreeing with the speaker may also impact what we remember. When we hear something that we disagree with, we tend to stop listening. This is what happens in the case study *Words Shut Down the Conversation.*

It is important to listen and be open to hearing what others are saying. Listening involves our whole body—ears, eyes, brain, emotions. Many of us do not think of body language as part of the conversation. Yet, we are constantly sending nonverbal messages, both positive and negative, that can easily change the tone of a meeting.

Listening is the other side of speaking. Everyone's voice needs to be a part of the conversation. Having deeper conversations, rather than simply sharing information, gives us the ability to move from "power over" others to "power with" others (Glaser, 2016). We cannot have meaningful conversations unless we listen to what is being said.

During a conversation, listening leads to asking targeted questions. Although people may ask questions, as we have already alluded to, most people do not always listen to the answer. Yet, by asking questions, parents and educators can develop a more complete understanding of the details of the student's educational experience and what the child needs. It also helps them understand the other person's perspective.

All questions are important, however, *why* and *how* questions are considered to be more powerful than *what* questions because they encourage the speaker to dig deeper and explain their thinking in more detail. *Why* questions are more likely to lead to great conversations because one *why* question often leads to another *why*. Effective conversations are dependent on the type of questions asked.

Let's consider two types of questions and see how they would impact the conversation. A low-level question requires a yes/no response: *Does* the student bring their homework to school every day? Whereas a higher-level question encourages the speaker to share information: *Why* does the student consistently forget to bring their homework to school? or What might be causing the student to forget their homework although they completed it?

We consider yes/no questions to be conversation stoppers and why/how questions to be conversation starters. Higher-level questions always provide the listener with more information. We have found the more you listen, the less questions you have and the less confused you are.

LISTENING VERSUS AGREEING

We want to remind everyone that listening does not mean agreeing. Listening to what the other person is saying allows you to hear their point of view and opens up the conversation. Sometimes we confuse active listening with critical listening. They are not the same. If you are critically listening, you are evaluating what is being said. If you are actively listening, you are trying to understand the other person's perspective and are building on their thoughts and ideas or asking for clarification. Being an active listener leads to meaningful conversations and helps people with differences of opinion find a way to compromise and then reach consensus.

Listening is hard work, which is why we might find ourselves listening intermittently. When we are actively listening, we have to physically attend to the conversation, which means consciously minimizing any distractions. This can be exhausting. Yet, active listening is rewarding because it allows you to be an integral part of the conversation. Building on what is being said and asking meaningful questions makes the dialogue productive.

The old adage about "two ears and one mouth" reminds us that it is important to listen twice as much as we speak. Mastering the *art of listening* helps to build trust, demonstrates transparency, and is the best way to avoid miscommunications. Although listening can be tiring, the results are worth it!

Did you know that our emotions can impact our ability to listen? Our natural tendency is to listen for what we want to hear, rather than everything that is being said. Many times, as soon as we hear something that differs from our opinion we stop listening, which can lead to communication breakdowns. This is what initially happened in *Words Shut Down the Conversation*. Mr. and Mrs. Cashman stopped listening and participating when they didn't like what was being said.

Sometimes we remember or hear *what we want to hear* rather than what was actually said. Research suggests when we hear or see an event, our memories may be modified or changed due to new information that is introduced (Loftus, 2016). To avoid this happening it is important to practice being an active listener throughout the entire conversation. We also suggest taking notes during conversations as a way to help you remember what was said.

The purpose of any conversation is to share ideas and/or feelings. In order to be an effective communicator, it is important to understand the key attributes of speaking and listening. For some reason people hone their speaking skills, yet they don't try to improve their listening skills. Listening strategies are often embedded in a speaking curriculum. However, there are almost no courses developed solely to being a good listener, which we believe is an important skill set.

Like all skill sets, active listening takes honing and practice. It is the best way to avert misunderstandings and misinterpretations. All listening begins with being attentive and looking at the speaker. Eye contact lets the other person know you are listening to them. It makes them feel important and valued. It has been said that former President Bill Clinton built his career around his ability to listen to others. He looked you in the eye when listening and responding. Many people we have spoken to confirm that Clinton made you feel as though no one else was in the room when he was speaking to you.

We are going to present eight active listening strategies that we suggest you learn and practice so that you will be ready to use them at your next Individualized Education Plan (IEP) meeting. These strategies will help you process the conversation, know how to respond, and increase your ability to remember what was said. We want to remind everyone that we listen to both what is said and how it is said. That is why tone and body language impact what you hear, how you listen, and what you remember.

ACTIVE LISTENING STRATEGIES

Paraphrasing

When it is your turn to speak and before continuing the conversation, it is important to repeat (paraphrase) a thought or idea the speaker said in your own words. Your statement should contain the exact same information but be said using your own words. This is an effective way to let others know you understood what they said.

Once you have paraphrased what was said, you are ready to build upon the speaker's idea or statement. Suggestions on how to paraphrase: "It sounds like you're saying …" or "What I heard you say was …" If you misunderstood or misinterpreted what the speaker said, they can immediately clarify it before the conversation continues. This avoids communication breakdowns.

Summarizing

Another listening strategy is summarizing. You don't repeat verbatim what the speaker said or paraphrase it. Instead, you provide a short but detailed summary, filtering out the less important information and only presenting the key ideas stated. If the listener misunderstood something, it is incumbent upon the speaker to clarify what they said. The speaker can repeat verbatim or restate their idea by either explaining it differently or providing more detail. Summarizing differs from paraphrasing because it abbreviates what was said.

Asking for Clarification

At any point during the conversation, if a listener does not understand something, it is very important for them to ask for clarification. By asking for more information, the speaker recognizes that the listener didn't fully comprehend their message. By not asking for clarification, it is possible that there will be communication breakdowns.

Keep in mind, *there is no such thing as a stupid question.* However, there are incomplete statements. Providing clarification (i.e., answering questions) allows the speaker to give new or additional information, which will hopefully explain what was said and avoid any misunderstanding or miscommunication.

Perspective-Taking

A crucial part of active listening is perspective-taking, which encourages everyone to both hear and understand the other person's point of view. Keep in mind that just because you understand another person's perspective doesn't mean you agree with them. Think of perspective-taking as part of the journey to reaching consensus and/or co-creating a new plan.

A strategy to use to help you understand the person's perspective is to focus on both *what* they are saying and *why*. Since asking *why* is the important piece of the equation, we suggest adding this strategy to your listening repertoire. It will improve the quality of your conversations and your ability to collaborate and compromise.

S.T.O.P. (Stop, Take a Breath, Observe, and Proceed)

The acronym S.T.O.P. allows you to pause before speaking or reacting to what the other person said. It is like the old "stop and think" before speaking. By pausing, you give your mind and body a chance to think, reflect, and understand what was said before responding. This strategy assists you in processing the other person's perspective. Then, when you are ready to respond, you can build on what they said, which will lead to more productive conversations.

Open-Ended Versus Yes/No Questions

Open-ended questions begin with the words *what, why, when, where, how* or are driven by descriptors such as *tell me, describe, explain.* These types of questions or requests open up conversations, rather than shut them down. Questions that can be answered with one word, especially *yes* or *no,* tend to stifle or end a conversation. On the other hand, open-ended questions provide insight into the *what, why,* and *how* and lead to more productive conversations.

- *Closed-ended question:* Parent to teacher: Is my child reading on grade level?
- *Open-ended question:* Parent to teacher: Tell me about my child's reading skills.
- *Closed-ended question:* Teacher to parent: Does your child independently complete their homework?
- *Open-ended question:* Teacher to parent: Describe what happens when it is homework time.

Answer With "Yes, And ..." Rather Than "Yes, But ..."

Yes, and ... informs the speaker that you were listening to what was said and are going to build on their statement. However, when you say *Yes, but ...,* these words negate what the speaker said and tends to shut down the conversation. In addition, saying *Yes, and ...* allows the speaker to provide an easily understood reason for adding to or building on what was said. We encourage using supporting details that explain what and/or why.

W.A.I.T. (Why Am I Talking?)

The acronym W.A.I.T. provides an easy-to-remember self-talk strategy that can help you become a better listener. Using this strategy before you start to talk or interrupt someone will encourage you to *wait* while you take the time to consider *why you are going to talk and what you are going to say.*

Some thoughts to reflect on:

- Why am I going to speak now?
- Am I asking for clarification?
- Do I want to add something to the statement?
- Am I reacting to what the speaker is saying?

5

Setting the Tone of a Meeting

> *When the appropriate tone is set, parents, along with educators and administrators, are able to actively participate on the IEP team and discuss how to best address the student's needs.*

We believe the 5-C Model of Communication and active listening are the key skills that allow parents and educators to actively and effectively participate in Individualized Education Plan (IEP) meetings. These tools provide everyone with the ability to fully engage and respectfully contribute to conversations. They also are great ways to develop trust and build partnerships.

Most conversations begin with simple pleasantries, which (as you might recall from our first scenario) did not occur when Sammy's parents were

Bud, P. S., & Jacobson, T. L.
Navigating Special Education: The Power of Building Positive Parent–Educator Partnerships (pp. 59-66).
© 2023 SLACK Incorporated.

brought into the conference room. When parents are given the opportunity to speak at an IEP meeting, we suggest they begin by thanking their child's teacher for their hard work. We want to remind parents to listen to what the teacher is saying, recognize what they are doing, and acknowledge their effort. Acknowledgment doesn't mean agreement; however, it shows respect and appreciation.

In addition, everyone needs to remember to use active listening strategies and ask questions when appropriate. Questions drive the dialogue, whether they ask for clarification, additional information, or supporting information. For example, if the teacher did not present concrete data to support her assessment, it is okay for a parent to request supporting data (e.g., *Can we see how our child performed at the beginning of the year vs. now?*). On the other hand, when parents present concerns, it is just as appropriate for a teacher or administrator to ask them to present supporting details (e.g., *What happens when your child has a meltdown when they get off the bus, and how frequently do they occur?*).

Messages are more likely to be well-received when the speaker sounds confident, but not cocky. It is crucial that the person talking sends the same message verbally and nonverbally. We highly recommend that parents and educators come to all meetings prepared to present their concerns or demonstrate progress using data. We believe that using data takes the emotion out of the equation. It is much harder to argue with facts.

EVERYONE IS IMPORTANT! EVERYONE BRINGS VALUE!

Vince Lombardi, the football coach who successfully took a losing Green Bay Packers team and turned them into three-time champions, knew the value of teamwork and setting the tone. He recognized every person on a team, no matter how seemingly insignificant a role they had, contributed to the team's success. Each person brings different, but important skills, to the team.

Some parents are reluctant to actively participate on the IEP team; others feel, even when they participate, their voices are not heard. If asked why, they would all say they do not see themselves as important or valued members of the team. We want to say loud and clear—this is NOT true! Everyone on the team is important—parents and educators!

Parents see themselves as less valued team members because they are not trained educators. We disagree; all team members, including parents, are valued because they each bring a different expertise and perspective regarding what the child needs and how to best develop an educational plan. We think of the team as the co-creators of the child's IEP.

We suggest parents and educators reflect on their roles and responsibilities as if they were a member of the board of directors of a major corporation. Each board member has an equal voice and an equal vote. Each person brings different experiences and a different perspective, which is why they were asked to serve on the board. All voices are welcomed and valued as they discuss and vote on proposals and decisions vital to the success of the company. When they speak, the other board members listen respectfully to everyone's ideas and opinions. They are discussed and considered because each board member's voice matters.

In many ways the IEP team is similar to a board of directors. Each person brings a different expertise and perspective to the team, whose responsibility is to oversee the child's educational program. As the Individuals with Disabilities Education Act (IDEA) has outlined, parents and educators are expected to have an equal voice by equally participating in the decision-making process related to the development of the child's educational plan. This only happens when everyone's voice is heard and considered. Just like the board of directors of XYZ Corporation, parents and educators each bring relevant, important (although often very different) information to every IEP meeting.

THE TONE OF THE MEETING

Often, the chairperson sets the tone of a meeting. In the case of an IEP meeting, the chairperson is usually a school administrator who has knowledge about both general education and special education. They might be the director of special services, the assistant director of special services, a supervisor of special services, or the student's case manager, whereas the principal or vice principal usually chairs the 504 meeting, which is a meeting held for a general education student who might require accommodations rather than modifications to assist them in school. The chairperson of this meeting doesn't require special education knowledge, since the 504 accommodations are not a special education service. It is important to know that who chairs either meeting may vary from district to district even within the same state since the chairperson is a district decision rather than one dictated by law.

Ensuring everyone feels welcome is the best way to begin a meeting on a positive note. In addition to greeting the parents, we encourage the chairperson to actively ensure they contribute to the discussion by asking for their input at multiple junctions during the meeting. We recognize parents may feel conflicted, worried their voices really don't matter, or think their questions are silly so they are embarrassed to contribute to the conversation. We remind everyone there is no such thing as a silly or stupid question. Actually, asking questions is a sign of empowerment rather than a sign of weakness. Therefore, if parents are involved in the conversation, they are sending a message to the team that they want to be active participants.

> *Questions are what drive conversations.*
> *Answers provide everyone the knowledge needed*
> *to make thoughtful data-driven decisions.*

In addition to the chairperson setting the tone of a meeting, there are other factors that may contribute to and/or impact tone, such as the presence of an attorney at the meeting. We want parents to be aware that the tone of the meeting changes if they bring an attorney to an IEP meeting. In addition, if parents bring their lawyer, many districts will have the board attorney attend the meeting. We understand that the parents' attorney may be acting as "another set of ears at the meeting" and helping them effectively advocate for their child. However, since it affects the tone of the meeting, we suggest parents invite a friend or consultant instead.

Sometimes a school district will invite the board attorney to the IEP meeting to explain or interpret the district's legal responsibilities. If the board attorney is present at an IEP meeting and parents did not bring legal representation, we strongly recommend the parents ask for the meeting to be postponed until they can bring their attorney. *Please understand the optimum choice and the full purpose of this book is to avoid getting to a point where the school district or the parents need to bring legal representation.* We believe that if both parties respect one another, have ongoing meetings, develop a shared vision, and embrace the 5-C Model of Communication the need for legal action will be greatly reduced and even avoided.

Using the 5-C Model of Communication encourages everyone's full participation and can positively affect the tenor of a meeting. The goal is for parents and educators to work in partnership. The foundation of a partnership is conversations, which is why we suggest the chairperson acknowledge that educators and parents may have differing opinions that need to be heard, discussed, and considered. However, unless parents feel their voices will be heard and all options will be genuinely considered, the tone and tenor of the meeting is affected.

Sometimes a specific option is not discussed because the chairperson does not have the authority to allocate funding for the program or service. We believe in the name of transparency; it is incumbent upon the administrator to explain that some recommendations require the expenditure of resources, which they cannot approve. We also suggest they agree to schedule a follow-up meeting with an administrator authorized to allocate funds. This type of honesty builds trust and helps the parents and educators form a partnership. It also ensures the meeting tone remains positive.

Parents or administrators may try to affect the tone of the meeting by bringing food. Food often relaxes the tone, invites conversations, and opens up the possibility of creative thinking. Whether home-baked goodies or purchased snacks, the purpose is to try to build and cement a home–school partnership. We like to think of this as an off-shoot of the biblical idea that "breaking bread" symbolizes community and fosters meaningful connections and cooperation.

BEING PREPARED

We encourage parents to come to every IEP meeting prepared, on time, and ready to participate, which includes bringing relevant information that can be used to drive the conversation. Being prepared helps to decrease anxiety. When parents arrive a few minutes early, they feel less rushed and they send a message to the school staff that attending the meeting is of top priority. We also suggest all school officials arrive on time, as it demonstrates to parents that they too are committed to the process.

Although the IEP process is driven by federal law, every school district runs their meetings a little differently. However, no matter the state or the district, the team must consider and discuss the core components of the IEP. As part of the conversation, we again recommend the administrator or meeting chairperson set a positive tone by reminding every team member that they have an equal voice in the discussion and decision-making.

In some districts, copies of the IEP are handed out at the beginning of the meeting as a way to drive the conversation. Best practice says that the IEP should be labeled draft as another way to ensure the tone of the meeting is positive. The word draft is saying to the team, *here is our thinking, now let's discuss it.* Whereas, if the document isn't labeled draft, parents often feel like the district is presenting them with a finished document. They interpret this to mean that they were left out of the process and their concerns, opinions, and voices don't matter.

We want to remind the team that if a district actually presented a completed IEP to the parents, they would be out of compliance. In our experience, no district has intentionally done that! We believe if a district omits the word draft, it is a procedural oversight that can be quickly and easily corrected. In fact, the special education process requires all IEPs remain in draft form until after the IEP meeting, since the purpose of the meeting is for parents and educators to consider, discuss, and make changes to any or all parts of the *proposed* IEP. The standard procedure is that following the IEP meeting, an administrator makes the agreed-upon changes, creates a meeting summary (i.e., a list of changes agreed to and rejected), and writes minutes that reflect what happened at the meeting. Only after all changes have been made can the IEP be finalized.

Best practice recommends parents are provided with draft copies of the goals and objectives about a week prior to the IEP meeting. If the district does not initiate this, we suggest parents request draft goals and objectives. Having a chance to review the goals and objectives, which are used to drive all other parts of the IEP, is an easy way for the district to establish trust and show transparency. It also gives parents an opportunity to review what is being proposed, determine if there are additional concerns they would like to discuss, and/or if they have questions. It also gives the family an opportunity to confer with other professionals, such as outside therapists, their pediatrician, an educational psychologist, and/or an educational consultant, prior to the IEP meeting.

We realize that it is standard protocol for the administrators to ask parents if they received a copy of their Procedural Safeguards and if they have any questions. We also know that this question may affect the tone of the meeting because parents may find the document intimidating. As mentioned previously, parents are often reluctant or afraid to ask questions. It is important for parents to understand, from an administrator's perspective, they are merely following protocol. By referring to the Procedural Safeguards document, their intent is to ensure the parents are ready to fully participate in the meeting. They are not trying to shut down the conversation; in fact, we believe their intent is quite the opposite.

Most of the time parents don't ask questions, whether or not they understand. As we suggested earlier, inviting parents to a one-on-one intimate first meeting with an administrator, school psychologist, or case manager is a great way to encourage parental participation and begin to build a parent–educator relationship. The purpose of the pre-IEP meeting is to review the special education process, explain the meaning of the Procedural Safeguards, and discuss basic educational terminology. It is our hope that as a result of this pre-meeting, parents will become familiar with the language and procedures used at the IEP meetings.

> *We want to remind parents that at the end of the day,*
> *the purpose of the IEP team is to develop a program to address*
> *your child's educational needs. Your voice is crucial to the process!*

WHAT MAKES A MEETING SUCCESSFUL?

We believe collaboration leads to success! Therefore, whenever parents and educators collaborate in the development of the student's IEP, we consider the meeting to be successful. On many levels, parents know their children better than anyone else in the room. They have vital information to share, and we discourage parents from deferring all decisions to the school. On the other hand, we suggest parents listen to the educators sitting around the table as they are educational experts. They work with the child every day and have a vast knowledge about how children learn. Their education and experience provide them with a toolbox full of strategies. No one person has all of the answers, which is why we encourage educators and parents to work collaboratively and embrace each other's perspectives.

There is a direct link between respect and how you communicate. If everyone speaks respectfully and recognizes each person has knowledge to share, the meeting will be successful. Respect happens when the team embraces the 5-C Model of Communication (see Chapter 2) and uses active listening strategies. Now the doors are open to collaboration and cooperation. We want to remind everyone that even though they may bring knowledge and experience to the meeting, we suggest they refrain from sounding arrogant or demanding. Of course it is important to sound confident, which is conveyed through words, tone, demeanor, posture, and evidence.

A collaboratively functioning team will lead to successfully developing a mutually agreed upon IEP, which is the overarching goal of the special education process. Through collaboration, parents and educators can begin to form positive partnerships. That only happens when each team member, including the parents, is ready and willing to share their concerns and perspective, actively listen, and participate in all aspects of the conversation. We might be sounding repetitive, however, to develop a mutually agreeable program it is crucial that everyone comments, asks questions, and shares ideas about how to best address the student's educational, social-emotional, or behavioral needs.

Let's think of it this way, each member of the IEP team brings their own special knowledge and passions to the table. Teachers and administrators have degrees in education. Parents have a PhD in their child. Sometimes meetings turn adversarial because parents and educators disagree about what is in the best interest of the child. We believe teachers and administrators are genuinely trying their best to ensure the student is successful. As educational professionals, they care deeply about *their student's* success. Of course, parents always believe they are advocating in their child's best interest. This is the reason we encourage everyone to voice their concerns and share what they believe the student needs.

> *Everyone has the child's best interest at heart, even though their perspectives may be different. Conversations are what open up possibilities. Partnerships lead to and encourage compromise. The goal is to reach consensus on how to provide the student the most appropriate program.*

PARTICIPATION STRATEGIES

When everyone embraces the virtues and behaviors required to effectively participate and is actively engaged in the process, they can co-create an IEP to meet the child's academic, social-emotional, and behavioral needs.

1. Begin by developing and strengthening your knowledge about the process. As a parent or educator of a student with disabilities:
   - Be familiar with all aspects of IDEA and special education policies and procedures.
   - Participate as equal partners in all meetings.
   - Come to all of the meetings prepared.
   - Listen to all team members with an open ear and mind.
   - Ask questions if you do not understand or need clarification.

2. Next, hone your effective communication skills. As a team member:
   - Speak with confidence—you bring value and expertise to the team.
   - Use data to support what you say—leave your emotions at the door.
   - Collaborate on the IEP development—share ideas, voice concerns, and attend all meetings.
   - Have deep conversations that allow you to know all of the team members.

3. Finally, remember the importance of documentation. Parents and educators:
   - Maintain an active file on the student.
   - Keep all documents and correspondence between home and school.
   - Send meeting follow-up summaries—this helps avoid communication breakdowns.
   - Maintain a phone log.
   - Send thank you notes for participation and cooperation (see Appendix).

How to Respectfully Disagree

> *When the appropriate tone is set, parents, along with educators and administrators, are able to actively participate on the IEP team and discuss how to best address the student's needs.*

WHAT TO DO WHEN YOU DISAGREE

People find it easier to agree than to disagree because they don't like conflict. Many parents worry that disagreeing will have a negative impact on their child's education or even their parent–teacher relationship. We want parents and educators to understand that disagreements happen. They usually arise from misunderstandings, different points of view, or incomplete information. We believe that disagreement can play an important role in a conversation.

Bud, P. S., & Jacobson, T. L.
Navigating Special Education: The Power of Building
Positive Parent–Educator Partnerships (pp. 67-75).
© 2023 SLACK Incorporated.

I Didn't Know What I Was Agreeing To

Adrian's parents, Mr. Rogers and Mr. McNeil, entered the conference room and were greeted by Mr. Tannenbaum, Adrian's case manager. He handed them a packet that said draft, which contained the Individualized Education Plan (IEP) goals and objectives the district was proposing. Adrian's parents hadn't had a chance to review the goals prior to the meeting.

After the team reviewed Adrian's present level of performance and got input from Mr. Rogers and Mr. McNeil, the special education teacher, speech pathologist, and occupational therapist reviewed the proposed goals and objectives. Parents listened respectfully, not knowing what to ask or what to suggest since this was the first time they were hearing the new goals and objectives.

When Adrian's teachers finished presenting, the principal, Miss Johnston, turned to Mr. Rogers and Mr. McNeil and asked if they agreed with the proposed goals and objectives. Both parents thought they were expected to say "yes," which was their response, and their agreement was recorded into the minutes.

Several months later, Mr. Rogers and Mr. McNeil decided that Adrian wasn't making meaningful progress. In fact, they felt that he appeared to be regressing. At that point, they compared his current IEP goals and objectives with those from the previous year. It appeared that the team had recommended the exact same goals from the previous year without the slightest revision.

They questioned whether disagreeing with the school team would affect their relationship with Adrian's educators. Would the situation turn adversarial? Up until now, they always went along with whatever the IEP team proposed. They never questioned their recommendations. They were worried about what would happen if suddenly they questioned Adrian's program.

Mr. Rogers and Mr. McNeil requested an IEP meeting and shared their concerns. Mr. Tannenbaum listened respectfully and then said, "You agreed to these goals and objectives at the last IEP meeting." He spoke loudly, intimidating Mr. Rogers and Mr. McNeil.

continued on next page

They immediately became defensive since Mr. Tannenbaum had raised his voice. Both Mr. Rogers and Mr. McNeil raised their voices, shouting that it appeared Adrian was regressing. Mr. Tannenbaum referred to the minutes from the most recent IEP meeting and read "parents agreed to the proposed goals and objectives."

This infuriated Mr. Rogers and Mr. McNeil. They didn't know what to do or how to respectfully disagree after having agreed at the last IEP meeting. They realized their responsibility was to ensure their son was getting an appropriate education and making meaningful progress. How could they do that without the tone of the meeting turning adversarial? They had to find a way to disagree without being disagreeable.

In their hearts, they believed Adrian's teachers knew he hadn't mastered last year's goals. Why hadn't they shared the information at the previous IEP meeting? Why had they merely presented the same goals for the following year without any explanation? Mr. Rogers and Mr. McNeil knew the right thing to do was to respectfully disagree. It was the only way to ensure Adrian would get what he needed.

In the case study, when there was a disagreement, both the case manager and the parents raised their voices. Yelling tends to alienate others and may even cause them to stop listening. That is why we suggest before verbally disagreeing, it is important to get your emotions in check. You don't want to say something you will regret, which can happen when you are emotionally upset.

Disagreement can put our bodies into a fight or flight mode. It causes us to feel angry and frustrated. Mr. Rogers and Mr. McNeil became defensive and distrusted the educators because they felt excluded from the development of Adrian's IEP. Their reaction caused them to automatically decide the proposed goals and objectives were not appropriate. They even questioned why the school had recommended them in the first place.

When any recommendation is made, it is possible that someone at the table will disagree. We encourage all team members to voice their opinions and their disagreements respectfully. Yet, being able to respectfully disagree can be challenging. Only when we can speak respectively, which includes our tone, words, and body language, are we able to *respectfully disagree*. We can then engage in open, honest, and productive conversations, which will lead to finding solutions to the problem.

Of course, disagreements lead to feeling disappointed, annoyed, and even infuriated, none of which will solve the problem. What is imperative is to always remain open to reaching a compromise. When we aren't sure how to disagree, we often just agree. Mr. Rogers and Mr. McNeil had wanted to disagree at the annual review. However, they were not prepared to have a conversation about the goals and objectives and didn't have any data to support their disagreement. The first time they saw the proposed goals and objectives was at the annual review meeting. That is why we suggest giving parents a draft of the goals and objectives at least 5 days prior to the IEP meeting. Parents can then review them, which in the case of Mr. Rogers and Mr. McNeil would have meant comparing the "new" goals with the previous goals.

They had agreed to the goals because they thought that was what was expected of them and they didn't know how to respectfully disagree. It wasn't until they realized Adrian's goals hadn't changed for the past 2 years that they became angry and decided that the proposed goals and objectives were not appropriate. They questioned why the school would recommend the same goals for a second year.

When we aren't sure how to disagree, we often just agree. Although Mr. Rogers and Mr. McNeil had wanted to disagree at the annual review, they felt ill prepared to have a conversation about the goals and objectives since the first time they saw them was at the annual review. They did not have any data to support their disagreement. This is one of the reasons we have previously discussed the importance of giving parents a draft of the goals and objectives at least 5 days prior to the IEP meeting. Then they will have an opportunity to compare last year's goals with those being recommended for the coming year.

Disagreements may send our bodies into a fight or flight mode. *Anger management experts recommend you think before you speak.* Remind yourself that "silence is golden" and begin by taking charge of your emotions. Say nothing! Do nothing! Take a deep breath and focus on your body and count until you feel your body relaxing. Label your feelings and, if need be, take a break ... which might mean asking to pause the meeting so you can leave the room and get some air. However, it will also mean that you will be ready to continue the conversation.

The best way to keep the situation under control during a disagreement is to move the conversation toward a solution by listening and then responding. Everyone has a chance to process what is being said and is in a better position to respond rationally and respectfully. Phrases such as *"I hear what you are saying," "Let me clarify my thinking," "I understand ...,"* and *"In my opinion, the student (my child) needs ... because ..."* are ways to respectfully disagree.

After Mr. Tannenbaum yelled at the parents that they had agreed to the goals and objectives, Mr. Rogers or Mr. McNeil could have calmly said, "Let me clarify our thinking. We had not been given the goals and objectives prior to the meeting. We were not prepared to comment on them. However, we have now had a chance to review the proposed goals and realize they were the same goals from Adrian's prior IEP."

By using these phrases, it is possible to prevent the conversation from shutting down, becoming emotional, or everyone getting defensive—like in the case study. The goal is to have a productive conversation so that everyone understands the other person's perspective and is agreeable to working collaboratively to reach a compromise. When we *respectfully disagree,* conversations are more likely to lead to the best way to address the problem or difference regarding how to meet the student's needs.

HOW TO DISAGREE WITHOUT BEING DISAGREEABLE

> *Most importantly, take control of your emotions.*

Disagreements happen. They usually stem from misunderstandings or miscommunication. The goal is to use strategies and techniques that will avoid a situation turning adversarial. When everyone works collaboratively, disagreements are less likely to be disagreeable. It is also helpful to use active listening strategies because they open up the conversation and create a path to reaching a solution or compromise. Also, when parents and educators identify a shared vision, it is easier for the team to find a way to address disagreements and differences of opinion.

If you want to disagree without being disagreeable, try not to yell. Nothing gets accomplished when voices are raised. In fact, when the volume increases, everyone stops listening. Therefore, we recommend that it is important to separate the people sitting around the table—the IEP team members—from the problem being discussed. As the saying goes, a lot more is accomplished with honey than vinegar.

Disagreeing without being disagreeable happens when educators and parents have productive conversations that revolve around listening and understanding the other person's perspective. Of course, there are those times when the most respectful thing you can say is *"let's agree to disagree."* However, even when that happens, it is still crucial to try to reach consensus since the goal is for the team to develop an appropriate IEP.

Getting upset changes the tone of the conversation. The negative undercurrents are what will be remembered. This happens because parents or educators become frustrated and/or feel threatened. Educators feel parents are making unreasonable requests. Parents believe the educators' recommendations aren't providing the child with what they need. In both cases, the productivity of the meeting stops and the conversations disintegrate.

We recommend when parents disagree with a recommendation or statement, they clearly restate their concern, request their disagreement be entered into the minutes of the meeting, and send a follow-up note (within 24 hours after the meeting) to the meeting chairperson stating their unresolved differences or concerns. We suggest all team members can avert disagreements by being overly specific when making recommendations and linking them to concrete data. It is much harder to disagree when the data support the recommendation.

If in *I Didn't Know What I Was Agreeing To* the educators had discussed Adrian's lack of progress and why they recommended using the same goals for a second year, then the parents would have understood what they were agreeing to. Being honest and transparent helps to drive the conversation even if it means that parents and educators disagree.

LISTENING STRATEGIES HELP YOU RESPECTFULLY DISAGREE

In Chapter 4, we discussed how to be an active listener and proposed specific strategies and techniques. We are going to explain how to use the active listening strategies presented earlier when *respectfully disagreeing*. Using these strategies can reduce or avoid disagreements, misunderstandings, or misinterpretations.

"Yes, And ..."

Saying *"Yes, and ..."* or acknowledging that you heard what the person said serves two purposes. First, it highlights that you were listening. Second, it demonstrates that you are open to building on what was said.

For example, after the teacher presents the proposed goals and objectives, a parent can begin by saying, "I know that [teacher's name] is proposing these goals based on her expertise in [subject matter] and that these are skills my child needs to work on." This respectfully acknowledges why the educators made their recommendation.

When the parents speak, they will build on what has been said when they share their concerns/point of view. "I also believe that my child has [state the areas of concern] and agree that they need to work on the proposed skills. In addition, we believe our child is struggling with [state new subject or areas of concern] and requires [explain concerns and suggestions regarding addressing those concerns]."

In this conversation, the disagreement suggests the proposed goals are not all-inclusive. It also reflects the parents' perspective that their child has other significant needs than should be addressed. This response allows the parents to respectfully voice their concerns. It isn't that they are disagreeing, rather they are building on what the educators have stated.

If the parent had said, "Yes, but ..." it would have negated the recommendations, which were educationally appropriate. The parents' disagreement was linked to their concern that the proposed goals and objectives were not addressing *all* of their child's needs.

In *I Didn't Know What I Was Agreeing To*, Mr. Rogers and Mr. McNeil requested another IEP meeting because they had now had a chance to review Adrian's proposed goals with those from the previous IEP. At that meeting, they told the team they no longer agreed. They should also request that the teachers share data to demonstrate Adrian's progress on the last year's goals and objectives and why they were recommending the same goals and objectives. Data is a powerful tool and can help during any disagreement. It is hard to argue with data. Goals and objectives should be written with the intent that they can be mastered in 1 year and the previous year's goals and objectives be closed out at the end of each year (U.S. Department of Education, 2000). If the student hasn't mastered a goal or any of the objectives, the team is expected to discuss how to best address them. In Adrian's case, the educators had not done that; however, the next IEP meeting rectified all concerns. In fact, the data showed that Adrian was making progress. When the parents were presented with the evidence, trust was somewhat restored.

Having *"Yes, and ..."* conversations are more productive and will more likely produce the results both sides want. When everyone is respectful, verbally and nonverbally, the IEP team is better positioned to co-create a solution, if there are disagreements. We want to remind everyone that words make up a small part of any verbal message because the listener hears and sees the speaker's nonverbal communication. Therefore, if your words and body language don't send the same message, the listener will more likely remember what you said nonverbally.

Saying *"I hear what you are saying and that is why I believe ..."* is a way of getting a point across. However, it is more powerful and believable when tone, volume, and body language all send the same message. When you include the *why* behind your statement, it backs up what you say with data and provides additional support if you need to *respectfully disagree*.

"I" Statements

Casting blame does not solve the problem and does not allow you to *respectfully disagree.* Blaming others is likely to create more problems. Instead, we suggest focusing on the power of "I" statements. When beginning with *"I feel...,* *"I think ...,"* or *"I believe the child needs ...,"* the use of "I" allows the speaker to take responsibility for their thoughts or feelings. We recommend that along with the "I" statement, you use supporting details that tell *how, what,* and *why you think, feel, believe, etc.* Supporting your "I" statements with concrete data offers credibility and objectivity to your feelings or beliefs.

The power behind any statement are data, which is why we suggest parents and educators come to meetings with evidence to support what they are going to say or propose. Evidence is always necessary, whether a statement is a concern, accomplishment, or recommendation. There is less chance for disagreement when using concrete evidence. Examples of data include, but are not limited to, student portfolios, test scores, work samples, videos, and audio recordings. This type of information highlights the student's strengths and areas of need; it also documents progress and/or regression.

Perspective-Taking

In order to have productive conversations, it is important to listen to and understand everyone's perspective. The best way to let the other person know you understand their point of view is to paraphrase or summarize what they say. If you are able to restate and/or explain the other person's perspective, it means you heard and understood what they said. Remember, it does not mean you agree with it. However, it may set the stage for you to *respectfully disagree.*

After repeating, summarizing, or paraphrasing what the other person said, it is best practice to wait 3 to 5 seconds before continuing the conversation. This gives the other person an opportunity for them to acknowledge that you heard and understood their perspective. It also provides them an opportunity to correct any misunderstanding.

Following the pause, it is your turn to state your perspective, using data or evidence to back up your statements. Now you are ready to have deeper and more meaningful conversations. Hopefully they will lead to new possibilities on how to address the child's needs. If there is disagreement, understanding everyone's perspective provides a foundation for compromise and consensus building.

Remain Calm

Having a meaningful conversation and remaining on an even keel is hard. We suggest keeping a conversation constructive is the best way to have a meaningful discussion. It is easier to *respectfully disagree* when you are calm. It is also the way to open yourself up to listening. We want to reiterate that from disagreement comes compromise, but—even more importantly—co-creation! Coming up with a collaborative plan that considers everyone's perspective helps address disagreements. None of this is possible unless all participants in the conversation remain calm.

Note: If the conversation becomes confrontational, take a deep breath for 10 seconds before responding or request a 5-minute break. Walk around, get some air, and process what has been said. Sometimes the most effective tool is the gift of time.

All IEP team members need to know when to hold them, and know when to fold them. There are occasions when the blood starts to boil on the part of the school or parents. Tempers may flare, yet nothing good comes if there is shouting, rolling eyes, or insisting "your" position is the right way to go. Getting agitated will accomplish nothing.

We recommend asking to end a meeting and reconvene in a few days when there is shouting and disagreements. By taking a break, everyone has a chance to calm down and reflect on what was said. Then, when the meeting is reconvened, all team members will be ready to come to the table with an open mind. We like to think of this as a way to give the conversation a fresh start so the team can address the problem, come up with a compromise if needed, and then reach consensus.

Recapping and Summarizing

Using this strategy when *respectfully disagreeing* allows the key points of the conversation to be outlined and reviewed. Recapping, paraphrasing, and/or summarizing is a good way to have everyone's opinions and perspectives be incorporated into the conversation. It is important for the person who recaps the conversation to ask the other team members if they believe the essence of the conversation was clearly conveyed. This is referred to as *member-checking*. This strategy encourages others to add something that might have been overlooked or forgotten. It also ensures that everyone's perspective is considered. In many situations, when everyone hears a clearly articulated summary of an argument, it crystallizes the conversation and becomes a catalyst for compromise.

Partnerships Build Trust

The way a team plays as a whole determines success.

—Babe Ruth

THE POWER OF PARTNERSHIPS

To paraphrase Aristotle, think of a team as the "sum of the parts." When parents and educators build strong, successful partnerships, the team is able to develop an appropriate educational plan.

Working together opens up opportunities for everyone to share information along with their expertise. We believe that a shared vision helps to build a strong home–school partnership. By being partners in the process, it reduces competitiveness. It also encourages each person on the team to bring their

Bud, P. S., & Jacobson, T. L.
*Navigating Special Education: The Power of Building
Positive Parent–Educator Partnerships* (pp. 77-94).
© 2023 SLACK Incorporated.

unique knowledge and perspective to the conversation while valuing everyone's voice. From our perspective, total team involvement is the best recipe for ensuring a child's success.

Home–school partnerships flourish when teams effectively communicate, collaborate, and cooperate. The development of the National Parent Teacher Association and The National Standards for Family Partnerships framework supports that when everyone is working together it maximizes the student's development, learning, and success in school (National Parent Teacher Association, 2009). These frameworks identify key components necessary for families and districts to develop meaningful relationships that lead to partnerships. We believe they are also crucial to ensuring Individualized Education Plan (IEP) teams effectively address the student's needs.

Breakdown in Trust: A Story

Charlie's parents, Mrs. and Mr. Malone, and their educational consultant, Mrs. Bernstein, were escorted to the conference room by the assistant principal, Mr. Nuy. He welcomed them to the meeting. Then, to their surprise, Ms. Alvarez, Charlie's case manager, handed them an IEP. As they reviewed the document, they realized that they had been given a completed IEP. They did not understand why all the sections were filled in, including the program model, goals and objectives, and hours of special education and related services.

Both Mrs. and Mr. Malone were angry that their voices had not been included in the development of Charlie's IEP. As they reviewed the document, it appeared that the district was making all the decisions about their son's education without getting any input from them.

The parents were familiar with the IEP process and knew that the Individuals with Disabilities Education Act specifically outlined the parents' roles and responsibilities, which required them to be part of the decision-making process. They were not sure what to say or how to react.

They knew that the purpose of an IEP meeting was for the team to develop the IEP and that parents were integral members of the team. However, their school district appeared to be leaving them out of the process. Furthermore, as they looked around the table, it appeared that the team was patiently waiting for them to review the document and approve all the recommendations.

continued on next page

At past IEP meetings, Mrs. and Mr. Malone had felt their voices were not valued. However, they had never been so blatantly excluded from collaborating on the development of Charlie's IEP. They were glad that they had hired Mrs. Bernstein and that they had invited her to attend the meeting to help facilitate the conversation. They also felt that Mrs. Bernstein could fairly and unemotionally advocate for Charlie's needs and be his voice at the table.

When Mrs. Bernstein noticed that the IEP wasn't labeled as a draft, she immediately collected all the copies. She asked Mrs. Alvarez, the case manager, to write draft on the cover of all the IEPs. This was her way of alerting the district to the fact that their proposal would not be approved without the parents' voices being heard. Mrs. Alvarez apologized for the oversight, marked the copies draft, and redistributed them so that Mr. Nuy could continue the meeting.

The tone of the meeting didn't change. The educators continued to review the IEP without asking Mrs. and Mr. Malone for their input. This caused them to disengage from the conversation and stop listening. They felt their voices didn't matter. Although they had not collaborated on the development of the document, Mrs. Bernstein noted that for the most part, the IEP appropriately addressed Charlie's educational needs. She also suggested some changes the parents should request.

What Mrs. and Mr. Malone did request was that the meeting be adjourned and reconvened the following week. They felt this would give them an opportunity to review the proposed IEP. They stated they had not been included in the development of Charlie's IEP and therefore did not trust what the district was proposing. They also felt that anything they said would be discounted.

By asking to "take a break," Mrs. and Mr. Malone would be able to carefully review the draft IEP so that they could bring their questions and concerns to the next meeting. They hoped at that meeting the educators and administrators would be open to having a meaningful discussion and include them in the conversation.

At the next meeting, everyone—parents and teachers—was open to having a collaborative conversation about what Charlie needed. Mrs. and Mr. Malone felt included in the conversation. Their questions and comments contributed to the draft IEP being modified. This included adding another objective to the reading goal, 30 minutes of consultative sup-

continued on next page

port from the occupational therapist to address handwriting, and 1 hour of direct services to be delivered in the classroom.

Trust was restored. Parents and teachers now had developed a shared vision as to how to best meet Charlie's needs. This only happened because Mrs. and Mr. Malone felt confident and were willing to speak up. Sometimes the best approach is to take a break and reconvene. The gift of time helped parents and educators both become more open to having a meaningful conversation and work collaboratively.

Parents + Districts = Student Success

The following information is adapted from PTA National Standards for Family–School Partnerships (National Parent Teacher Association, 2009, p. 45):

- Districts effectively communicate with families, ensuring they feel welcome in the school community.
- Districts and parents are able to effectively communicate with each other.
- Districts and parents work together to support and celebrate student success.
- Districts and parents form meaningful partnerships related to the decision-making process.
- Districts and parents collaborate with the community at large.

The PTA Standards specifically list communication as a key component (National Parent Teacher Association, 2009, p. 45). We, too, believe successful partnerships, which lead to student success, are built on open and honest communication and teams embracing the 5-C Model of Communication. If parents or educators ineffectively or incompletely communicate, it causes a breakdown in the home–school relationship and can impact the child's academic achievement.

One of the reasons we wrote this book was to help parents and educators understand that partnering is a crucial element to the success of *all* students. Learning how to develop strong partnerships can be challenging, takes time, and is definitely a commitment on the part of parents and educators. However, we believe it is well worth both the time and effort. By doing so, everyone is giving the child a gift—the best opportunity for success!

Although there are different perspectives around the table, when teams form partnerships developing programs is easier. The key is having an open mind and honing a new set of skills: working together, listening and learning from each other, and understanding the other person's perspective. Co-creating a plan can then happen more organically because everyone comprehends and appreciates what others think and why. Compromise and eventually consensus are able to occur because different, but important, perspectives come together.

In many cases they actually create an entirely new perspective. *Parents look at the problem through a narrow focus—what their child needs. Whereas school districts are responsible for planning and programming for all students, so they look through a much wider lens.*

We do not want parents, teachers, or administrators to ever lose sight of the fact that building a partnership requires regular and reciprocal communication between home and school. Then everyone garners a clear grasp of the child's disability and abilities. Open and honest communication also helps to reduce stress and anxiety because the team's mindset is built on a foundation that values collaboration and cooperation.

Sometimes the Problem Is Parents Disagree With Each Other

We have been discussing the importance of parents and educators working as partners and reaching consensus. However, sometimes it is the parents who are undermining the process because they cannot agree with each other. When this happens, the only way for the team to function is for the parents to work out their differences. We suggest they do it outside of the purview of their child or the school. Children are very aware when there are tensions between their parents, often using it to their advantage and pitting one parent against the other. All this does is further complicate the situation and often increases the conflict between their parents.

It is important for parents to be aware that their conflict can undermine and/or sidetrack the IEP process. They are putting at risk both the team's ability to build a home–school partnership and their child's ability to be successful in school. As educators, we know that communicating with parents who are in-fighting can be challenging.

In-fighting between parents is likely to put the student's success at risk. When they struggle to communicate effectively with each other, they are less able to successfully advocate for their child. Their personal conflict interferes with their ability to address the child's educational needs. It also jeopardizes their willingness and ability to collaborate and compromise, let alone reach consensus.

Divorce can lead to additional communication breakdowns. When parents divorce, there is often an added layer to the fighting: custody. Often the court decides which parent has legal rights concerning educational decisions. This adds to the tension and may spill over into an IEP meeting. To help reduce this tension, we suggest the school administration allows both parents to have a voice at the meeting and to include them in the conversation, even though only one of the parents has the "legal" decision-making power.

We all know having a power struggle at the expense of the child does not accomplish anything. It may even be counterproductive, destroy trust, and destabilize the IEP process. Therefore, we would also like to suggest another way to reduce home–school conflict at an IEP meeting is to have both parents sign all educational documents. Of course, the only signature that is required is from the parent who has custody.

In-Fighting Sabotages Partnerships

Robin, a 16-year-old student, had just spent the last 10 weeks in a residential placement. The IEP team was now responsible for developing a transition plan that required "partnering" between home and school. It was necessary for everyone to agree on an interim out-of-district placement.

The problem was that Robin's parents, Mrs. and Mr. Wang, were now divorced. They had great difficulty communicating with each other, let alone being able to advocate for their son. They yelled at the school staff and their son. They had co-parenting rights, so they had to agree. Sadly, nothing was getting accomplished and the clock was ticking.

Robin had been struggling in school since seventh grade. At that time, he was diagnosed with oppositional defiant disorder, depression, ADHD, and anxiety. In addition, he was the victim of several bullying incidents at school and on the bus.

During Robin's eighth and ninth grade years, Mrs. and Mr. Wang were in the midst of a lengthy and contentious divorce. During that time, they both completely neglected their son's educational needs.

Robin became so depressed that he could not attend school, missing over 120 days of school in the 2 years combined. He couldn't relate to his peers and had difficulty making and keeping friends.

It was now crucial that Mrs. and Mr. Wang successfully partnered with the school district on his behalf. They needed to come to an agreement as to the most appropriate out-of-district placement and IEP for Robin.

continued on next page

This couldn't happen unless Mrs. and Mr. Wang stopped arguing and started to communicate with each other, the administrators, and teachers. Mrs. and Mr. Wang needed to put Robin's needs and priorities first. It was the only way the teachers, case managers, and therapists could work with the family.

Mrs. and Mr. Wang realized hiring a consultant was their best approach, since they needed to stop arguing and start parenting. This was something neither of them knew how to do.

In their hearts, they both wanted what was best for Robin, but they were so busy fighting that his educational needs were not being addressed. Thankfully, Mrs. Bono, the educational consultant, was able to teach Mrs. and Mr. Wang how to set their differences aside and put Robin's needs first. She helped them learn how to actively listen to each other—hearing the other person's perspective and building on what each person said.

Through many facilitated conversations, Mrs. and Mr. Wang learned to speak, listen, and then respond. It was about taking turns.

Mrs. Bono put time limits on how long each parent could speak before it was the other person's turn. This process helped Mrs. and Mr. Wang iron out their differences and reach consensus regarding how to best advocate for their son. Once they were on the same page, they were able to form a partnership with their district and also reach consensus on how to best address his educational needs.

Fast forward: Robin graduated from high school at the age of 21. He got a job, had a girlfriend, and started to build a positive relationship with his parents. His future looked optimistic. This was the result of parents working together and putting their child's needs first.

The Alphabet Soup of Education

It is difficult to work together as partners if you don't speak the same language. Like all professions, education has its own language that includes abbreviations, acronyms, and educational terminology. In our experience, many parents find that the *alphabet soup of education* creates a significant communication barrier between home and school. This affects their ability to have meaningful conversations with education professionals regarding their child's academic developments and learning needs.

Since some parents do not understand the educational lingo, we want to heighten teachers' and administrators' awareness that this can lead to communication breakdowns. As is true for all of us, if we don't understand something we become disconnected from the conversation. We probably remain quiet, reluctant to ask questions and ask for clarification. As educators, we might forget that parents don't have the same working knowledge of the jargon, terminology, or educational lingo we are speaking.

We suggest educators try to imagine the conversation from the parents' perspective. In some ways, it is like trying to participate in a conversation in a language where you have a limited vocabulary. Not understanding can be intimidating and may negatively impact trust. Therefore, we suggest school staff take the time to explain the program or service they are suggesting, along with the terminology they are using. Taking the time to do this will go a long way in avoiding miscommunication or misunderstandings and will demonstrate transparency.

Another strategy we believe can help to reduce communication breakdowns is for the school district to create a type of a "cheat sheet" containing easy-to-understand explanations of the terminology connected to an upcoming IEP meeting. We recommend providing this information to parents 24 hours prior to the meeting; then they will have an opportunity to familiarize themselves with the terms and concepts. In addition, we suggest having copies of this "cheat sheet" on the conference table to ensure everyone is speaking the same language. We believe this will help parents be better prepared to participate in the conversation. It will also reduce the chance of a communication breakdown because everyone will be speaking the same language.

Lack of understanding leads to distrust. Sadly, when parents don't understand what is being said, they often conclude the district is not telling them the whole story or the "truth." The goal is for parents and educators to trust each other, not to create suspicion. Again, we want to reiterate that speaking the same language is **key** to working collaboratively and forming partnerships. It also prevents parents from feeling that there is a hidden agenda. This is why it is so important to speak up and ask questions at any point during a conversation if you don't understand something.

In order for parents to navigate the special education process, it is important to develop a common language between home and school. To help bridge this gap, we have provided definitions of educational terms and jargon in the glossary at the end of the book. In addition, there are free resources, such as the State Parent Advocacy Center. Parents can also hire an educational consultant to help them understand the language and the special education process.

Trust Is a Must!

Gabi was 8 years old and in the third grade. She had severe health issues that required the district to develop a health care plan. The plan allowed her to independently leave the classroom and go to the nurse's office whenever she felt sick or wanted to take a nap.

Testing had indicated Gabi was performing about 2 years behind her peers in both reading and math. Her parents, Dr. and Mr. Gilbert, worked alongside her teachers to collaboratively develop a comprehensive program to address her academic concerns, yet Gabi continued to struggle. Dr. and Mr. Gilbert did not think she was making progress and were unsure of her ability to be on track to master her academic goals.

They believed Gabi was in crisis and thought that her academic needs would be best met if she attended a small, private, special education school. The one they had selected offered a nurturing, flexible environment and would provide Gabi with customized services to support her individual needs. However, Dr. and Mr. Gilbert felt certain that their school district would not support the request for outplacement, which meant they had a difficult decision to make.

The parents hired an educational consultant to help them communicate with their district. The consultant understood their perspective. However, she also understood the district's point of view, which was that "outplacement was not necessary." The district believed they were providing Gabi with an appropriate education in the Least Restrictive Environment (LRE).

Gabi's parents wanted her in an out-of-district placement. Should they request an IEP meeting and ask the district to outplace Gabi? Dr. and Mr. Gilbert worried that their request would be refused. If that happened, the question now was "Should they unilaterally place Gabi in the private school and then tell their school district?" In the end, that is what they decided to do.

After unilaterally outplacing their daughter, Dr. and Mr. Gilbert wanted the district to pay the tuition. They asked their consultant to facilitate the conversation. When the team met to discuss the situation, the district's response was that Gabi's parents had been "sneaky." Dr. and Mr. Gilbert broke trust within the parent–educator partnership when they didn't share

continued on next page

their intentions and instead placed Gabi in a private school without telling the district. The educators believed they had done everything to meet Gabi's special education needs as outlined in the IEP. The problem was that there were no data to back up their claim.

On the other hand, Dr. and Mr. Gilbert had data to support their request for a smaller class size, a readily available nurse, and a co-teaching educational model. They had previously shared these documents at Gabi's annual review and felt their requests were not considered.

Dr. and Mr. Gilbert had made their decision to unilaterally place Gabi in a special education school because they did not feel their voice mattered. Therefore, they did not trust the school to listen to their concerns and partner with them regarding addressing Gabi's educational and health needs.

The district accused Gabi's parents of being divisive and "hiding" information.

There was a lack of trust and transparency on the part of both parents and educators.

A few months after Gabi started attending the private school, the educational team at the private school recommended a change in her goals and objectives and increased the amount of one-on-one instruction she should receive. They also recommended that her class placement be changed and wanted to move her from a third-grade class to a second-grade class.

Dr. and Mr. Gilbert didn't want the district to stop paying for her placement, however, they were not in agreement with the changes. They felt they needed help and reluctantly shared all the information from the private school with the home school district.

Dr. and Mr. Gilbert still didn't trust the school district because when Gabi was in crisis they felt the district did nothing. They didn't review the goals and objectives, the amount of special education support, or the type of program she required. They also didn't agree to her outplacement.

The district felt that when Dr. and Mr. Gilbert unilaterally outplaced Gabi, their actions were devious. They outplaced her without having a conversation with any of her teachers or the school administrators. Gabi's parents had not been open to collaborating with the district or trying to find a compromise.

continued on next page

The district's downfall was that they did not have any data to support their belief that Gabi's program and placement were appropriate. Lack of data was the only reason they agreed to pay for her outplacement even though they didn't think it was providing her an education in the LRE.

Over time, the parents and district worked very hard to rebuild trust. The district observed Gabi in her special education school, and Dr. and Mr. Gilbert had several informal conversations. Together they were able to develop a shared vision on how to best meet Gabi's academic and health issues in the LRE. They collaboratively developed a transition plan to bring Gabi back to the district. Mending the break in trust took a lot of hard work on both sides. Trust is dependent on honesty and transparency.

Intended and Unintended Messages

In addition to the *alphabet soup of education,* words, along with vocal and nonverbal communication, send both intended and unintended messages. We all inadvertently send unintended messages, which might be said nonverbally. That is why we want to remind everyone that communication is both *what we say* and *how we say it.* How we communicate affects relationships, trust, and our ability to form partnerships.

Our words, or *what we say,* can cause communication breakdowns, which is what we just discussed related to educators' and administrators' use of educational jargon and terminology. However, most of us are less focused on the impact of *how we say it,* which is more likely to cause misunderstandings and misinterpretations. *How* is related to the vocal aspects of our speech, such as tone and volume, and our nonverbal language, such as hand gestures, facial expressions, and posture. The best way to avoid sending an unintended message is to make sure both *what you say* and *how you say it* send the same message. Otherwise, the listener is going to focus on the *how* and may not remember the *what.*

Did you realize when we shake someone's hand, pat them on the back, or even give them a hug, our body secretes oxytocin—commonly called the trust hormone? Prior to COVID-19, we usually shook hands or made some type of tactile connection when we met someone. Although you might not have realized it, this simple action helped people connect. Now many meetings occur virtually, so this little gesture we took for granted was removed from the equation.

Since it is still important to welcome others and connect, even on a virtual call, everyone needs to learn how to give a "virtual handshake." It is quite easy. As soon as you see others, smile, wave, and look into the camera, which is the virtual version of eye contact. This action helps you connect and is a way to welcome others as they join the call. Did you realize that eye contact increases your level of oxytocin (whether virtual or face-to-face) and decreases your cortisol level? (Cortisol is a hormone that increases when we feel stressed.) Beginning online meetings with a virtual handshake sets a welcoming tone and builds trust, in our opinion.

As is discussed in *Trust Is a Must!,* a breakdown can cause anxiety for both parents and educators. In order to alleviate this anxiety, parents, teachers, and administrators need to have open and honest conversations and use evidence to support their ideas, opinions, or recommendations. We realize that parents and educators may feel that transparency presents risks. For example, administrators do not feel comfortable telling parents exactly what programs the district can and cannot offer the child. Yet this lack of transparency and trust is what often leads to a breakdown in communication and prevents parents and educators from working as partners.

Building trust is part of the shared vision conversation. We suggest the initial IEP conversations focus on deciding what the child needs, rather than identifying which program the district has to offer. This way parents and teachers are collaborating and cooperating as they create a student's IEP.

Trust begins when everyone honestly discusses the concerns and needs of the child. It is also linked to the quality and quantity of data parents and educators provide to support their suggestions. Data not only increase trust but establish transparency and help to decrease anxiety.

The school district in *Trust Is a Must!* did not have data to support their claim that the district's program was appropriate, which was why they had to pay for Gabi's outplacement. We think of data as the cornerstone of a strong partnership and an excellent way to reduce communication breakdowns. It is much harder to argue with facts.

We like to think of conversations as a way to share information and build trust vs. a one-sided rant that causes people to stop listening. We believe that parents may interpret the district's actions as self-serving if teachers and administrators do not encourage them to engage in a dialogue. Trust happens when everyone's input is valued. We agree with Dorothy H. Cohen (2015), educator and author, who suggests no school program will be successful unless parents and teachers act in partnership on behalf of the child's best interests.

Parents trust teachers when they understand what their child is being taught and why. We suggest teachers openly share this information with parents without fearing prejudicial judgment. We also believe it is important for parents to be open and honest with the IEP team at all levels, from what is happening in the home to why they agree or disagree with what is happening at school.

When educators and parents effectively communicate the child wins! Yet, open and honest communication can only happen when there is a high level of mutual trust between home and school. We have found that when educators give parents a voice, they (parents) are more likely to accept the district's proposal. Without a voice, parents may reject an excellent plan. Therefore, we highly recommend including parents in all conversations. If the conversations embrace the importance of the 5-C Model of Communication, the conversations can lead to the formation of a home–school partnership.

We all want to be heard and our ideas to be considered. That is why we encourage educators to listen to what parents have to say, to honestly consider their recommendations. It is also crucial that parents listen to the district's proposals and to reflect on the value of what they are offering. We believe everyone's suggestions represent what, in their opinion, provides the student with the most appropriate program.

Best practice recommends parents and educators operate under the assumption that everyone is being totally truthful, that the evidence they are sharing is accurate. However, if at any point the data show parents or educators are manipulating information to fit their own narrative, trust will be broken. Partnerships rely on mutual respect and total transparency as the best way to ensure the child gets the support and services needed to access the curriculum and be successful.

Honesty is a key factor, which is why we encourage parents to focus on clearly identifying their concerns. Vague references or incomplete and inaccurate information causes their concerns to be less credible. For example, if the child is struggling to complete homework, parents need to accurately explain what is happening, rather than merely say "my child isn't able to do their homework." The ambiguous statement doesn't provide the teacher with enough information to provide insight or support. The same is true when a teacher reports on the student's progress and provides incomplete, inflated, or subjective data. Parents do not place a lot of value in a subjective report saying "your child has made good progress this semester." That is why we highly recommend holding parents and educators to the same standards, whether sharing information or voicing concerns.

Honesty, trust, and transparency are interconnected, which is why the most successful conversations are dependent on total transparency. Whether something is said or written, it must be data driven. We can't stress enough the importance of not exaggerating, omitting information, justifying, or excusing the child's behavior or performance by telling half-truths. Facts don't lie; the use of reliable evidence will help the team make appropriate, objective decisions.

Integrity and respect are core factors that educators, parents, and administrators should use to build and maintain trust. They occur when there are data to back up what is being said or proposed. In a study by De Jong et al. (2016), team performance was found to be directly affected by trust. Therefore, we remind everyone of the importance of evidence. It is the best way to build trust. With trust, the IEP team is ready and willing to co-create an IEP.

> Having open and honest conversations involves both courage and risk.

Perspective-Taking

Parents feel since their understanding of the IEP process is limited, their voices won't be valued. However, since everyone comes with a unique perspective of the child's needs, all voices provide indispensable information. Parents *know their child and how their child performs outside of the classroom and the school day.* Parents bring a different perspective to the IEP team: the home perspective. Their input adds crucial information that helps the team make appropriate programing decisions and recommendations.

Teachers and administrators view the student through a school perspective. They also share information critical to the conversation and decision-making. Only when both parents and educators share their perspectives does the team get a complete and accurate picture of the student. Then everyone's insights, along with objective data, will be used to create a program that addresses the child's unique needs.

Parents (and sometimes educators) report that they *don't know what they don't know.* Some parents reported that due to their lack of knowledge and understanding of the special education process, they struggled to find the right words to communicate with their child's team. This meant they said nothing! Others said they were simply confused so they remained silent. Many families reported there were topics they were reluctant to discuss because they didn't feel like they were a part of the team. In all cases, the parents' perspective impacted their openness and ability to form a home–school partnership on behalf of the child.

Educators also reported there were taboo topics, such as emotional, behavioral, and friendship issues, that they were reluctant to discuss. A lack of trust, honesty, and transparency contributed to everyone's hesitancy to broach certain topics. Yet they are important to understanding the total child and their needs. If conversations aren't open and candid, the home–school relationship may turn adversarial. Of course, when the team doesn't have all of the information, they are less likely to be able to provide the student with appropriate support or services.

We believe there is a direct link between trust and one's ability to effectively communicate. Ineffective or poor communication negatively impacts trust building. That is why we encourage parents to ask questions and educators to be open to listening to the questions and answering them honestly. Some parents are reluctant to ask questions about their child's IEP goals, diagnosis, and/or services. They worry their questions won't be welcomed. They are also concerned that broaching these topics will affect their relationship with the school-based team. We want to reiterate that "questions drive conversations" and "conversations are the gateway to partnerships." The perspective of some educators is that they are the professionals in the room and they know best what the child needs to be successful. We understand that educators may feel their professionalism is challenged when parents question their recommendations. However, from our perspective, questions are what drive the conversation and open up new possibilities. We want to remind the team that everyone, including the parents, is an important team member. That means it is crucial that parents actively participate in all conversations. It is the meeting dialogue that leads to new ideas and the ability for the team to co-create a program and to develop services that may be far better than the ones originally proposed.

We have found that the best decisions emerge from productive conversations. Asking questions and having deep conversations are *always* in the student's best interest. Trust and partnerships require answers that are complete, accurate, and easily understood. A lack of trust discourages participation, which may cause team members to doubt the veracity of what is being said and to question, openly or silently, if the program that is being recommended truly meets the student's needs.

The people, when rightly and fully trusted, will return the trust.
—Abraham Lincoln

When the team forms a partnership, they understand how trust and transparency translate into the embracing of diverse viewpoints that lead creative solutions. When everyone feels they have a voice in the process, or "skin in the game," they are more likely to embrace the perspectives of others. Parents know their child better than anyone else and bring a different, but important, viewpoint to the team, which includes how the child is performing outside of a structured classroom. These important conversations only happen when there is two-way trust.

You're a Lady of Your Word

Julie was diagnosed with high-functioning autism. Her parents, Mr. and Mrs. Andersen, enrolled her in the school district's integrated pre-K program, which they believed would provide the early intervention she needed. When she turned 4, Mr. and Mrs. Andersen felt the district was not addressing Julie's needs. They based this on the limited number of services she was being given: 30 minutes of speech therapy and 30 minutes of occupational therapy weekly.

Mr. and Mrs. Andersen felt the integrated pre-K program and the IEP goals did not appropriately target Julie's language and learning needs. They believed she needed one-on-one instruction throughout her day. Hostility developed between the family and the district, leading Mr. and Mrs. Andersen to unilaterally place Julie in a private special education school. Her daily program consisted of mostly one-on-one support and a variety of therapies. After a battle—but prior to going to due process—the district agreed to fund the out-of-district program and placement.

Julie attended the private special education program for 2 years. Quarterly reports indicated she was making steady progress toward mastering all her goals and objectives. However, after the district reviewed these reports and observed Julie in her out-of-district placement, they unilaterally decided to no longer fund the placement.

Mr. and Mrs. Andersen felt certain the private school was providing Julie with what she needed. They believed she wouldn't make the same level of progress in her home school. Both parents were ready to fight the fight; they were committed to providing Julie with the education she deserved. The district's reason for refusing to pay for the private special education program was because they believed Julie would get a more appropriate program, in a LRE, if she returned to her home school.

At this point, Mr. and Mrs. Andersen hired an educational consultant, Mrs. Cohen. They asked her to review Julie's IEP, observe Julie in her current program, and help them convince the district to continue to fund the out-of-district placement. Mrs. Cohen shared with the family her philosophy, "the child is my client, not the parents." She assured Mr. and Mrs. Andersen that she would assist them in getting their daughter what she believed was necessary.

continued on next page

After meeting with Mr. and Mrs. Andersen, the consultant reviewed past files, observed Julie during several one-on-one therapy sessions, and met with the private school staff. Based on her review of the records and Julie's present level of performance, the consultant determined Julie would be educationally better off in her home school district.

The private placement, which used a one-to-one student teacher ratio, was building dependency rather than fostering independence. Julie appeared to be more capable than the peers she was being paired with. She had no typical peer models, and the curriculum was being taught in a very rote manner. It was not designed to push Julie to develop higher-level thinking skills. Instead, Julie became the model for the other students. Almost all questions were "what" based, rather than asking her to explain her thinking—which she could do.

The consultant met with Mr. and Mrs. Andersen to discuss recommendations. They had many questions. If their daughter returned to the school district, would she be isolated? Would the district be able to develop her socialization skills? They were worried about having her be in a class with typical peers—would these children make fun of her, bully her, or totally reject her? Where was the safety net? The parents held on to their past beliefs that the district would not be able to meet their daughter's educational needs as identified on the IEP.

After Mr. and Mrs. Andersen explained their fears and concerns, Mrs. Cohen asked them to trust her. Together they went to the IEP meeting. They reviewed all the findings, using data to support their statements. Julie had made significant progress over the past 2 years. Mrs. Cohen explained why she thought it was time for Julie to return to her home district. During the meeting, Julie's parents continued to voice their concerns. If they agreed to this plan, how did they know Julie would continue to make progress?

Mrs. Cohen facilitated the conversation, outlining the types of support Julie required and how the district's program could provide those supports in her LRE. She coached the team on how to work as partners, which included having the private school help with the development of the IEP goals and objectives to help with the transition.

Together, parents and educators developed a transition plan, which included the type of data needed to be collected to measure progress.

continued on next page

Mrs. Cohen created a formal and informal meeting schedule that would keep everyone in the loop regarding what was happening at school. She educated the family about the importance of creating a balance between developing the child's independence and giving the child one-to-one support across her entire day.

Mrs. Cohen was slowly able to build Mr. and Mrs. Andersen's confidence and trust using data-driven recommendations. Julie's parents began to understand the educational and social importance of attending a less restrictive program. In the end, the district and parents agreed to trust the consultant's judgment. The district worked with the family to implement recommendations. Through a carefully outlined transition plan, including a thoughtfully developed IEP, Julie successfully returned to the district, made steady and measurable progress, became more independent, and developed a few friendships.

During the last week of school for that academic year, Mr. and Mrs. Andersen called Mrs. Cohen to thank her and say she was "a lady of her word." They said she had asked them to trust her, and in the end they did. They had just left Julie's end-of-the-year IEP meeting, and they shared Julie's successes. Mr. Andersen said Julie had never done that well before. Mrs. Andersen said she had never been so happy. Mr. Andersen voiced his pride in Julie's accomplishments. They ended the conversation with "thank you."

When the parents hung up the phone, they both had tears in their eyes. Julie's parents realized through the development of mutual trust, data-driven working meetings, and a strong home–school partnership, their daughter was the winner!

The Importance of Teamwork

BEST PREDICTOR OF STUDENT SUCCESS—PARENTAL INVOLVEMENT

Research has found that parental involvement is twice as predictive of academic success than socioeconomic status (National Parent Teacher Association, 2000). Thus, it is essential for parents to participate in all aspects of their child's Individualized Education Plan (IEP) development. Participation means sharing of ideas, concerns, and attendance at all meetings. It seems that parents who actively participate in their child's education have a far greater understanding of the special education process. The saying "knowledge is power"

Bud, P. S., & Jacobson, T. L.
*Navigating Special Education: The Power of Building
Positive Parent–Educator Partnerships* (pp. 95-101).
© 2023 SLACK Incorporated.

is quite apparent here. Yet, for many parents, they see their lack of knowledge about the special education process as a major barrier to involvement in their child's education. Since parental involvement is the best predictor of a child's success, we encourage parents to learn as much about the process as possible.

First impressions matter, and it takes no more than 7 seconds to make a first impression. Often parents are brought into the conference room after the school staff has arrived. We want to remind them that they are important members of the IEP team, and it is important that they make a good first impression. We suggest they send a message of confidence, connecting with other team members through a smile and eye contact as they take their place at the table. When speaking at the meeting, their collective verbal and nonverbal message needs to say, "I'm ready and able to actively participate in this meeting." Where and who you sit next to at a meeting can make a difference. We realize that seating arrangements are often not an option. In the best of all possible worlds, conference tables would be round or oval rather than rectangular or square. Then there wouldn't be a head of the table, and we have found that where people sit can affect the tone of a meeting. Often the person who sits at the head of the table directly influences the group's dynamics.

Since we realize circular tables aren't usually an option, we propose educators vary where they sit in meetings and who they next to, as it can affect the power structure of the team. When possible, parents should select a seat in the middle of the table rather than at the end. By sitting in the middle, they are sending a nonverbal message that they want to be integral and approachable team members. Another desirable seat would be next to an administrator, who is often a key IEP decision maker. We also recommend educators and parents change where they sit from meeting to meeting. It is an easy way for everyone to feel they are on equal footing and see themselves as equal members of the IEP team.

It is important that everyone understands the roles and responsibilities of those attending the meeting. If parents are unsure why a person is attending the IEP meeting, it is okay to ask their name and job title. Best practice suggests everyone introduces themselves at the beginning of very meeting. It helps parents become familiar with all of the IEP team members. We also recommended parents introduce themselves to the school team. We believe introductions are a great way to get to know each other, which is a first step in building partnerships and developing a sense of community. It is important for parents to introduce themselves to the school team, since introductions are a great way to get to know each other and the first step in building partnerships and a sense of community.

ROLES AND RESPONSIBILITIES OF THE INDIVIDUALIZED EDUCATION PLAN TEAM MEMBERS

Board Attorney

They advise the school administer on special education law and protocols.

School Administrator/Director of Special Education or Special Services

They oversee the special education department and advise the school board and superintendent on all special education programing, services, and fiscal responsibilities.

Case Manager

Special education teacher, social worker, or psychologist who assumes responsibility for ensuring everything written in the IEP is correctly recorded and carried out with efficacy.

Classroom Teacher

Child's current general education teacher. Responsible for reporting on the child's current academic, behavioral, and social-emotional level of performance in the classroom. All information should be objective and data driven (test scores, writing samples, math quizzes, etc.).

Special Education Teacher

A teacher with special education certification who provides academic special education instruction. Delivery of services depends on the program: coteacher model, self-contained teacher, or push-in/inclusion model.

School Psychologist

The school psychologist conducts IEP testing, offers one-to-one counseling to students and parents, and provides input and instruction on social-emotional issues. They are able to interpret and explain the implications of all testing: cognitive, academic, and social-emotional.

Social Worker

In many districts, the social worker acts as the case manager. They address parent and student psychological and social issues and are the conduit between school, parent, and outside agencies. They often assist families when considering an out-of-district placement.

Physical Therapist

They assess, report, and develop goals and provide physical therapy for students identified as needing physical therapy services on an ongoing basis.

Occupational Therapist

They can assess, report on, develop goals, and provide direct occupational therapy for students identified as needing occupational therapy services on an ongoing basis.

Speech-Language Pathologist

The speech-language pathologist assesses, reports on, develops goals, and provides speech and language therapy for students identified as needing speech services on an ongoing basis.

School Nurse

Collaborates with the district's physician, reads recommendations from the student's primary physician and specialists, and creates an individual health plan to present to the family and their physician for approval. The school nurse is the keeper of this plan, which is stored securely and kept confidential.

Special Teachers (Art, Music, Library, Physical Education)

They report on the progress of students who attend their general education classes in relation to general education peers and their goals. They work in conjunction with a special education student's one-on-one aide or co-teacher to ensure they are included in general education art, music, library, and physical education. Adaptive special education classes may be created when needed.

Parents and Students

Parents should attend all IEP meetings and be prepared to articulate and advocate on behalf of their child. Students over the age of 13 should attend all IEP meetings when/if they are able to articulate their concerns and advocate for the programs and services needed, including specialized accommodations and modifications.

WILLINGNESS TO COMPROMISE SCALE

An important part of the 5-C Model of Communication is compromise. When differences of opinion drive the discussions, the way to reach consensus is through compromise. It also leads to the team's ability to co-create, since built into compromises are new possibilities. When everyone listens with an open mind, what they hear may spark an idea or provide insight into how to modify what is currently being proposed. We like to think of conversations as a springboard to compromise.

We recommend everyone remains open and willing to give in a little and make some concessions. We discourage parents, educators, or administrators from digging their heels in and refusing to compromise. It accomplishes nothing. No one really wins in that situation. What is most important is to listen and understand the other person's perspective. This sends a clear message that you are open to the possibility of compromise.

Using a "start at the end" philosophy can be a great strategy for reaching a compromise. Where do you want to end up? How do you hope to solve the problem? Too often parents and educators begin with defining the problem, then identifying the child's needs rather than focusing on solutions. *What do you want the end result to be? What does the student **need** in order to be successful?* Once the end game is established, then the IEP team should find it easier to reach a consensus on how to get there. Of course, it might mean everyone needs to compromise a little.

By considering the end game at the beginning, it allows all team members to stay focused on what they hope to accomplish. Success requires listening, not just hearing the words, but understanding the intent as to what everyone's thinking and saying. It means maintaining an open mind at all times, collaborating and cooperating in order to be open to compromise, which will result in consensus.

We cannot stress enough the importance of parents and educators remaining open to compromise. This means being willing to have difficult conversations. Embracing the 5-C Model of Communication provides the team with tools and strategies and the ability to negotiate respectfully. We believe having a collaborative mindset means being willing to compromise. By embracing this philosophy, everyone demonstrates an awareness that compromise might be required before consensus can be reached.

We want to share with you the Willingness to Compromise Scale, which originally appeared in the *Journal of Career Assessment* (Wee, 2013). The purpose of the scale was to provide a reliable and valid way to measure a person's readiness to compromise. The scale's original use was related to making career decisions. However, the scale, which was also used in the workplace, was able to predict and demonstrate an understanding of career-related decisions because it measures personality traits such as regret, dealing with uncertainty, and career adaptability.

We suggest parents, administrators, and educators step back and look at their own readiness to compromise when faced with situational dilemmas. We know there is a strong possibility that at some point team members will be asked to compromise. By using the compromise scale, you can self-reflect as to the degree to which you are open to compromise. This scale looks at both positive and negative feelings toward compromise, and how you feel about changing your preliminary opinions. The Willingness to Compromise Scale can also help everyone to understand how prepared they are to work together and reach an agreeable compromise.

Where Are You on the Compromise Scale?

The questions below will help you find the answer (Wee, 2013).

- Are you someone who avoids conflict?
- Do you try to accommodate the other person?
- Do you think your ideas are competing?
- Do you see yourself as highly assertive or aggressive?

Think about your answers to these questions as they relate to the chart. Do your answers pave the way for collaboration and compromise, or do they create roadblocks? We suggest parents and educators try to move their "willingness" in the direction of compromise, because it is often the only way a team can reach consensus (Figure 8-1).

A willingness to compromise affects decision-making. This scale visually highlights a person's willingness to compromise by looking at the degree of assertiveness or cooperation (from low to high) and what they do when presented with the need to compromise. The most successful compromises occur when everyone is either accommodating or collaborating. When collaborating, everyone is more assertive; when accommodating, everyone is more cooperative.

Figure 8-1. Willingness to Compromise Scale. (Adapted from Wee, S. [2013]. Development and initial validation of the Willingness to Compromise Scale. *Journal of Career Assessment, 21*[4], 487-501. https://doi.org/10.1177/1069072712475281)

PART II

ANALYSIS OF AN IEP

I Do Not Like These IEPs

Do you like these IEPs? I do not like these IEPs.
I do not like them, Jeez Louise.
We test, we check, we plan, we meet, but nothing ever seems complete.

Would you, could you like the form?
I do not like the form I see. Not page one, not two, not three.
Another change, a brand new box, I think we all have lost our rocks.

Could you all meet here or there?
We could not all meet here or there. We cannot all fit anywhere.
Not in a room. Not in a hall. There seems to be no space at all.

Would you, could you meet again?
I cannot meet again next week. No lunch, no prep. Please hear me speak.
No, not at dusk and not at dawn. At 4 p.m. I should be gone.

Could you hear while all speak out? Would you write the words they spout?
I could not hear, I would not write. This does not need to be a fight.
Sign here, date there, mark this, check that, beware the student's
ad-vo-cat(e),

You do not like them so you say.
Try it again! Try it again! And then you may.
If you let me be, I'll try again and you will see.

Say!
I almost like these IEPs. I think I'll write 6003.
And I will practice day and night. Until they say, "You've got it right."

—Author Unknown

9

IEPs Versus 504 Plans

An IEP and a 504 Plan are legally binding documents that outline how a child with a disability receives educational services. The major difference is an IEP outlines the child's entire special education experience and a 504 Plan outlines the accommodations and modifications a student receives to remove barriers to learning.

Bud, P. S., & Jacobson, T. L.
*Navigating Special Education: The Power of Building
Positive Parent–Educator Partnerships* (pp. 107-116).
© 2023 SLACK Incorporated.

THE INDIVIDUALS WITH DISABILITIES EDUCATION ACT

It is important to understand the history of the Individuals with Disabilities Education Act (IDEA) and the due process relevance for both educators and parents. One of the key concepts presented in IDEA is the protection given to students with disabilities, which guarantees a Free Appropriate Public Education (FAPE) with neurotypical peers in the Least Restrictive Environment (LRE). Please note that IDEA only applies to public school students.

In 1975, Congress passed the Education for All Handicapped Children Act (initially referred to as Public Law 94-142). This bill aimed to ensure children with disabilities would be afforded the same opportunity to receive FAPE as their typically developing peers. Again, these statutes only apply to students who attend public schools. A private school is not held accountable to the regulations outlined in IDEA, because they do not receive federal money. Only when a school receives federal funding are they eligible for both the benefits and scrutiny of IDEA.

In 1990, this law was amended and renamed the Individuals with Disabilities Education Act, commonly referred to as IDEA. The law has been updated and revised several times to reflect our changing education system. In 2015, it was amended through Public Law 114-95 and called Every Student Succeeds Act (U.S. Department of Education, 2022).

SUMMARY OF THE SPECIAL EDUCATION LAW

An Individualized Education Plan (IEP) provides a student with a disability an individualized program to address their unique educational needs. The student must have a disability, the disability needs to be preventing the student from accessing their learning environment, and it must require specialized instruction. Special education services provide both academic and related service support, such as speech therapy, occupational therapy, physical therapy, and assistive technology. All aspects of the special education program are provided to the student free of charge.

Although all students with disabilities in the United States are granted the right to special education services, each state has the right to interpret the law. This means that special education may look slightly different from state to state. We realize that this might cause parents to be confused or frustrated if they move to a different state. What is crucial to know is that a state cannot provide a student with less than what is outlined in the law. However, it is legally acceptable for the state to provide the student more.

The tone and intent of the federal law must be the same at the state level, although it may look different state by state. The law says that *every school district provides all identified students with an appropriate program in the LRE.* However, there are some aspects of the IEP process that are not up for state interpretation, such as who serves on the IEP team. The federal law is very clear that parents are required to be members of the IEP team and that decisions cannot be made without their knowledge and input (IDEA, 2004). IDEA also requires parental consent, in writing, before the district is allowed to evaluate the student and before implementing the IEP. There are also guidelines as to how parents can resolve disputes, which include mediation, due process, lawsuits, and state complaints and are explained in the Procedural Safeguards document.

Disability and exceptionality are terms that are sometimes confused as they are related to special education, yet it should be noted that these terms are not interchangeable. The word disability is used to refer to any of the 13 categories of physical or mental impairment identified in IDEA. However, when a child's exceptionality is referred to, it means the student's assets and deficits. Although gifted and talented students may not have a disability, they may require individualized education or specific teaching strategies to address their high level of performance. In some school districts an IEP is developed for gifted students as well as students with a specific disability.

INDIVIDUALIZED EDUCATION PLAN

Before the IEP team develops an individual educational plan, they are required to determine the student's disability (U.S. Department of Education, 2000). This is done through formal educational, psychological, and sometimes medical assessments, along with anecdotal observations and work samples. The IEP team uses the results of the evaluation along with checklists to determine a student has one of 13 categories of disabilities. Federal law IDEA (2004) identifies the following categories: (1) Autism Spectrum Disorder, (2) Deaf-Blindness, (3) Developmental Delay (3- to 5-year-olds only), (4) Emotional Disturbance, (5) Hearing Impairment (deaf or hard of hearing), (6) Intellectual Disability, (7) Multiple Disabilities, (8) Orthopedic Impairment, (9) Other Health Impairment (includes attention-deficit/hyperactivity disorder [ADD/ADHD]), (10) Specific Learning Disability, (11) Speech or Language Impairment, (12) Traumatic Brain Injury, and (13) Vision Impairment.

Determining disability includes identifying areas of concern affecting the child's ability to perform academically, social-emotionally, and/or behaviorally. It also means identifying how these concerns are affecting the student's ability to access the curriculum. Lastly, the team identifies the type of specialized instruction the student requires due to the identified disability. It is at this point that the IEP team determines eligibility for special education.

Once the team determines eligibility, it is incumbent that the team develop an IEP. This document outlines the customized program and comprehensive services the student requires in order to successfully participate in their school day. Although IEPs may look different, on paper, from state to state, they always contain the same core sections: present level of performance in academic, behavioral, and social-emotional areas; measurable goals and objectives; service hours for both special education instruction and related services such as physical therapy, speech therapy, or occupational therapy; location of services; and educational teaching model. This information will be discussed in more detail in other parts of the book.

We want parents to know the IEP is a legally binding document that drives their child's program and services. If parents move to a different town or state, the district is required to continue to deliver the IEP, as written, until the new district convenes an IEP meeting. The team will discuss the current IEP and determine how to best address the student's needs in the new district. Changes may occur because the type of programs and services vary from district to district.

Once the IEP is developed and agreed upon, the district is required to deliver it to the student with efficacy. All IEPs are written for 1 year and must be reviewed and updated annually. However, if at any time during the school year parents or educators believe the IEP is not addressing the student's needs, they must request an IEP meeting. The purpose of the meeting is to review and revise the current document.

IDEA also requires a student to be reassessed at least once every 3 years, which includes re-determining disability and eligibility for special education services (U.S. Department of Education, 2022). This assessment is often called a triennial review. It is important to understand that a student's disability and/or the reason they require special education services may change from year to year. It is worth noting that some children have more than one disability. The IEP team is required to determine which disability is driving the child's primary need for special education and that disability is what is listed on the cover of the IEP. If during the assessment/reassessment process, there is not enough information to determine a student's disability or eligibility, yet the team continues to suspect a disability, we suggest the IEP team requests additional testing.

SECTION **504** OF
AMERICANS WITH DISABILITIES ACT

We want parents and educators to be aware that all students who qualify for special education are protected under Section 504 of the Rehabilitation Act of 1973. This act protects anyone with a disability from discrimination. The 1990 Americans with Disabilities Act provided civil rights protection to anyone with a disability and barred discrimination against them, whether in private industry, higher education, or the government, due to their disability. Unlike IDEA, this law is not specific to students who attend public school (2004).

Section 504 outlines the rights of students with disabilities. It specifically states, "No otherwise qualified individual with a disability in the United States … shall, solely by reason of her or his disability, be excluded from participation in, be denied the benefits of, or be subjected to discrimination under any program or activity receiving Federal financial assistance …" (Rehabilitation Act, 1973). The purpose of Section 504 is to provide accommodations to students with disabilities by removing obstacles that prevented them from accessing the curriculum or participating in school-sponsored activities.

Before a student is found eligible for 504 accommodations, the team has to identify a documented mental or physical disability that substantially interferes with their ability to learn in a general education classroom and limits one or more major life activities such as seeing, hearing, learning, communicating, concentrating, speaking, reading, or thinking (Rehabilitation Act, 1973). Examples of disabilities that might impact a student's ability to receive FAPE include hearing impairment, mild dyslexia, ADD/ADHD, or medical conditions such as allergies, asthma, epilepsy, cancer, diabetes, or mental illness. Sometimes school districts create a 504 Plan when a child returns to school following an injury or illness and requires specific accommodations needed to access the school environment (U.S. Department of Education, 2020).

504 Plan

The 504 Plan is a blueprint for giving students with disabilities accommodations. These students require specific accommodations to address barriers (in the classroom and in school-sponsored activities) in order to ensure successful participation in general education classes (U.S. Department of Education, 2020). Examples of accommodations include physical modifications, such as wheelchair ramps and handrails; policy modifications, such as snacks for students with diabetes to fidget toys for those with ADD/ADHD; learning aids, such as calculators, iPads, FM systems; classroom modifications, such as enlarged print, extended time on assignments and tests, and preferential seating; or oral testing. Once in a while a one-on-one aide is considered to be an accommodation because the person helps the student participate in school sports or after-school activities. Examples of barriers include focusing, hearing loss, severe illness, visual impairments, and difficulties with daily organizational skills.

A team develops the 504 Plan, which consists of the school's 504 coordinator and teachers, parents, and the student, when appropriate. It is important to be aware that a 504 team's composition may vary depending on the type of disability and could include the principal and support staff such as a counselor, social worker, school nurse, speech therapist, or occupational therapist (U.S. Department of Education, 2020).

A 504 Plan is developed for a student with a disability that requires a specific type of accommodations. These include medical accommodations, classroom accommodations to ensure access to the curriculum, instructional accommodations, testing accommodations, or some type of communication plan (Rehabilitation Act, 1973). As part of the identification process, the 504 team reviews the child's records, grades, behavior charts, communication books, and any modifications or accommodations that have been tried and then determines the specific barriers that are preventing the student from being able to participate (equally) in a general education classroom. Like the IEP, the 504 Plan must be reviewed and updated each school year (U.S. Department of Education, 2020).

INDIVIDUALIZED EDUCATION PLAN VERSUS 504 PLAN

Similarities and Differences Between a 504 Plan and an Individualized Education Plan

Similarities

Both plans are designed to ensure that students with documented disabilities are able to fully participate in programs and activities with typically developing peers to the maximum extent possible. Federal laws, which states interpret, drive both the 504 Plan and the IEP and provide protections to the student as well as identify how parents can resolve disputes or disagreements with their school district. Some parents ask if a 504 Plan is a prerequisite for an IEP or if parents can choose which one the student receives. The answer is "no" to both questions.

Another similarity is that both a 504 Plan and an IEP require that the student has a documented disability. In both cases, parents are members of the team that develops each program. However, eligibility is not a parental decision or choice—it is a team decision. Parents are always key members of the team and have a voice in the process (Office of the Student Advocate, n.d.).

Overall Differences

A student is eligible for an IEP when they have a documented disability or are struggling to access the general education curriculum and require specialized instruction. On the other hand, a student is eligible to receive a 504 Plan when they have a documented disability and require accommodations to overcome barriers that are affecting their ability to successfully participate in the general education classroom (Office of the Student Advocate, n.d.).

In both cases, a student with a disability is ensured access to FAPE. Often checklists are used to assist the team in reviewing the documentation, determining eligibility, and the developing an education plan.

Individualized Education Plan

A subtle but important difference is that IDEA's procedural requirements drive an IEP; these requirements clearly and specifically outline every step of the process. IEP services are for students from age 3 through high school graduation or age 21, if indicated due to their disability. The law dictates all aspects of the child's program, from eligibility to the monitoring of progress. To be eligible for an IEP, the student must have one of the 13 disabilities identified under IDEA (2004). Their disability must significantly affect their educational performance, their ability to learn and benefit from the general education curriculum, and require specialized instruction.

One of the major differences between an IEP and a 504 Plan is students with IEPs require *specialized instruction,* which means they need to be taught differently (U.S. Department of Education, 2000). The student's educational program and specialized instruction is determined through targeted goals and objectives. Progress on goals and objectives must be measured and reported to parents at least as frequently as progress is reported to all parents in the school.

The IEP describes the teaching model that will be used to address the student's individual needs. It also identifies where teaching and learning will take place. A student with an IEP may receive their academic instruction outside of the inclusive classroom. The IEP also states specific modifications and accommodations required to address the student's learning environment (U.S. Department of Education, 2000).

Does My Child Require an IEP or a 504 Plan?

Scenario #1

Mrs. and Mr. Murphy noticed that their son Harry seemed to be easily distracted and was struggling completing his homework. They were concerned he had ADHD. They thought he might also have some executive functioning difficulties because he seemed to be disorganized.

What did this mean? Was his distractibility happening in the classroom? Was it affecting his school performance? Did what they see at home mean that Harry's recent difficulties were going to require specialized instruction? Did he need some accommodations to help him remain focused and organized? Should Harry be evaluated for special education?

We suggest the first thing parents do if they have concerns is to set up a meeting with their child's teacher and/or the school psychologist. We recommend parents bring some concrete evidence that supports their concerns to begin the conversation. Mrs. and Mr. Murphy could make a short video of Harry doing his homework. They could also keep a chart to record how long he can attend to a task before losing focus, bring a photo of Harry's messy room, and/or share samples of homework or classwork that is of concern to the parents.

Providing this concrete evidence helps the parents and teacher have a meaningful conversation. By being open and transparent, the teacher is less likely to feel that the parents are casting blame. Honest home–school conversations are the best way to build a partnership and work collaboratively and cooperatively with the teacher.

The question is does the teacher see the same things happening at school? Sometimes they do and sometimes they don't. What is key is for parents and teachers to brainstorm strategies. If the teacher is already trying things, especially if they are working, it would be helpful for the parents to implement the same strategies at home.

Since a 504 Plan requires a documented disability, we suggest Mrs. and Mr. Murphy get professional support to determine if Harry has ADHD. They could reach out to their pediatrician, the school or private

continued on next page

psychologist, or a therapist regarding an ADHD diagnosis. In most cases, determining ADHD is done by using standardized checklists.

An executive function diagnosis requires a licensed psychologist to conduct formalized testing. If parents suspect this type of disability, it is helpful to collect evidence that supports their concerns before reaching out to the teacher. If the teacher sees the same concerns at school and strategies are not working, we suggest Mrs. and Mr. Murphy discuss having Harry evaluated. This would require convening an IEP meeting and requesting the school district do a comprehensive evaluation to determine if Harry has a documented disability that requires specialized instruction or if his disability merely requires specific accommodations.

Scenario #2

Emma and Ivan Roman wanted to know if their daughter, Brenda, who was a fourth grader with a documented moderate bilateral hearing loss, required special education or a 504 Plan. Each year, Brenda is finding it increasingly more difficult to understand large group instructions and to socialize with her peers.

During a parent–teacher conference, the parents and classroom teacher discussed their concerns. Brenda already has a documented disability. The parents wanted to discuss how a 504 Plan could provide their daughter with specific accommodations to help her successfully learn in the inclusive classroom setting.

Since Brenda has an identified disability, we suggest parents discuss with the classroom teacher her overall academic performance. The question is whether Brenda needs some specific accommodations or specialized instruction to be better able to participate in class. If the teacher believes that Brenda only needs accommodations, a 504 meeting should be convened. If there is a question as to whether she requires specialized instruction, Emma and Ivan should request an IEP meeting. Then the team can discuss whether a comprehensive evaluation is indicated, based on whether they suspect Brenda's disability requires special education services.

In either case, we want to remind teachers and parents that it is crucial to bring data to either a 504 or IEP meeting. Data will help the team review the current accommodations and strategies being used to determine

continued on next page

how to best meet the student's needs. Since it was Brenda's parents who brought the concern to the teacher, any documentation from home that they have gathered would be extremely helpful to the team. The goal is to pinpoint how she is struggling during large group instruction due to her bilateral hearing loss and what has already been tried. It is important to have documentation regarding what is working and what isn't.

504 Plan

On the other hand, a 504 Plan is developed for a student who has an identified disability and *only* requires accommodations to access the inclusive classroom setting. A student with a 504 Plan does not require specialized instruction. This plan provides accommodations for any student from kindergarten through college. Accommodations may be required for the student's total education or may be needed for a specific period of time. A 504 Plan outlines not only the accommodations but how they will be provided in order to ensure the student's equal access to the general education classroom and curriculum. These accommodations do not remove the student from the general education classroom (U.S. Department of Education, 2020).

Although students eligible for a 504 Plan have a documented disability, they are on a broader spectrum—so the 13 disabilities identified by IDEA do not dictate their eligibility. What *is* necessary is that their educational needs require and can be met solely through accommodations; they do not require specialized instruction (U.S. Department of Education, 2020). Examples of 504 disabilities also include severe allergies, ADD/ADHD, epilepsy, executive functioning disorder, and some physical disabilities such as hearing loss and visual impairment.

A 504 Plan may be created for short-term use because a student requires accommodations due to illness or injury (U.S. Department of Education, 2020). Examples include broken bones that require a wheelchair, crutches, use of the school elevator, or support of a scribe. Sometimes a severe illness may require the development of a 504 Plan to provide short-term accommodations such as snack breaks or a shortened school day. Other times, the 504 Plan is a long-term approach that provides specific accommodations to help the student overcome barriers that are preventing them from successfully accessing the general education classroom.

10

Fair Access

The Importance of an Individualized Education Plan

The Individualized Education Plan (IEP) team is responsible for developing the IEP—the legal document that drives the student's special education program. It consists of goals and objectives, type of services and hours required for each service, and modifications and accommodations. The Individuals with Disabilities Education Act (IDEA) states the document should be written at the IEP meeting with input from teachers and parents. The school-based team may bring a draft IEP to the meeting with the intent of using it to drive the

Bud, P. S., & Jacobson, T. L.
Navigating Special Education: The Power of Building
Positive Parent–Educator Partnerships (pp. 117-141).
© 2023 SLACK Incorporated.

discussion. However, there needs to be a clear understanding that the document is a draft and will be edited based on the input of parents and staff, which includes conversations related to the student's present level of performance.

In many cases, the draft IEP outlines the student's present level of performance and how areas of weakness are impacting their ability to access the curriculum. In many cases, the school-based team probably includes suggested goals and objectives. However, IDEA is very clear that a majority of the IEP needs to be written at the IEP meeting.

Best practice recommends the district provide parents with a copy of the draft goals and objectives prior to the IEP meeting. If parents haven't seen the proposed goals, it is more difficult for them to process what is being recommended. This is what happened in the case study *I Didn't Know What I Was Agreeing To* in Chapter 6. Mr. Rogers and Mr. McNeil were reluctant to trust the district's recommendations because they had not received the goals and objectives prior to the IEP meeting. If draft goals are provided, which can and probably will be edited at the meeting, the district is creating a level of transparency. This leads to a higher level of trust and a meeting where everyone is part of the decision-making process. It also demonstrates that all team members understand they are morally and legally obligated to work together to create an appropriate IEP for the student.

INDIVIDUALIZED EDUCATION PLAN

Stakeholders in Attendance

IDEA is very clear about who must be in attendance at any IEP meeting. For that reason, all IEP meetings begin with recording the names of all those in attendance and their titles, which appears on the cover of the IEP. Usually there is a sheet that all those in attendance sign. *Educators and a parent or guardian must be present at all IEP meetings, otherwise the meeting is not considered to be a "legal" meeting.*

Here are possible team people who could be in attendance:

- An administrator or administrative designee in the role of meeting facilitator
- A general education and a special education teacher
- At least one pupil services representative (e.g., psychologist, speech pathologist, occupational therapist, physical therapist, guidance counselor, or social worker)
- Parent(s) of the child

- Students between the ages of 12 and 21 are invited to every IEP meeting, and it is recommended they attend
- Students 18 years or older retain all rights the parents had *(unless parents obtain legal guardianship),* and they must attend the IEP meeting or it is not a legal meeting (IDEA, 2004; U.S. Department of Education, 2000)

Frequency of Meetings

IDEA requires that an IEP meeting be held at least once a year. The meeting is referred to as the child's annual review. The purpose of the meeting is to review the student's progress, to review or revise the program, and to develop new goals and objectives. In some cases, monitoring progress and adjusting the program, services, or goals may need to happen more frequently, quarterly or semi-annually. IDEA also requires that at least once every 3 years the student is reassessed to redetermine eligibility and disability. This is referred to as the student's triennial review.

We encourage parents to request to meet with their child's teacher or case manager if they have questions, concerns, or want to discuss progress between IEP meetings. Having open and ongoing dialogues between parents and educators is the best way to build partnerships. The IEP team may recommend these meetings be outlined in the IEP or they may occur at the request of the parents or teachers at different points during the year. We like to think of these meetings as either team meetings or conferences because the purpose is to discuss progress, but not to change the IEP. Some districts allow minor changes they call amendments to be made outside of an IEP meeting with parental approval. However, in most cases and in most districts, all changes to the IEP must be made at a legally convened IEP meeting.

Procedural Safeguards

At the beginning of every IEP meeting, parents are asked if they have gotten a copy of their Procedural Safeguards and "if they have any questions regarding their rights." This is standard protocol and we recommend parents take this question very seriously.

If parents want to find out more information about the components of Procedural Safeguards, they can visit the U.S. government site https://sites.ed.gov/idea/regs/b/e/300.504. Parents can also locate a copy of the Procedural Safeguards for their state by going to their State Board of Education website and typing in Procedural Safeguards for Special Education. For example, Connecticut parents would visit the link https://portal.ct.gov/-/media/SDE/Special-Education/Prosaf.pdf.

Procedural Safeguards are given to parents at the beginning of the special education process because they outline their parental rights. According to the law, parents are supposed to receive a copy of the document at least once a year. Many districts send them with an invitation to the student's annual review IEP meeting. This varies from state to state and district to district; in some districts they are sent prior to all in-person meetings.

Although the Procedural Safeguards document is filled with important information, it is unfortunately written in legalese and uses a lot of educational jargon. It can be intimidating, difficult to understand, confusing, and even overwhelming. However, we recommend all parents read it in its entirety and ask questions when they don't understand something. Most parents receive a copy of their Procedural Safeguards even before the first IEP meeting is convened.

According to IDEA (2004), all states must provide parents with their Procedural Safeguards in writing. This document, which is not part of the IEP, outlines the regulations that protect the rights of children with disabilities (and their families) and ensures students with disabilities have access to a Free Appropriate Public Education (FAPE). The Procedural Safeguards document outlines the parent's role and rights in the IEP process and provides information on how to resolve disputes if they occur.

In addition to parents, sometimes general education teachers are only marginally familiar with the IEP process and find the procedures confusing. That is why we cannot stress enough the importance of everyone understanding the language, jargon, and the inner workings of the special education process. Knowledge is what assists the team in working collaboratively on behalf of the child. We recommend that teachers and administrators read the document to ensure they understand the parents' rights.

In addition, we suggest an administrator meets with parents outside of the IEP meeting to explain the document and the special education process prior to the parents attending their first IEP meeting. We envision this as a short, one-on-one meeting that is not currently part of any school district's protocols. It is our own concept, which we believe to be best practice. It is an easy way to introduce parents to the language, procedures, and protocols of special education. The meeting would reduce the parents' anxiety and be a first step in building a home–school partnership. Parents would then be better prepared to actively participate in their first IEP meeting.

Even if parents are prepared to attend an IEP meeting, we know they will probably have lots of questions. We cannot emphasize enough that *asking questions is **not** a sign of weakness*. We encourage parents to ask questions at all IEP and school meetings. It is the best way to learn about the process and the only way to actively participate as vital and vocal members of the team.

The Procedural Safeguards recognize that parents are a part of the IEP team. We suggest as a way to ensure all meetings maintain a collaborative tone, educators and administrators periodically reinforce the importance of the parents' voices by welcoming and encouraging their questions and urging them to voice their concerns. Then the IEP meeting becomes a conversation, which we see as another step to building positive parent–educator partnerships.

We know the special education process is complicated, and since most school districts do not invite parents to a pre-IEP meeting, we suggest they contact their school district and request to meet with an administrator or the case manager prior to attending their first formal IEP meeting. Again, this meeting would prepare parents, reduce anxiety, and ensure they were able to actively participate in the IEP meeting. We also want to remind parents that it is crucial to continue to ask questions and get clarification at every IEP meeting. There is always something new to learn or something that needs to be clarified or more clearly explained.

Note: If parents do not receive a copy of their Procedural Safeguards, we encourage them to contact their school and request one. We also encourage families to ask questions about their rights. We want to emphasize that receiving a Procedural Safeguards document is mandatory (Bureau of Special Education, 2021). A copy of "Parents Procedural Safeguards" can be found on every state education website. Some parents contact an educational consultant to answer their questions and get an unbiased, detailed explanation.

In many states, this document is available in both English and Spanish. We suggest if English is not the parents' first language, they reach out to the director of guidance in their school district and request a copy be translated into their native language. We remind districts to make sure that a translator is available to assist parents at IEP meetings when they are not fluent in English. If parents don't fully understand what is being said because English isn't their first language, they will not be able to actively participate in the IEP meeting (Bureau of Special Education, 2021). Administrators are aware of the fact that getting and paying for translators is sometimes costly or difficult. We recommend creating a list of school staff who speak multiple languages and can assist parents at meetings as translators.

In summary, in addition to outlining parents' rights and how they can exercise due process, the Procedural Safeguards document reinforces the right of every parent to participate in all meetings, to examine all educational records, and to obtain an Independent Educational Evaluation (IEE) for their child if they disagree with the findings of the district's assessment. Parents also have the right to a written notice when the school proposes to refuse to change the identification, evaluation, or placement of a child (Wrightslaw, 2019).

We want to emphasize that if parents disagree with how their school district is meeting their child's needs, they can and should exercise any of the procedures outlined in the document. The law allows up to 2 years following a dispute to file for due process. Once the family files for due process, "stay-put" will go into effect, which means the student continues in the program and placement they are currently attending until the dispute is resolved. Although there are legal procedures that parents can follow to address disputes, we believe the quickest and most effective way to resolve disputes is by forming parent–educator partnerships.

Individualized Education Plan Meetings

In the case study *How Is My Child Reading?*, Sammy's parents initiated an IEP meeting. They were not aware that requesting an evaluation started the special education process. The school-based team probably thought his parents understood the process, since along with an invitation to an IEP meeting, Sammy's parents received a copy of their Procedural Safeguards. As reflected in the case study, his parents did not understand the process or their rights. (This is why we are recommending a pre-IEP meeting before the first IEP meeting.) In most cases, parents feel intimidated and/or they don't know what they don't know and so they do not contact the school to ask for clarification.

Parents and educators have the right to initiate an IEP meeting at any time and for any reason. Requesting an evaluation is just one of the many reasons. Other reasons include referral for special education services, (re-)evaluations or reviewing evaluations, annual review of the child's program, and developing and revising the IEP. It is important to note that no change can be made to a student's IEP outside of an official IEP meeting. Therefore, if any team member, including parents, believe the child's current plan needs to be revised, they should request an IEP meeting.

No matter who initiates the meeting or why it is being called, the school district always schedules the meeting and sends a formal invitation to the parents and all members of the child's educational team. The purpose of the meeting must be stated on the invitation. (See Appendix for a sample invitation to an IEP meeting.) If a parent requests a meeting, the reason is listed as "parent request." It is incumbent on parents or educators, when they suspect a student requires special education services, to begin the "special education process" by requesting an IEP meeting.

The purpose of the initial IEP meeting is to discuss concerns that appear to be preventing the student from successfully accessing the curriculum. If the team agrees that they suspect the student has a disability that requires special education services, they will design an evaluation. The results of the evaluation will be used to help the team determine eligibility.

In the case study *How Is My Child Reading?*, Sammy's parents suspected he had a disability so they requested an evaluation. The problem was they did not understand the special education process. In addition, they were not aware of the need to provide the team with evidence that supported their concerns. Sometimes concerns are observable, which we call "red flags." These issues are another reason to suspect a disability that might require special education services and, of course, a reason to request an IEP meeting.

Coming to an IEP meeting prepared means bringing evidence that documents concerns, demonstrates the student's strengths, or highlights successes related to academic, social-emotional, or behavioral performance. All data drive the conversation about *what might be impacting the child's ability to successfully perform in school?* If Sammy's parents and/or the teacher had provided data, the meeting would not have turned adversarial. It is hard to argue with clear documentation. It is also important to recognize that a student may perform differently at home than at school. If this is the case, the IEP team needs to unpack what is happening and why.

Observable Factors That Could Trigger Requesting an Individualized Education Plan Meeting

- Failing grades, significant regression academically, school avoidance, or any dramatic change in academic or social-emotional behavior
- Depression or self-injurious behavior
- Display of irregular social-emotional behavior, inappropriate language, or avoidance behavior
- Poor eating habits or use of substances such as vapes, drugs, alcohol
- Behavioral changes linked to dislike of school, parents, siblings, and friends
- Consistent crying or rolling on the floor

Setting the Stage: Everyone Has a Voice

We cannot emphasize enough that IDEA requires parents, educators, and administrators to be equal and vital members of the child's IEP team. We believe equal participation can only happen when everyone is given an equal voice, which means all team members are able to clearly and honestly state their concerns, ask questions, and/or make comments. The goal is for the team to have deep conversations and develop a shared vision, which leads to the cocreation of an appropriate educational plan for the student.

We encourage all conversations to be friendly in both words and tone and for everyone to engage in active listening and perspective taking. We know this may be difficult, especially when changes are being recommended. Using some of the active listening strategies outlined in Chapter 4 will help facilitate the conversations. We know that if someone disagrees with what is being said, they might stop listening. This leads to shutting down conversations and is likely to prevent the team from effectively collaborating and cooperating on how to best meet the student's needs.

From our perspective, a sense of urgency to effectively and appropriately address the child's needs should encourage initial conversations to focus on shared vision. Most of the time, when teams have deep and meaningful conversations, they lead to the generation of lots of opinions and recommendations related to all aspects of the IEP—including possible changes. That is why it is important to give everyone a chance to speak, comment on what others say, and ask questions. It also ensures the IEP team is ready and willing to collaborate, cooperate, compromise, and reach consensus.

We can't stress enough the need for parents, educators, and administrators to be honest, transparent, and willing to speak candidly. Conversations are how information is shared and should be a welcoming platform for asking and answering questions. We believe that the most effective discussions will begin with the team talking about *what does the student need to be successful*, which leads to developing a shared vision. These conversations lay the groundwork for forming a partnership. Partnerships also require everyone to be open and ready to embrace the different perspectives related to what the child needs and to best address those needs. It opens up opportunities to work collaboratively on the development of the student's IEP.

We want to remind educators and parents about the importance of the student's voice in the IEP process. IDEA identified the need for students to attend IEP meetings beginning at age 12. We suggest encouraging students to participate in their own IEP meeting so their voices are heard. We believe that the student's input is priceless because it provides the team with another, often overlooked, perspective. We have found students are often able to identify needs and suggest strategies that the team may have not considered or may have discounted. We also encourage everyone to factor the student's thoughts and feelings into their decision-making. Another important reason for student participation in the IEP process is that it teaches them self-advocacy skills, which is a life-long skill.

DETERMINING SPECIAL EDUCATION ELIGIBILITY

In addition to the formal assessments that the district does, we recommend including input from parents as part of the assessment process. We recommend that the psychologist, social worker, or guidance counselor interview the parents to obtain background information. In addition, we suggest parents provide names of books the child reads, homework samples of math and writing that highlight the child's performance at home, and any other data related to behavior or social-emotional concerns that the parents have compiled. Then parents are providing additional information that is vital to determining eligibility.

Eligibility for special education is an IEP team decision. Following the administration of a comprehensive evaluation, the team reconvenes to review the reports and determine if the student has a disability that requires specialized instruction.

Three-Pronged Approach to Eligibility

The special education eligibility process uses three prongs:

- Identifying a documented disability
- Determining the disability adversely affects the student's ability to access the curriculum
- Agreeing the student requires specialized instruction in order to access the curriculum

---

Sometimes the team agrees the student has a disability, but their disability does not require specialized instruction and can be easily addressed through accommodations. This would suggest the child requires a 504 Plan. That means the team ends the IEP meeting and recommends convening a 504 meeting. This may or may not happen immediately following the IEP meeting, because in most districts the IEP team and 504 team include different administrators and often different staff members.

According to IDEA, a district has up to 60 days to complete an evaluation; however, in many states this timeline is between 30 to 45 days. In all cases, once the school-based team has completed their evaluations, an IEP meeting is convened to review the assessments and to determine eligibility. We want to remind parents that the professionals who assessed their child cannot recommend special education without convening an IEP meeting and having you participate in the decision-making process.

Even though eligibility is a team decision, evaluators are allowed to include in their report general education recommendations and strategies to be implemented by the classroom teacher. What they aren't allowed to do is to state that based on the assessment, the student qualifies for special education services. Best practice suggests the evaluators' reports will clearly state areas of concern, rather than a diagnosis of a specific disability. It is the IEP team that makes that determination. We also suggest reports include the statement that *all the results of the evaluation will be shared at the IEP meeting.*

It is important to reiterate that eligibility for special education is not solely based on the child's disability. The team is expected to look at three different criteria, with identification of a disability being only one of them. The other two criteria include determining if the disability is impacting the student's ability to learn and if the student requires specialized instruction. When the team has looked at all three criteria, they will have the information needed to determine eligibility. The next step is to design appropriate programming along with modifications and accommodations.

We believe best practice is to provide parents with a written copy of each assessment report prior to the IEP meeting. We also suggest that all evaluators meet individually with parents prior to the IEP meeting to share test results and to review their reports. When parents meet with the individual staff members, they have a chance to ask questions and are then better prepared to participate in the IEP eligibility conversation.

In addition, if the school-based professionals have presented their reports to parents prior to the IEP meeting, it is appropriate for them to present a summary of the testing at the meeting. We have found when the testing information is shared with parents prior to the formal IEP meeting, it also reduces parental anxiety. Parents are better able to listen, ask questions, and actively participate in the development of the IEP.

After the team reviews the assessment results, they discuss the evaluation results, along with other factors, to determine if the student has a disability and if it requires specialized instruction. In many states there are checklists the team is required to use as part of the eligibility process. In order to determine the student's specific disability, the team considers the 13 categories outlined in IDEA. They select the one that is most appropriate. Sometimes determining the child's disability creates tension in the meeting, because parents believe their child has one type of disability and the district believes the child has a different disability. It is important for parents to be aware that students can actually have more than one disability; this is called comorbidity, which means there is the presence of more than one disorder. The team needs to determine which of the disabilities drive the need for special education.

Sometimes it is helpful for parents to obtain a medical identification code, which could be used to identify or support the diagnosis of a disability, especially when related to "health issues." For example, if a student has a medical diagnosis of ADD/ADHD that is impacting their ability to learn, a medical diagnosis could help the team qualify them for special education. Other examples include auditory or visual processing difficulties or an executive functioning disorder, although they may also be identified through the school evaluations. Additional information could help the team not only determine eligibility but also ways to provide the student appropriate support and services such as an FM system or specific organizational support.

For purposes of developing the IEP, the team must identify what they consider to be the student's primary disability and what is driving the need for special education. Sometimes parents worry that labeling their child may have a negative impact (Mueller, 2019). At one time, there were more negative implications and stigmas associated with various disability labels, including teacher expectations, bullying, and social implications. Today this has changed, but it has not vanished.

Most parents accept that a disability label is part of the identification process for special education. The label is what opens the door for the student to receive the support needed to be successful in school. Educational scholars Banks and Banks found in some cases that labeling students helped in assessing the student's capabilities and needs (2012). What is important to keep in mind is that children grow and change. These changes can affect the reasons they require special education and/or their label.

Determination of eligibility is based on the results of the assessment, which are more than the results of the standardized tests. Other important information that is gathered and considered include background history, a review of the student's school records (work samples, grades), and any other clearly documented anecdotal data. The team needs to also consider information shared by the family, such as the child's medical history, outside assessments, and outside therapy providers' reports. Since data are used to drive the eligibility conversation, parents and educators are less defensive and are better able to reach consensus on both eligibility and disability.

Note: The determination of the student's disability is based on a review of the assessments, school performance, and anecdotal information gathered during the assessment process. The team may agree the student has a documented disability but does not require specialized instruction, which means they would not qualify for special education.

WHAT NEXT?

Once the student is found eligible for special education, the special education teacher and the appropriate related service staff (i.e., speech pathologist, occupational therapist, physical therapist, counselor, psychologist, social worker) present draft goals and objectives and discuss their appropriateness. The team—parents and educators—design the child's educational plan, which includes goals and objectives, type of program, and service hours. The service hours recommended are based on the amount of time required to master goals and objectives.

We encourage the team to have a conversation to ensure that everyone agrees that what is being proposed is appropriate. Some districts require parents to sign a document before special education services can begin. Others develop the program but do not require a signature. Instead, the parents have the right to refuse services or disagree with what is being recommended within 10 days of receiving the IEP. If they disagree, they send a note to the school documenting their concerns and/or disagreements.

Additional Types of Deficits and Disorders

In addition to the documented disabilities identified in IDEA and that are used to determine eligibility, some students are diagnosed with other types of disorders or deficits that also affect their ability to fully participate across the school day. We encourage parents and educators to become familiar with these disabilities and understand their implications. They will then be better prepared to address all of the student's needs when developing the IEP. The school psychologist, counselor, social worker, or pediatrician can be helpful in providing information and resources to assist the IEP team.

Cognitive-Communication Disorders/Deficits

In addition to having a disability, some students are diagnosed with a cognitive-communication disorder. The cause of this type of deficit is the result of a variety of factors, including emergency birth, major injury, hypoxia, traumatic brain injury, Down syndrome, or autism spectrum disorder. Some of the observable factors related to this disorder include reduced awareness, delayed memory, language sequencing difficulties, social language deficits, and an overall difficulty initiating effective communication. These deficits may affect the student's ability to master vocational training goals, participate in vocational training, and impact employment after graduation.

Motor Dysfunction Disorder

In both school and the community, motor dysfunction disorders can be a barrier to learning and inclusion. Students who fall under this category may not be able to fully participate with their peers because they have difficulty performing tasks, such as packing up their belongings at the end of a school day. In the community, children with motor dysfunction disorders might not be able to participate in social activities (such as birthday parties) because of their difficulty performing many age-appropriate motor tasks like bowling, miniature golf, or gymnastic activities.

Parents and educators should be cognizant that it is not always obvious that a student has motor dysfunction disorders. However, they have difficulty keeping up with their peers since they are in a wheelchair or wear leg splints. It can be upsetting to students when they struggle with the motor skills to do what their peers can do, making them vulnerable to bullying or peer exclusion.

School-based physical therapy or adaptive physical education, which can be built into the student's IEP, helps to address these issues. Other suggestions include targeted assessments or programs to support participation in extracurricular activities and counseling to address self-esteem or friendship issues. For older students, programs in the community and job training are effective ways to bridge their motor gap.

OUTSIDE EVALUATIONS

Usually, the IEP team designs the assessments that determine eligibility and the district's professional staff conducts the tests (see Data Collection chapter). However, we realize that there are some parents who have their child privately assessed, with the hope that providing the district with the assessment will get their child special education services. This almost never happens! In our opinion, most of the time this is not the most efficient way for parents to get their child identified as a special education student.

What usually happens is that following having an outside evaluation done, the child's parents share it with their school district. Now the district is required to convene an IEP meeting in order to review the assessments with the team. In almost all cases, the school district exercises their right, under IDEA, to conduct their own assessments before discussing eligibility.

Of course, in the name of transparency, whenever parents have any outside testing done we encourage them to share the report with the district. This is also true about medical reports and progress notes from outside providers. It helps build trust, assists the team in determining eligibility, reduces redundancy, and ensures test reliability. Now parents and educators are working in concert.

Sometimes parents request an IEP meeting because they believe their child requires special education services based on an outside evaluation. However, they are not demonstrating trust or transparency if they withhold sharing the report until they are at the IEP meeting. Understandably, this action would be off-putting to the school staff.

When parents share an outside evaluation with the district prior to the IEP meeting, it is a first step in working as a team. It also gives the educators a chance to review the report prior to the meeting, so they will be better prepared to discuss the findings. This will ensure the team is able to have a meaningful conversation at the IEP meeting. The school staff can bring data to the meeting to either support or refute the report. In addition, being able to review the report prior to the meeting allows the educators to gain a clearer picture of the parents' concerns and perspective.

Even though parents have had their child assessed, the district has the right to conduct their own evaluation. The district will review the outside evaluation at the meeting and then design their own evaluation. The district's assessments should address the same areas and skills found in the outside evaluation. However, they need to use different assessment tools and standardized measures. Best practice says the same tests cannot be administered multiple times, in less than a year, because it impacts test reliability.

Parents sometimes feel their qualified professional's opinion is being questioned. This is not the intent of the school district. We want to remind parents that although there are many professionals who can identify disabilities, according to IDEA only the IEP team can find a student eligible for special education services. We understand that this frustrates parents when they see their child struggling. However, it is part of the special education process outlined by IDEA that every school district who gets federal funding is obligated to follow.

Following the completion of the district's assessment, the IEP team reconvenes, reviews their assessments, and discusses special education eligibility. Parents have the right to disagree with the results of the district's evaluation, and the school district is obligated to inform the parents of their right to request an IEE. The two most common reasons parents request an IEE are that the outside evaluation and district evaluation have totally different conclusions or that the district has not been able to identify a disability and the parents continue to believe that their child has a disability. We encourage the family to provide data that support why they continue to believe their child requires special education and therefore are requesting an independent evaluation. Again, it is much harder to argue with evidence/data.

A qualified professional, such as a psychologist, neuropsychologist, special education teacher, or speech-language pathologist, administers an IEE. The evaluator is not connected to the school district, but both parents and district agree to the person. In most cases the district pays for this evaluation. The overall purpose of the IEE is to provide objectivity to previous assessments or clarification of them, which will then either validate or invalidate previous testing.

Sometimes districts recommend an IEE if they continue to suspect a disability but do not have enough information to determine eligibility, disability, or to develop an appropriate IEP. Another reason to request an outside evaluation is if the district does not have qualified staff to administer specific types of tests, such as a neuropsychological evaluation, a psychiatric evaluation, or behavioral assessments.

THE VALUE OF AN AGENDA

We acknowledge that most parents are nervous about attending their child's IEP meeting. A feeling of stress, anxiety, or just being overwhelmed happens because parents do not fully understand the process or know what to expect. This is especially true at the beginning of the process. We suggest using an *agenda* as a way to help parents understand what is happening. We also suggest that prior to each agenda item, the administrator explains what is going to be discussed and why. This will help parents gain a better understanding of the conversation and keep the team focused. By adding this process to the IEP meeting, we believe it will help to build trust and demonstrate transparency. The team is then more open to collaborating and building partnerships.

Being able to ask questions and ask for clarification are key to having meaningful IEP conversations. When an agenda is driving the conversation, it ensures everyone is on the same page and knows both what is being discussed and why. We remind parents to always ask questions, and if they feel their questions are not fully answered in the IEP meeting to request a follow-up meeting with school personnel. Only if parents fully understand the conversation can they actively participate in the process.

IT'S ABOUT CREATING THE BEST INDIVIDUALIZED EDUCATION PLAN!

It is our hope that parents and educators embrace the words of former Green Bay Packers' Coach Vince Lombardi. He said, "Perfection is not attainable, but if we chase perfection, we can catch excellence." We believe all students can reach their highest potential, whatever that looks like. All it takes is everyone using grit, motivation, positivity, and mentorship.

To us, demanding excellence in all things related to education will ensure that all students reach their highest achievement levels, which includes any student with a disability. It is important that every team strives to create the best plan in order to maximize the student's success. This can only be accomplished when parents, teachers, and administrators have open and honest conversations, monitor progress, and make recommendations based on data and objective evidence.

When adults set high bars for themselves, they are on the road to achieving success. We suggest school districts embrace this same philosophy and design programs that ensure every student will be able to reach their highest level of achievement. In the case of Endrew F. v. Douglas County School District, the U.S. Chief Justice John Roberts wrote, "A student offered an educational program providing merely more than '*de minimis*' progress from year to year can hardly be said to have been offered an education at all" (Harmon et al., 2020; Yell et al., 2020). Although Roberts's opinion highlights that a student should receive more than minimum support, it is disappointing that the Supreme Court has not been willing to elaborate on what *appropriate progress looks like*. This vague description of support and progress provides challenges to school districts.

We suggest that everyone maintain a positive attitude and growth mindset. We think this can help teachers and parents take education to a different level. This includes striving to deliver services to all students in the Least Restrictive Environment (LRE), which is outlined in Section 300.114 of IDEA. The IEP team decides what environment would be least restrictive, which varies from student to student. After considering the student's placement, and using the Least Restrictive Environment Checklist (which can be found in the Appendix), the team is required to check the box on the IEP that says LRE.

ADDITIONAL INFORMATION ABOUT THE INDIVIDUALIZED EDUCATION PLAN PROCESS

Always Read the Individualized Education Plan!

We cannot stress enough that when the IEP is finalized and distributed, parents and educators must **read** the document. *If there are incorrect statements and/or information in the IEP that do not reflect what occurred at the meeting, it is incumbent upon all team members to bring this to the attention of the administrator.* After reading the completed IEP, it should be filed and referred to over the course of the year by all those who are involved with the student. This is the only way to ensure the student's program is being delivered with efficacy.

We have heard parents tell us that they did not keep their child's IEP. In fact, some parents have actually thrown the document away after receiving it in the mail. **Parents, please do not throw away the IEP!** It is a legal document. File it along with other documents that support your child's education—reports, report cards, testing. Think of the IEP as a legal contract between the district and the student. It drives the child's placement, program, and services for the coming year.

An Ah-Ha Moment: Parents Realize the Importance of the Individualized Education Plan

The McHugh family hired a consultant, Mr. Sullivan, to help them advocate for their son Liam in conversations with their school district. Morgan and Patrick McHugh felt their seventh-grade son Liam was not getting the support he needed. He was smart, but he was suddenly drifting farther behind his classmates academically. It did not appear that his teachers were sure how to best help him.

He was no longer happy going to school and reported that he felt isolated within the general education classroom. Liam's parents did not think he was making meaningful academic progress, despite his teachers labeling his progress as "satisfactory." There was no evidence to support the claim that Liam was struggling. Mr. and Mrs. McHugh thought the special education support was supposed to teach him skills and strategies so he could successfully access the curriculum. However, at this point, they could not see the benefits.

Liam had been identified as a student with a specific learning disability in third grade, and his parents have attended his IEP meetings annually. After 5 years, they still were unable to understand the importance or power of the IEP. They knew it drove their son's special education services and outlined the goals and objectives. They had hired Mr. Sullivan to help them understand how to get Liam the help he needed. His first request was to see Liam's IEP. Mrs. McHugh said since she did not understand it, she threw it away. Mr. McHugh was surprised to learn that the IEP was a legal document and the school district was required to deliver the program outlined in the IEP with efficacy.

Mr. Sullivan was totally surprised that after 5 years, the McHughs had never asked the school staff or administrators to help them understand the special education process or the meaning of the IEP. After having in-depth conversations with the family, he realized Liam's parents simply did not see themselves as vital members of the IEP team. They did not think their voices mattered.

continued on next page

The McHughs thought if they questioned the school's recommendations, they would be creating problems for their son. Even though they had been concerned that Liam wasn't making progress and perhaps the program was not appropriate, they felt obligated to accept all recommendations because they did not want to appear adversarial. In fact, all they wanted was for Liam to learn and feel better about himself.

Mr. Sullivan explained to Liam's parents that each year's IEP created a road map for his educational journey. He familiarized the family with the IEP process, the sections of the IEP, and the importance of measurable and achievable annual goals. He encouraged them to request an IEP meeting, which he agreed to attend as a facilitator of the conversation.

The parents called their district and requested an IEP meeting for the following week. They said that their consultant, Mr. Sullivan, would be attending the meeting. Mrs. McHugh requested that Liam's teachers bring all data related to progress on goals and objectives to the meeting.

At the IEP meeting, the team reviewed the parents' concerns, work samples, and the data related to goals and objectives. The team, including the parents, agreed to adjust Liam's program, including adding a note-taking goal and an organizational skills goal that would address breaking down long- and short-term assignments. It seemed that the demands of middle school presented new challenges for Liam.

A few weeks later, Mrs. McHugh called the case manager to report that Liam was much happier. She thanked him and the rest of the team for making the changes to the IEP. With the help of Mr. Sullivan, she was also able to organize all of the educational paperwork, including the revised IEP.

WHAT IS A DRAFT INDIVIDUALIZED EDUCATION PLAN?

Throughout the book we have often referred to draft IEPs. We want to take the time to clarify what that means. Many IEP teams present sections of the IEP or the entire document at the beginning of the meeting as a way to drive the discussion, which includes concerns, questions, and input from all team members. Since all decisions regarding the IEP are team decisions that require parental input, we want to remind school districts to label these copies draft. *(It is important to note that any copy of the IEP written prior to the IEP meeting*

must *be considered a draft, whether or not labeled so.)* The intent of the law is that the student's educational plan cannot be fully developed prior to the IEP meeting. Parents cannot be presented with an IEP that is considered to be "fait accompli."

If a district writes an IEP without parental input, the district is considered to be out of compliance with IDEA procedures. It is within the parents' rights to file a complaint with their state. Of course, we recommend that parents have a conversation with the school administrator prior to filing such a complaint, as not labeling the document draft was most likely an unintentional oversight. That being said, we encourage all districts to check that the IEP is marked draft before sharing it at the meeting. It will help to build trust and avoid parents even thinking the IEP was created without their input.

As we have said previously, it is helpful for parents to be able to review the goals and objectives prior to the IEP meeting. That is why we encourage districts to create draft goals and objectives and share them with parents at least 24 to 48 hours prior to the meeting. This provides the family with an opportunity to review what the district is recommending. Sometimes parents will share the draft goals and objectives with a consultant, private professional, or friend to help them determine if the proposed goals are appropriate.

After reviewing the school's recommendations, some parents decide to propose additions or changes that will be shared at the IEP meeting. We continue to stress the importance of transparency. We therefore encourage parents to provide a written copy of any proposed changes/suggestions to the case manager or school administrator prior to the IEP meeting.

We have found when the team has open conversations, everyone is given a voice, concerns and opinions are discussed, and the team is more willing to make minor or major changes to the IEP. Following the meeting, all agreed-upon changes are added to the IEP document, along with a meeting summary and minutes to reflect what was talked about and by whom. At this point the IEP is finalized, which means it is now the official document that will drive the student's special education program for the coming year. The district is legally obligated to deliver the finalized IEP with efficacy.

CAN THE INDIVIDUALIZED EDUCATION PLAN BE REVISED?

The short answer to the question regarding revising an IEP is "yes." However, this can only be done at an IEP meeting. The finalized IEP is the road map for the child's educational program. It identifies where the student is starting and where the team believes the student will be performing

12 months later. If for any reason during the course of the year any member of the team believes there is a need to change or revise any part of the IEP, the team must convene an IEP meeting. We suggest that concrete data drive all changes. Think of changes as detours or side trips necessary for the student to master the proposed goals and objectives. If the team agrees to the changes, the district will rewrite the IEP to reflect agreed-upon changes.

INDIVIDUALIZED EDUCATION PLAN COMPLIANCE

Most of the time, school districts deliver the program and services outlined in the IEP with total efficacy. However, there are times when parents or educators suspect that the district is not complying with the terms of the IEP. We recommend parents immediately discuss their concerns with the case manager or administrator and try to resolve the problem before taking legal action. We suggest the conversation identifies *what* part of the IEP is not being appropriately delivered, *why*, and *how* to move forward.

Examples of a district being out of compliance (i.e., not following IDEA's outlined procedures) include, but are not limited to, not sending the IEP invitation 10 days prior to the meeting, not holding an annual review, or not completing an evaluation within the mandated 60 days. Sometimes, parents agree to waive their rights, then the district is not considered to be out of compliance. When parents waive their rights, it is important to document it in the IEP minutes.

Once the IEP has been developed and the entire team agrees upon it, it is the district's obligation to deliver it in its entirety, without exception. If there are data or documentation that are not being delivered as written, parents have the right to file a compliance complaint with the state. The state then reviews the complaint and sanctions the district if they found them out of compliance. When parents are concerned about how the IEP process is being delivered and what constitutes a compliance violation, we suggest they refer to the Procedural Safeguards document, discuss their concerns with a school administrator, or speak to an educational expert.

Part of rectifying a complaint includes reconvening an IEP meeting and recording the changes. At the meeting, we encourage the parents to thank the district for correcting the problem. Remember the goal is to create a partnership and work together. Through the use of positive communication, trust and transparency can be restored. The good news is now the compliance issues have been resolved.

Conversations Ensure Compliance

The IEP team had recommended that all of Thomas's services be delivered in his general education classrooms. His parents, Mrs. and Mr. Spinelli, had agreed to the team's program recommendations. However, after several months, they became concerned that he was not making progress social-emotionally, academically, or behaviorally.

The Spinellis were understandably confused. They had taken an active role in the development of Thomas's IEP. They thought the teachers were delivering the program that the IEP team had created, but it did not appear to be working. Thomas's parents were unsure if the problem was his program or placement.

Mr. and Mrs. Spinelli decided the problem was where he was receiving services rather than the services themselves. They met with his case manager, Mrs. Chu, and shared their concerns, which included work samples to highlight areas where he was struggling. Following their conversation, Mr. and Mrs. Spinelli were convinced that Thomas's placement was the problem. They asked if having him pulled out of his general education classes would be the best solution. Her immediate response was "not yet, we are going to begin by making changes to Thomas's program."

At an IEP meeting held the following week, Thomas's parents again shared their concerns along with the data they felt highlighted their son's stunted progress. Thomas's teachers also shared data that showed (1) Thomas's progress on his IEP goals and objectives and (2) evidence to highlight his social-emotional, academic, and behavioral performance in his general education classroom. The teachers' data confirmed that Thomas was on target for mastering many of the goals outlined in the IEP. The data also highlighted a few areas that could be "tweaked." Overall, his teachers did not believe his placement was the problem.

During the discussion at the IEP meeting, his teachers noted that Thomas appeared to be struggling to understand directions, especially in math class. Both his special education teacher and general education teacher reported that if they took the time to break down the question or task into small steps, Thomas was successful. However, if he had to do the tasks independently, Thomas would lose focus. They reported that he never asked for help.

continued on next page

Based on the data-driven observations and the parents' concerns, the team recommended a teacher aide help Thomas chunk his assignments into manageable parts. The team recommended adding an objective to teach Thomas the skills needed to break large tasks into easily manageable components. They also added extended time as a modification related to math homework completion and preferential seating away from distractions.

Mrs. Chu reviewed the most recent state assessments and noted that Thomas had some gaps related to reading comprehension. He was decoding on grade level but struggling to answer questions related to what he read. She concluded that this too might be interfering with his ability to understand directions. The team discussed the pros and cons of Thomas participating in a reading program outside of the classroom for 6 weeks to give him some reading comprehension strategies.

This open and honest conversation with the classroom teacher, case manager, and the entire IEP team resulted in service and instructional changes to Thomas's IEP. However, Thomas remained in the LRE—a general education classroom—for most of his academic day. The team also agreed to reconvene in 6 weeks to review progress and determine if the recommended changes were appropriate and effective.

When parents and teachers work as partners and discuss the child's needs openly and honestly, they identify a shared vision: what the child needs and how best to ensure the child's success. In the case study *Conversations Ensure Compliance*, everyone agreed that Thomas should receive his instruction in the inclusive classroom. By using data and having meaningful conversations, the team reached consensus on how to change the IEP.

Guide for Successful Participation

This guide provides simple to follow steps on how to successfully participate in an IEP meeting.

- **Always be prepared.** Know and be prepared to discuss the student's strengths. Bring data/evidence.
- **Both parents attend all meetings (if possible).** Otherwise consider bringing a second person to listen and take notes.
- **First impressions count.** It takes 7 seconds to make a first impression. You don't get a second chance.
- **Arrive promptly.** This shows you are ready to actively participate.
- **Be friendly—smile.** Introduce yourself, separate the people from the problems.
- **[Parents] Sit with other team members.** Send the message of being an equal partner in the process.
- **Effectively communicate.** Speak slowly and clearly. Have eye contact when talking and listening. Make positive statements such as "My child needs" and "I understand." Ask open-ended questions and ask for clarification when you don't understand. Sound confident both verbally and nonverbally.
- **Stay focused.** Be flexible but firm regarding your opinion as to what is best for the student. Don't get sidetracked by past experiences or issues. Meetings that aren't productive should end and reconvene at a later date.
- **Follow up and say thank you.** We suggest that at the end of the meeting parents and educators thank each other verbally and, if possible, summarize any key take-aways. In addition, we suggest that parents write a thank you note that summarizes the key take-aways from their perspective via email, text, handwritten note, or thank you card.

Preparation Makes for Best Practices

Chloe's parents, Mr. and Mrs. Richards, met with an educational consultant, Mrs. White, the evening prior to her annual IEP review. Mrs. White prepared Chloe's parents for the meeting by reviewing the key points she wanted them to make the next day.

She noticed that each time she made a point, Mrs. Richards wrote "I want ..." The third time Mrs. White saw Mrs. Richards write "I want," she stopped her. Mrs. White respectfully explained that many parents want their children to get everything that is available in the district, even if their child doesn't require it to be successful. She explained that although it wasn't wrong for her to want the best for Chloe, it was important to tell the district what Chloe needed and why.

Mrs. Richards immediately crumbled up her notes, took out a clean piece of paper and began writing, "Chloe needs ... because ..."

With the help of Mrs. White, Chloe's parents successfully prepared for the IEP meeting the next day. They listed their key points in a clear and organized manner. Then, they made sure they had evidence to support each of their requests. They also practiced articulating their points so that they sounded confident.

When Mr. and Mrs. Richards arrived at the IEP meeting, they were presented with a copy of Chloe's IEP for the coming year. They were surprised to see everything was already filled in and the document was not labeled draft. From their perspective, the school-based team had written the IEP, which included goals and objectives, the type of program, and the service hours, without any input from them. They had arrived ready to share their concerns and were taken aback.

However, before they could say anything, the administrator, Dr. Gross, asked everyone to mark their copy of the IEP draft. The tone in the room immediately changed. Mr. and Mrs. Richards felt that the administrator recognized that they were important members of the IEP team and not labeling the document draft was merely an oversight.

continued on next page

Mr. and Mrs. Richards had come to the IEP meeting prepared. They knew their rights and had a list of what they believed Chloe needed to be successful, along with data to support their reasoning. After carefully reviewing the draft IEP, Chloe's parents acknowledged that the district's goals and objectives were appropriate, but also incomplete. They took out their list and highlighted each of their points, along with supporting data. When given a chance to speak, they explained what they thought Chloe needed to be academically successful and why.

As they advocated for their daughter, Mr. and Mrs. Richards spoke with confidence, used a pleasant tone, and made direct eye contact with the other IEP team members at the table. Their actions led to a productive conversation, with educators and parents working to develop an appropriate IEP. After the parents shared what they thought Chloe needed and why, everyone agreed on the best way to adjust the IEP to safeguard her success.

Revising the IEP in a collaborative manner requires that both educators and parents are prepared. Mr. and Mrs. Richards came to the meeting prepared. Their preparation gave them the confidence to share their ideas without sounding aggressive. Their goal was to ensure the educators understood what Chloe needed.

We want to point out that if the parents had come to the meeting unprepared, they might have been intimidated. It could have shut down the conversation. Once the IEP was labeled draft, they used it to drive their conversation and work collaboratively with the school-based team. Success!

The What and Why of
S.M.A.R.T. Goals

Goals and objectives drive the student's special education program. Federal law, as outlined in the Individuals with Disabilities Education Act (IDEA), says academic and functional annual goals are written to include what the student will be able to do, under what circumstances, and with what support systems (U.S. Department of Education, 2022). Goals address all areas of concern (academic, behavioral, social-emotional, and functional) and are written with the intent that they will be mastered within one academic year. They are presented at the Individualized Education Plan (IEP) meeting in draft form, and should include performance and evaluation criteria as outlined in the IEP as the way to measure progress.

Bud, P. S., & Jacobson, T. L.
Navigating Special Education: The Power of Building
Positive Parent–Educator Partnerships (pp. 143-148).
© 2023 SLACK Incorporated.

We recommend using the S.M.A.R.T. goal format when writing all goals and objectives (Table 11-1). The goals are developed to address specific concerns identified and recorded on the IEP under the Present Level of Academic Achievement and Functional Performance (PLAAFP). Without a specific concern, there is no reason to write a goal or objective. After developing each goal, the most important consideration is how progress will be measured. We discourage using terms such as "improve" because it cannot be measured. We suggest replacing "improve" with words such as *increase, decrease, maintain, stop,* or *start,* which allow progress to be precisely measured. For example, many academic skills are written with the expectation that the student will *increase* their ability to perform a specific skill. Whereas, some behavioral goals might measure a student's ability to *decrease* a behavior, such as yelling out or inappropriately touching others.

Table 11-1
S.M.A.R.T. Goals Definitions and Example

SPECIFIC (S)
Describe the deficit area—what, why, when, and how

MEASURABLE (M)
Identify the data/evidence used to measure progress

ATTAINABLE (A)
Viewed within a 1-year time frame

Directions of action: Increase, decrease, maintain

Goal and levels: Reading, writing, math, communication, social skills, fine motor; grade/age level, with/without prompt, independent

REALISTIC (RELEVANT) (R)
Achievable in 1 year, otherwise unrealistic and must be rewritten

TIMELY (T)
Written as a 1-year plan

We recommend using baseline data, or data that identify where the student is currently performing, to drive all goal development. Terms like *at grade level, age level, independently, with prompts,* or *at a percentage* are objective ways to measure attainment. Proposing data-driven S.M.A.R.T. goals leads to meaningful and productive conversations, since it is easier to agree to something that is data driven.

As we previously suggested, it is best practice for the school-based team to share draft goals and objectives with parents prior to an annual review. It allows the team (parents and educators) to have more meaningful conversations when discussing the proposed goals and objectives at the meeting. When parents have an opportunity to review the goals ahead of time, they can come to the meeting prepared to ask questions and discuss their concerns regarding the appropriateness of the proposed goals and objectives.

We want to remind parents they can propose goals and objectives, which should be data driven. We encourage them to share their goals with the case manager prior to the IEP meeting, to ensure the school-based team is prepared to discuss them.

What Is a S.M.A.R.T. Goal?

The S.M.A.R.T. goal format incorporates a baseline (where the student started or their current level of performance) and mastery criteria of at least 80% accuracy, in most cases. This structure drives outcomes, supports performance, enhances learning, and provides teachers with evidence as to what is or isn't working. We believe it is harder for parents to argue with a data-driven progress report. Therefore, we suggest teachers present objective data along with the subjective reporting system outlined in the IEP—*limited progress, satisfactory progress,* or *mastery.*

PROGRESS REPORTING FOR INDIVIDUALIZED EDUCATION PLAN GOALS AND OBJECTIVES

The following abbreviations typically denote progress on goals and objectives on the IEP.

M = Mastery, S = Satisfactory progress,
L = Limited progress, and NI = Not introduced

If progress is reported without tangible evidence to back up the statements, we encourage parents and educators to request the appropriate staff to provide data, which were identified in the IEP as the criteria to be used to measure progress. We believe that if a performance procedure is listed as "anecdotal," it is incumbent upon the educator, who is using anecdotal evidence, to provide documentation as part of the progress report (see Table 11-1).

EXAMPLES OF S.M.A.R.T. GOALS

Writing goals and objectives using the S.M.A.R.T. goal format will prove to be beneficial to both parents and educators. It helps teachers more effectively drive instruction. The baseline information helps parents monitor their child's progress. When writing goals using this structure, it also allows educators and parents to more easily revise and adjust the student's goals and objectives for the coming year because they are directly linked to data. IDEA requires that the IEP includes "a statement of measurable annual goals, including academic and functional goals, designed to meet the child's needs that result from the child's disability to enable the child to be involved in and make progress in the general education curriculum" (2004, §1414). S.M.A.R.T. goals allow the IEP to meet federal regulations and provide a way for parents and educators to use data to discuss a student's needs.

Format 1

- When given a graphic organizer, the student will *increase* the quality of their paragraph writing skills, *going from* writing one sentence *to writing two five-sentence paragraphs,* with a topic sentence and three supporting details.
- The student will *increase* their ability to participate in class discussions, ask questions, and make requests by *going from* inappropriately calling out or only raising their hand one time per day to raising their hand five times across the school day *without a physical or verbal prompt.*
- When given a two-step math problem, the student will go from needing teacher support in identifying the correct first step of the problem to independently beginning the problem and solving it 80% of the time.

Format 2

- **Goal:** The student will increase their knowledge of community safety signs and symbols, such as the universal "hospital" or "wheelchair accessible" signs, going from demonstrating a knowledge of 5 symbols to at least 20 symbols with 80% accuracy in a 12-month period.
    - **Objective 1:** When presented with a vocabulary matching card activity, where the student must match cards depicting universal community safety signs and symbols to cards depicting related images, the student will go from matching 5 symbols to matching at least 20 symbols with 80% accuracy, in four out of five opportunities over the course of a 12-month period.

- **Objective 2:** When presented with cards depicting community safety symbols and a set of related real-life objects, the student will go from matching 5 symbols to their corresponding objects to matching at least 20 symbols with 80% accuracy, in four out of five opportunities over the course of a 12-month period.
- **Objective 3:** When presented with a functional community and safety symbol, the student will demonstrate knowledge of the symbol by going from being able to verbally identify 5 symbols to verbally identifying 20 symbols with 80% accuracy in four out of five opportunities over the course of a 12-month period.

- **Goal:** The student will increase oral motor competence, going from accurately eating, drinking, and chewing 20% of the time to 80% of the time in a 12-month period, as defined and measured by the three following objectives:
  - **Objective 1:** The student will increase the ability to take a small amount of liquid into their mouth, swallow, and place the cup on the table for at least 3 seconds before taking another sip, going from requiring the instructor to prompt the sequence at least once to independently doing so 80% of the time, in four out of five opportunities in a 12-month period.
  - **Objective 2:** The student will put a bite-size piece of food in their mouth and use their tongue to push it to one side, chew at least five times, swallow, and repeat the same process on the other side of their mouth, going from requiring verbal and physical prompts to performing the task independently 80% of the time, in four out of five occasions over the course of a 12-month period.
  - **Objective 3:** The student will execute tongue, lip, and jaw movements (including sticking out the tongue, licking the top and bottom of the lip, and pushing the tongue against the inside of each cheek), going from requiring the visual aid of a mirror or by imitating an adult to executing the movements upon verbal instruction 80% of the time, in four out of five occasions in a 12-month period.

- **Goal:** The student will communicate during class discussions by raising their hand before speaking, going from requiring multiple prompts to independently raising their hand 80% of the time, in four out of five opportunities in a 6-month period.
  - **Objective 1:** The student will demonstrate a request to participate in the whole class and/or small group settings, going from requiring at least one verbal prompt to raise their hand to independently raising their hand 80% of the time, in four out of five opportunities in a 6-month period.

- **Objective 2:** The student will go from waiting for the instructor to provide a class break to raising their hand to request a break independently in 8 out of 10 opportunities over a minimum of 2 months over the course of a 6-month period.
- **Goal:** The student will go from requiring an adult to prompt them several times in relation to making a classroom-related decision to independently making a choice 80% of the time in an 8-month period, defined in relation to the decisions within the following three objectives:
  - **Objective 1:** When given a school lunch menu with two options available that day, the student will go from declining to select a lunch option to selecting their lunch 4 out of 5 days over the course of an 8-month period.
  - **Objective 2:** The student will go from being told where to sit, to selecting a seat in the classroom with no more than one verbal prompt 80% of the time over the course of an 8-month period.
  - **Objective 3:** When presented with five elective courses, the student will go from requiring multiple prompts to select a course to selecting one elective course with no more than one prompt 80% of the time over the course of an 8-month period.

PART III

DATA AND CORRESPONDENCE

Data Collection

> *Data are useful because they help drive instruction and monitor progress.*

THE IMPORTANCE OF DATA

Having knowledge can be powerful, but having data is even more powerful. It has been said that the person who has data also has power. We cannot stress enough the importance of parents and educators using concrete evidence to back up their concerns and recommendations. We believe decision-making should be an objective, data-driven process. It is more difficult to argue with data and easier to trust a request or recommendation when there is

Bud, P. S., & Jacobson, T. L.
*Navigating Special Education: The Power of Building
Positive Parent–Educator Partnerships* (pp. 151-167).
© 2023 SLACK Incorporated.

evidence to back up the statements, opinions, or recommendations of parents and educators rather than deferring to emotionality.

Data Are Collected on All Students

Data help both general and special education teachers adjust their instruction. The information gathered can be used to address the student's learning needs and provide insights on how to differentiate instruction, develop modifications, and identify accommodations. Data collection can be viewed as a tool used to help teachers customize instruction and determine effectiveness of their teaching. When using data-driven research-based programs, teachers are better able to identify appropriate strategies for teaching reading comprehension, reading fluency, math computation, and math reasoning.

Response to Intervention

Prior to being formally assessed for special education, many school districts use systematic and targeted interventions, referred to as RTI. The process begins when teachers identify students who they believe are at risk for learning. The students are provided with RTI assistance (Fuchs et al., 2003), which are targeted instructional strategies implemented to try to close the achievement gap. Instructional interventions identify concerns related to the student's learning (Fuchs et al., 2003).

Think of RTI as a systematic approach used to identify students who might require special education services. Classroom teachers identify those students who are performing significantly below grade level because they suspect the student's performance is due to a learning deficiency or disability. The student is then provided tiered instruction, presented as targeted and individualized interventions and used to help close the learning gap (Fuchs et al., 2003). Educators can use RTI strategies as a way to help them make decisions regarding consideration of special education services.

Progress Monitoring

Progress monitoring is a term used to determine if RTI is successfully addressing the student's academic needs. If it is not, then the plan is modified. The progress monitoring process collects data that can be used to drive instructional decisions. It breaks down the student's needs into different tiers and identifies ways to address academics and behaviors that may be interfering with the child's learning. We recommend parents discuss progress monitoring with their child's teacher, especially when they have concerns that their child isn't making appropriate progress. It is important to keep in mind that the type of progress monitoring and the tools used may vary from state to state and district to district.

Baseline Data

All data begin with the gathering of baseline information. The term *baseline data* refers to the student's level of performance on a task or goal prior to receiving any direct instruction or interventions. We believe the use of baseline data makes it easier to measure the student's progress and recommend it be incorporated into the development of all goals and objectives. However, we know that many districts do not identify the student's baseline when developing Individualized Education Plan (IEP) goals and objectives, although we believe it is best practice.

The Individuals with Disabilities Education Act (IDEA) does require goals and objectives to identify the student's baseline; however, it does require performance and evaluation criteria be included. We suggest that beginning each statement with the student's baseline on the task or behavior, such as not performing, requiring prompts, or performing 20% of the time, makes it easier to monitor progress and removes subjectivity from the equation. This removes any chance for disagreement related to progress, which helps parents and educators more effectively work together as partners.

When to Collect Data

Just like you need more than one tool to build a house, using a "tool chest" of data collection methods is the best way to document student progress. The purpose of data collection is to gather evidence as to the effectiveness of the supports and strategies the child is receiving and to measure progress. Data points provide information to the team that can be used to make objective, data-driven decisions and help teachers deliver the most appropriate instruction.

We encourage data collection to occur on an ongoing basis, which for some educators is a mindset shift. Data begin with baseline information, but that isn't enough. We suggest teachers collect information related to progress on a daily or weekly basis, rather than once a quarter or annually. We also encourage writing progress reports using data, which means the information in the report is unbiased. Objectivity builds home–school trust and demonstrates transparency. Data can be powerful when used to drive instruction because they clearly highlight what is working and what is not working. Using subjective statements such as "satisfactory progress" or "limited progress" when writing a report is okay as long as the statement is backed up with objective evidence.

We recommend teachers provide copies of data, along with explanations, to parents and other team members if appropriate. The frequency of data collection (daily, weekly, bi-weekly) and when to share the data can be agreed to at the IEP meeting. We recommend data be collected related to all goals at least several times a quarter. Parents may request data updates at any time, especially if they are concerned about their child's progress. If at any point the data suggest the child will not be able to master certain goals and objectives, we strongly suggest the team convene an IEP meeting rather than wait until the annual review.

If parents believe their child isn't making meaningful progress and/or questions the school data, we suggest they too gather evidence before requesting an IEP meeting and sharing their concerns. This way they will have evidence to share with the team in support of their concerns. We can't stress enough the importance of evidence when evaluating progress. Without it, the teacher's statements related to the child's academic, social-emotional, and behavioral growth are subjective. Subjectivity is open to interpretation, which may lead to arguments—the parents' opinion vs. the teacher's opinion. On the other hand, by using data, all statements are objective and build home–school trust.

Data are one of the best tools a teacher has in their tool box. It demonstrates what is or isn't working and helps parents and educators have more meaningful conversations. We recognize that data collection is time consuming; it is also a valuable and irreplaceable tool that becomes part of the student's educational record. Therefore, it is crucial to collect data legally and with efficacy. It is also important to carefully label it, which will ensure its reliability and validity.

Data collection can be done in many ways—recordings, videos, photographs, and work samples. When teachers share the data they collect, they are providing a statistical analysis of the student's progress. This information circumvents any surprises related to a learning gap, especially if teachers provide data updates on an on-going basis, such as every 4 weeks. Over our professional careers, we have seen data create many "ah-ha" moments.

It is very difficult to objectively support concerns or demonstrate progress without data. It is like trying to fix something without having all of the tools— hard and likely unsuccessful. Deciding what a student needs takes more than sharing anecdotal findings; it requires facts, data, and evidence. We also recommend that parents provide data related to how skills taught at school are or are not being carried over at home. This type of information can be very helpful to the team. It stimulates conversations, demonstrates collaboration and cooperation, and provides opportunities for compromise, if needed.

When data are driving the conversation rather than emotions, the bias has been removed from the conversation. It is hard, actually almost impossible, to argue with facts. There is a reduction of defensiveness on the part of both parents and educators since everyone is relying on evidence to evaluate student performance.

TYPES OF DATA COLLECTION THAT SUPPORT DECISION-MAKING

Formal and Informal Assessments

Think of assessments, both formal and informal, as the tools used to improve student performance, collect baseline data, and monitor progress. Educators use formal and informal student assessments to drive their instruction. Parents like to see both anecdotal assessments and formal tests because they both provide data to support learning and progress.

Formal Assessments

Standardized tests are considered formal assessments because they have predetermined evaluation criteria related to performance and achievement. Formal assessments are recommended at IEP meetings as part of a student's comprehensive eligibility evaluation. They are also used to document progress for an annual or triennial review. Professionals such as a psychologist, special education teacher, and speech-language pathologist administer these assessments in one-on-one settings. Formal assessments include, but are not limited to, IQ tests, language tests, and achievement tests. Behavioral data may be collected through a formal Functional Behavioral Assessment (FBA) or through targeted checklists, which look at the frequency and duration of behaviors. (See later in this chapter.)

The purpose of a formal assessment is to identify the student's needs, strengths, and weaknesses. A special education teacher administers the academic portion of the assessment, which includes standardized tests, observations, and work samples. The results provide insight and evidence regarding how the student learns, is performing academically, and identifies knowledge gaps. This information is used by educators to differentiate and customize the student's academic program and by the IEP team to assist in the development of goals and objectives, programing, and placement recommendations.

A licensed educational psychologist administers the psychological assessments, which include a structured series of interviews, standardized tests, and questionnaires designed to evaluate the student's strengths and weaknesses. These tests may also identify cognitive functioning, learning styles, and social-emotional patterns of functioning, which together provide a learning profile. These assessments are useful in understanding behavioral development beyond academia, which might require some types of therapy. The results of a formal assessment provide guidance to educators and therapists regarding strategies needed to support the child academically, social-emotionally, and behaviorally.

If the assessments identify concerns in articulation, language, communication, and/or the areas of fine or gross motor skills, additional targeted testing as part of the student's comprehensive evaluation is recommended. A speech-language pathologist, occupational therapist, and/or physical therapist would be responsible for doing the evaluations and presenting the findings to the IEP team. The results will be used to assist the team regarding programming and goal development.

Informal Assessments

Informal types of assessments are also used to gather information regarding the student's performance and/or progress. Both professionals and parents can collect data informally using audio or video recordings, anecdotal information recorded in a journal, and by creating a portfolio of the student's work. Data that are collected informally by the family and the IEP team would be formal and legal in cases of due process. Since anecdotal data are gathered through observation rather than with a data collection tool, we recommend parents and educators always rule out observer bias when sharing informal or anecdotal information.

Another factor that may affect informal data collection is the Hawthorne effect (Cook, 1968). This is when a student behaves differently when they know someone is watching them than when they think they are not being observed. The most reliable observations occur when the student is not aware they are being observed. Unless the student can be watched through a one-way mirror, this is often exceedingly difficult to accomplish.

Cumulative Files

Valuable information about the student can be found in the cumulative files school districts keep on every student. These files contain general school information, report cards, attendance records, discipline records, results of state and local testing, and school health records. Districts also have additional "special education" files for every identified special education student. This file contains all of the paperwork that state laws and federal statutes mandate, including IEPs and other special education process-related paperwork, IEP progress reports, and annual and triennial assessments.

We recommend parents also keep an easy-to-access 3-year file containing IEPs, all other documents related to the special education process, and any correspondence between the home and school. This provides parents with information and data that will help them evaluate the effectiveness of the special education services their child is receiving and can help them participate in meaningful conversations at their child's IEP meetings. We suggest the file be organized chronologically, with the most recent documents on the top, and older information filed separately but kept until the child is 21 years of age.

Parents' Cumulative File

We just discussed that school districts keep a cumulative file on all students and an additional file related to special education matters on all identified students with disabilities. We encourage all parents to keep a cumulative file. Listed below are all of the documents we recommend they include in the file. In the Appendix, there are details related to how to set up the file.

Documents to Keep and Why

- ***Comprehensive IEP or 504 packets.*** These are legal documents that identify the responsibility of the school district regarding all aspects of the child's IEP or 504 Plan, including goals and objectives, modifications, accommodations, programs, and services. They may look different from state to state, but contain the same content.
- ***Invitations to IEP or 504 meetings.*** An invitation to attend an IEP meeting is usually sent to parents 7 to 10 days prior to the IEP meeting. The intent is to provide parents ample notice so they will be able to attend. Best practice is to discuss with parents some proposed dates and times prior to sending out the invitation, which confirms parents' due process rights were not violated. Many districts send parents the Procedural Safeguards document in the same letter as the invitation to the IEP meeting.
- ***Report cards.*** Report cards and progress notes serve as a written record of the student's academic, social-emotional, and behavioral performance over a specified period of time. In most districts, report cards are sent home quarterly. In many school districts, elementary level report cards use

checklists, which can be subjective, as well as utilizing test scores, reading and math assessments, work samples, and anecdotal information. At the middle and high school level, report cards focus mostly on grades or percentages. Some schools also provide a written summary or comments along with the grades. In all cases, data-driven documents provide a clear and objective measure of the student's progress.

- We believe report cards should be objective and use data versus subjective statements such as "making progress." We encourage parents to have follow-up conversations with teachers if there is no evidence of data being used to back up grades or written progress reports.

- **District and state testing.** School administrators are required to oversee district-wide, state, and federal testing. Sometimes special education students are exempt to sit for these mandatory tests. Initial state and district evaluations for special education students can be conducted annually or triennially. The child study team and/or IEP team members are required to conduct mandated evaluations a minimum of every 3 years to update and address concerns of the IEP. The purpose is to ensure the student is keeping up with their IEP goals and objectives. All yearly testing by state and/or school districts will highlight the student's areas of strengths and weaknesses and identify current learning gaps.

- **Formal assessments.** Formal evaluations are used to collect information about a student's ability, knowledge, and present level of performance. The results are an important part of the data collection process, providing standardized information regarding the student's performance academically, social-emotionally, and behaviorally. They also give insight into the student's learning style as well as identify strengths and areas of concern.

- **Independent evaluations.** Information from all outside providers such as doctors, therapists, and aides.

- **Correspondence between home and school.** Make copies of all notes, emails, text messages, and postal mail.

- **Phone logs.** Phone calls between school and home, including date and time of call, who you spoke to, and why.

Yearly Academic Portfolio

In addition to cumulative files, we also suggest parents and teachers keep a yearly academic portfolio on each student. The portfolio can be kept in a binder or scanned and kept electronically. The folder contains the student's work for the academic school year and is another way to help educators and parents objectively monitor the child's progress. Current schoolwork is an effective way to identify strengths and areas of weakness or concerns related to the student's academic, social-emotional, or behavioral progress.

Examples of information kept in a yearly portfolio include handwriting samples, homework, writing or math assignments, and a list of books (title and author) the student has read within the last year. In addition, include tests, report cards, and progress notes to support the student's progress or lack thereof. Creating 30- to 60-second videos, such as the student reading a book, is another way to document the student's present level of performance.

Parents who are reading this section and realize they do not have a complete copy of their child's educational records can request one from their school district in writing. The request would be sent to the building administrator or director of special education. The 1966 Freedom of Information Act (FOIA; 1966) provides full disclosure of information and documents controlled by the U.S. government upon request, which includes the student's educational records. The updated FOIA (2000) states public schools are obligated to comply with the FOIA, which means parents have the right to access all records pertaining to their child. We want parents to know the first copy of their child's educational record is usually provided free of charge; additional copies are usually charged per page.

Disciplinary Records

All schools have codes of conduct and disciplinary rules that guide both suspensions and expulsions (Framework for Revising School District Codes of Student Conduct, 2014). If there are behavioral violations, the incident is written up, a disciplinary action report is filed, and the report is placed in the student's cumulative file. These reports can provide insight into patterns of behaviors. The disciplinary report includes a description of the incident (date, time, and location) and a detailed narrative that describes what happened, who was involved, and background information regarding the frequency of the behavior and other actions taken (Framework for Revising School District Codes of Student Conduct, 2014). The report usually contains information that reflects a variety of perspectives related to the incident—students involved, witnesses, teachers, and administrators.

Any student who violates school rules may be disciplined. This misbehavior can happen during the school day, at a school-sponsored activity, or at the bus stop. IDEA outlines how to address disciplinary actions regarding students in special education. This process is followed when a child's behavior significantly violates the Student Code of Conduct and the disciplinary actions taken are suspension, expulsion, or change of placement. When disciplinary actions involve a special education student, the procedure is called a *manifestation determination hearing*. It is held when the student's behavior led to removal from school for more than 10 school days or a change of placement was required.

At the manifestation determination hearing, the team (which includes the parents) reviews the child's behaviors that led up to the disciplinary action. Then the team determines if the child's behavior is a manifestation of their disability. In addition to reviewing all the documentation related to the incident, the team reviews psycho-educational and psychiatric evaluations, current and past IEPs, and all academic records and then determines if the behaviors were the result of inadequate student support.

If the team determines the student's behaviors were due to their disability, the suspension cannot be for more than 10 days, and the child cannot be placed in a different program. In addition to the manifestation determination hearing, the district convenes an IEP meeting to discuss how to monitor the student's behavior and if there needs to be changes made to the IEP to address the behaviors.

Records Speak Volumes

Sean, a third grader, has a diagnosis of emotional disturbance, ADHD, and other specific learning disabilities. He receives special education services in the general education classroom and sees the guidance counselor twice a week to address his emotional outbursts. He has difficulty following directions, with math being particularly challenging.

During a recent math class, Sean was working with manipulatives to try to complete his math assignment. The students who were finished with their work were goofing off since it was almost lunchtime, and one student accidentally bumped into Sean's desk. All the manipulatives fell on the floor. Sean got upset, picked up a large block, and started hitting him on the head.

The teacher, Mrs. Randall, quickly intervened, and Sean was escorted to the principal's office. The damage had been done: a child suffered a concussion from the blow to his head. This was not the first time Sean lost his temper, but it was the first time he ever seriously hurt another child. Since the school has a zero-tolerance for violence policy, Mrs. August, the principal, suspended Sean for a month based on school policy.

Sean's parents, Mrs. and Mr. Bradley, were called and were asked to come to school. When they arrived, Mrs. August told them she was suspending their son for 30 days. This news was disheartening. Based on Sean's Behavior Intervention Plan (BIP), they thought supports were in place to prevent such outbursts from happening.

Following a behavioral incident, such as discussed in *Records Speak Volumes*, the district is obligated to convene a manifestation IEP meeting as soon as possible. The purpose of this type of IEP meeting is to review the incident, the student's IEP, and other educational records to determine if the behavior was a manifestation of their disability. In *Records Speak Volumes*, Sean's parents felt his outburst was a manifestation of his disability; however, this is a team decision. If a team determines the behavior is a manifestation of the child's disability, they are required to amend the IEP. In Sean's case, that would mean creating goals to address his behaviors and ending his suspension. However, if the team decided Sean's behavior was not related to his disability, he could be suspended according to the zero-tolerance school policy just like any neurotypical student. In either case, our recommendation would be to request an FBA and develop a BIP.

Individualized Education Plan Progress Reports

Under the Elementary and Secondary Education Act of 1965, also known as the Every Student Succeeds Act (ESSA), school districts are required to report on every special education student's academic progress several times a year. According to IDEA, students with IEPs must receive progress reports related to their goals and objectives at least as often as the general education population receives report cards (2004).

The Family Educational Rights and Privacy Act (FERPA; 20 U.S.C. § 1232g: 34 CFR Part 99) protects the privacy of a student's education records. This law applies to any school that receives funding from the U.S. Department of Education. After reviewing the student's records, parents have the right to request that a school district correct any records they believe to be inaccurate or misleading. FERPA gives parents rights with respect to their child's education records, and FOIA gives parents rights related to privacy issues. When a student turns 18 or attends a school beyond high school, the student is considered to be an "eligible student," and the rights that FERPA gave to the parents are now transferred to the student.

Schools may disclose, without consent, information such as a student's name, address, telephone number, date and place of birth, honors, awards, and dates of attendance. However, schools must tell parents and eligible students about directory information and allow parents and eligible students a reasonable amount of time to request this information is not disclosed. Schools must notify parents and eligible students annually of their rights under FERPA, with the type of notification left to the discretion of each school.

DATA COLLECTION
METHODOLOGIES AND TOOLS

Parents and educators can use these tools to document progress or highlight concerns.

Logs

Data collection logs help parents and educators easily and efficiently collect data (see Appendix). They provide multiple ways of documenting the student's performance academically, social-emotionally, and behaviorally. Each method has a different purpose, such as collecting data to highlight specific concerns, organizing information, or gathering and documenting a performance at home and in the community. They can also target different types of measurement—frequency, intensity, or duration of a specific task or behavior. In all cases, using data leads to more productive conversations and more appropriate IEPs.

Data also lead to stronger home–school partnerships because they create a level of trust and transparency. Although we agree that data collection is time consuming, it is a crucial component of teaching and learning and ensures home–school conversations and decisions are able to be objectively made. We know using evidence takes the emotion out of the discussion. It makes it easier to develop assessments, strategies, and programs. It also reduces disagreements. It is harder to argue with facts.

We suggest IEP meeting conversations identify the type of data to be collected, the frequency, and how data will be shared with the family. Collecting data from different sources allows all teachers' views to be part of the conversation—classroom teachers, special education teachers, and related service providers. Bringing all of the information together through the use of metrics and data is the most effective way to track student progress. It looks at student performance under different circumstances and with different teachers.

Recordings

As the following case study shows, a video presents an unbiased account of the student's progress. Using both video and audio recordings are effective tools that clearly identify a student's strengths, successes, or areas of concern. Recordings are powerful data collection tools, and we suggest they are made across a variety of settings (home, community, therapeutic, and school). They are able to document the type of support being provided to the student, whether the student is able to perform a task independently, and the student's behavior across a variety of settings.

I Can't Believe It!

The administrator for outplacement, Mrs. Scott, was attending Devon's annual review IEP meeting. Devon's current placement, at a private special education program, had been made several years ago. Although it had been a difficult decision, the team, parents, and school district had agreed the smaller setting would be better able to address her academic, social-emotional, and behavioral needs.

Although her parents, Mrs. and Mr. Rusk, had agreed to the placement, they usually challenged all recommendations and decisions. Every meeting was a battle because they did not believe their daughter's needs were being appropriately met. They felt she was not making progress!

At today's annual review meeting, as is usually the case, Devon's parents arrived, did not greet anyone, and took a seat at one end of the table. They avoided eye contact with everyone and sat expressionless as the school-based team described Devon's progress over the past 12 months.

About 15 minutes into the meeting, the school director, Mrs. Mahoney, said that she wanted to share a video clip with the team. The first 2 minutes of the video had a date stamp of a year earlier. Devon was being argumentative and noncompliant, unable to follow any directions.

As the team watched the video, it was unclear whether Devon was unable to follow the directions or just being noncompliant. Then Mrs. Mahoney paused the video and said, "The next clip will show you how much progress Devon has made this year."

The next section of the video showed Devon following directions. She was performing simple tasks and interacting with her teachers. Mr. and Mrs. Rusk went from frowning to smiling. In fact, their entire body language changed. They were leaning in and watching with awe.

Devon had made progress over the last year! By the time the video ended, the parents were crying.

Presenting a visual rather than a written summary at the meeting proved to be a powerful tool. Mr. and Mrs. Rusk witnessed their daughter's progress with their own eyes. It is hard to argue with data. They realized the program was working.

When creating a recording, it is helpful to use a clock to document the start and stop time as a way to add additional context. We suggest that most videos are no longer than 2 minutes. When creating a video, due to confidentiality requirements, teachers are not allowed to film or photograph the faces of other students. If another student appears in a video, before sharing it with parents, the teacher is required to get parental permission (U.S. Department of Education, n.d.).

Student Portfolios

Portfolios are a collection of work samples used to demonstrate a student's present level of performance. They include tests, writing samples, titles, and dates of books read. Other information that is part of the student's yearly portfolio would be examples of academic assignments, report cards, tests and quizzes, and the most recent school and state standardized test results. Think of data as objective evidence used to document progress or lack thereof.

It is our opinion that best practice means collecting 3 weeks of schoolwork in the areas of concern. We recommend that teachers and parents bring their portfolios to the IEP meeting, as they can be a springboard for authentic conversations. Sharing home and school data is a way for the team to see the home and school perspectives related to progress. In addition, we encourage parents and educators to keep anecdotal records, which describe what has been tried and the results, whether successful or unsuccessful. The goal is to develop a consistent home-and-school approach to learning and work completion.

Data Collection Tools for Behavioral Concerns

We suggest parents and educators collect data related to all physical or emotional behaviors the student displays. This can be done by using a variety of checklists and/or recording anecdotal comments in a journal. It is important to gather baseline information—where the behavior occurred, when it occurred, and how frequently it occurred. This follows the same procedures that are used when completing an FBA. It is also important to use this same methodology during all on-going data collection. The use of data is objective, which makes it effective way to measure progress. (See Tables 12-1 through 12-3.)

Table 12-1
The Where, How, and When of Behavior

Where behavior occurs	Home, school, after school
How frequently behavior occurs	Hourly, daily, weekly
When the behavior occurs	Morning, afternoon, evening, weekends

Table 12-2
Physical and Emotional Behaviors

PHYSICAL BEHAVIORS	EMOTIONAL BEHAVIORS
Hitting	Lying, cheating, stealing
Spitting	Anxiety, depression
Kicking	Self-harm (cutting)
Constant rocking	Experimental or excessive drug use
Head banging	Eating disorder
Screaming	Class/school attendance and difficulty getting up
Temper tantrums	Focus/hyperfocus
Excessive crying	Distractibility/difficulty sitting
	Bullying/fighting
	Procrastination
	Long-term academic regression
	Short-term academic regression
	Poor personal hygiene
	Difficulty sleeping

Table 12-3

Data Collection Template

DATE	TIME	LOCATION	CONCERN	INTERVENTION TRIED	WORKED?	
					Yes	No
					Yes	No
					Yes	No
					Yes	No
					Yes	No

Functional Behavioral Assessment

The FBA is a powerful assessment that provides school staff advice and suggestions related to all aspects of the student's behavior, which may be interfering with their ability to learn and/or is causing them to disrupt classroom instruction. The purpose of this assessment is to understand the biological, social, affective, and environmental factors linked to the child's actions. A school psychologist, independent psychologist, or psychiatrist conducts an FBA by observing the student, identifying and analyzing their behaviors, and then making targeted suggestions. These suggestions can be implemented by the classroom teacher.

The three parts of an FBA are indirect assessment, direct observation, and functional analysis. The person conducting the assessment is observing the student through either direct observation (in the classroom, home, or community) or indirect observation (through a glass). An FBA is a vital data collection tool that assists educators and families and helps them understand the child's behaviors related to the antecedent, behavior, and consequences.

The basic components of this assessment include pinpointing observable and measurable behaviors, determining factors that predict when the behaviors will occur, identifying the context in which they occur, and labeling the purpose they serve for the child. These components help the team unpack the situation. An FBA includes the following sections: background information, formal observation, data collection, problem behaviors, pattern analysis of the problem behaviors, functions of the problem behaviors, and recommendations.

The professional conducting the FBA uses a variety of methodologies to understand what is causing the child's behavioral challenges, since children act in certain ways for different reasons. Through an in-depth analysis, the assessor looks at when the behaviors occur, the triggers across multiple settings, and under what circumstances/locations (including home, school, therapy sessions, and extracurricular activities). The IEP team then uses these data to identify effective ways of addressing the child's behaviors. We encourage parents to also collect data related to their child's behaviors outside of the school day and share the data they collect with the IEP team.

Following the completion of an FBA, the IEP team convenes to review the results and determine how to best address the child's needs. This may include supports beyond IEP goals and objectives, such as the development of a BIP. The purpose of this plan would be to specifically address the concerns identified in the FBA. The BIP lists the behaviors and why they occurred (triggers) and recommends strategies and supports to address them.

Phone Logs

A phone log is a data collection tool that documents the adult actions rather than student behaviors. We recommend parents and educators maintain phone logs as they are the best way to document all conversations (Table 12-4). The types of phone log vary according to the frequency of calls you make and with whom you are speaking. When calling people multiple times in a month, keeping "monthly logs" for each person is appropriate. Otherwise, using a more general phone log to track calls between parents and educators should be implemented. If you are making calls to outside providers frequently or infrequently, a different phone log should be used.

Table 12-4
Phone Log Template

DATE	TIME	SPOKE TO	SUMMARY OF CONVERSATION

Written Correspondence

Communication between educators and parents is key to the success of the student. Often home–school communication takes place as written correspondence rather than a face-to-face conversation or phone call.

The first written communication related to the Individualized Education Plan (IEP) process is the letter inviting parents to an IEP meeting. We have included a sample invitation to an IEP meeting in the Appendix. The letter parents receive varies from state to state in its format, but the tone and intent are the same. We want to remind parents that along with this invitation, parents often receive a copy of their Procedural Safeguards, which were outlined in an earlier chapter.

Bud, P. S., & Jacobson, T. L.
*Navigating Special Education: The Power of Building
Positive Parent–Educator Partnerships* (pp. 169-179).
© 2023 SLACK Incorporated.

WHY WRITE A LETTER?

The purpose of all correspondence is to share information, voice concerns, make a request, or summarize an interaction. We suggest adding positive comments, such as *how everyone is working collaboratively* or a simple *thank you,* as a way to put a positive spin on the correspondence. It is important that parents and educators copy and file all written correspondence because communication between home and school is considered part of the child's educational record.

We highly recommend parents, educators, and administrators follow up on all parent–school communication, whether phone calls, face-to-face, or virtual meetings and conversations with a written response. Having a paper trail is the most effective way to prove the communication took place and to ensure there is follow through on all recommendations. A written summary of all interactions is the most effective way to ensure everyone is on the same page and understands the intent of requests and conversations. Sometimes the response can be a one-sentence email that says, *"As a follow-up to our conversation, I am confirming that we agreed to ..."* Written follow-up avoids misunderstandings, miscommunications, and builds perspective-taking.

Texting and Email

Texting and email have become popular forms of communication. Schools and school districts are using group texts as a way to communicate with families. They have found parents respond quicker to texting than email, voice mail, or flyers in the students' backpacks. Texting seems to be a fast and easy way to ensure parents are notified of school closures, delayed openings, or any type of emergency. Texting became even more popular as districts were trying to quickly and efficiently communicate with parents during COVID-19.

Although texting is a quick and easy form of communication, it is not always the best form of communication between teacher and parent, especially when it comes to discussing the child's academic, social-emotional, or behavioral needs. *(It should also be noted that many teachers are reluctant to share their mobile phone numbers with parents and sometimes vice versa.)* In our opinion, email is the most efficient way for parents and educators to communicate and provides a time-stamped record, which phone calls do not.

Misunderstandings and miscommunication can happen when emails go unanswered. We recommend the person receiving the email (whether teacher or parent) respond in a timely fashion. Our suggestion is within 24 to 48 hours of receipt of the message. If an email is not answered, we believe it is appropriate to forward the note to a building administrator or case manager with a copy to the person who sent the original email in the hopes of having the problem addressed. It also reduces the chance of a home–school communication breakdown.

Writing out your thoughts is an effective way to organize your thinking and may even help to clarify the issue. This easy-to-do strategy is recommended for parents, teachers, and administrators. Keep in mind that when something is presented in writing, it is more difficult for the request to be ignored or misunderstood. It also helps to ensure the matter is addressed in a timely manner.

In the case of the special education process, school districts are obligated to send parents a written invitation to an IEP meeting, along with a copy of their Procedural Safeguards, which formally begins the process. This is usually sent via the U.S. Postal Service. If parents want to initiate the process or request a meeting, we also suggest they put their request in writing. It can be hand-delivered, sent through the mail, or via email.

Correspondence Is a Legal Document

Putting all requests in writing is the best way to avoid any misunderstanding. We want to remind everyone that any written correspondence is considered to be part of the child's educational record, which is why parents and educators need to keep all correspondence, this includes email and texts. We suggest that they print all correspondence between home and school. Email and text messages can be either printed or saved in an electronic file. Either is fine, as long as they are easily accessible.

It is important to know if the correspondence was received, which is why sending letters by certified mail with a return receipt is advisable. There is nothing worse than believing your mail/email was received, when in fact it is lost or sitting in someone's spam folder. It is OK to request notification when an email has been received and read. We know that parents may hand-deliver a letter to the school or central office as a way to ensure it was received. When doing that, we suggest requesting a time-stamped receipt and then attaching it to a copy of the letter.

We have created easy-to-use sample letters, which can be found in the Appendix, since we believe it is best practice to follow up all meetings or conversations with some type of written correspondence. We also suggest if a communication breakdown occurs, parents and educators have a conversation as soon as possible. Problems are resolved through conversation, collaboration, and sometimes compromise.

It is best practice to have follow-up notes begin with saying "thank you." Then the parent or educator clearly states the purpose of the letter and what has been agreed to. The words "thank you" at the beginning of the note set the tone and help create positive feelings even when there are some disagreements.

Reasons for correspondence between home and school include, but are not limited to, requesting a meeting, requesting an evaluation, sharing concerns, and follow-up thank you notes for a face-to-face or virtual meeting or phone calls. Follow-up notes allow the teacher and parent to confirm what they were agreeing to at the meeting.

WHY REQUEST A MEETING?

Parent–teacher conversations are key to building partnerships. Procrastination in asking for a meeting only prolongs growing concerns and creates anxiety. Without a meeting, parents' or teachers' concerns cannot and will not be addressed. The purpose of the meeting is to alert others as to their (parents' or educators') concerns about the child's academic, social-emotional, or behavioral performance. It is highly recommended that the initial meeting is with the teacher and the purpose is to discuss concerns about the child's performance and to brainstorm initial strategies. It is suggested that this type of meeting occurs prior to requesting an IEP meeting or meeting with a building administrator. However, if the parents believe their concerns are connected to the teacher, then they should request a meeting with the building principal.

Follow up all meetings with a letter that outlines what was discussed and agreed upon at the meeting. This will avert future communication breakdowns or misunderstandings. It is best practice for teachers to meet with parents prior to bringing a formal request to the child study team or the IEP team because it helps to build trust and partnerships.

At the end of this chapter there are a few case study letters that model how to write home–school correspondence. In the Appendix, there are templates to assist parents creating a variety of different letters. Written correspondence is the best way to avoid any confusion or misunderstanding. We realize that most correspondence today is electronic. However, sending a follow-up handwritten note or email after a meeting or phone call goes a long way in cementing partnerships and building trust.

GENERAL INFORMATION ABOUT WRITTEN CORRESPONDENCE

- Correspondence should be short and to the point; if possible, no more than three concerns should be listed in the note.
- Begin by saying "thank you" to set a positive tone.
- Always send a thank you note, summarizing your discussion and acknowledging the person that took the time to listen.
- State the outcome of the meeting and what was accomplished.
- State what you agree with and what you disagree with.
- State what still needs to be accomplished.
- Reiterate the agreed-upon date or time line.
- Check for spelling and grammar before sending a note.
- Print a copy of all correspondence sent and received.
- Keep and file all correspondence.
- All correspondence is a part of the student's educational records.
- Date and sign all correspondence, include full outgoing signature (name, address, phone number, and email address).
- Requests to meet and discuss concerns can happen at any time of the year.

ELECTRONIC PROTOCOLS

- Emails are an appropriate and professional type of home–school correspondence.
- Emails and texting can be tricky; tone and message nuances may not be clear.
- Texting is informal and more appropriate between friends.
- Before texting parents, ask their permission.
- Many teachers do not want parents to have their mobile phone numbers.
- Email only one person at a time.
- If the classroom teacher does not respond after 1 to 2 days, resend the email and copy the principal.
- Only send group emails if you are thanking the team or reporting on a student's success.

SAMPLE LETTERS

Purpose: Requesting a Meeting With the Teacher

January 6, 2023

Dear Ms. Jones,

I am writing to request a meeting with you to discuss Ben's abilities and disabilities across his school day along with my concerns regarding their impact on his academic and emotional performance in the classroom and at home.

I know we have spoken several times since the beginning of the school year. However, my concerns have grown significantly since we last spoke on December 2, 2022.

I would like to set up a meeting with you as soon as possible. Please send me the date and time that you can meet, and I will arrange my schedule accordingly.

I look forward to hearing back from you in the next few days. Thank you.

Sincerely,
Mary Smith
Mary@MarySmith.com
204.123.4567

Purpose: Requesting a Meeting With Parents

February 24, 2023

Dear Mr. and Mrs. Kennedy,

I believe parents are a vital part of their child's educational team.

I would like to schedule a meeting to discuss Paul's overall performance. I will be sharing with you test scores and work samples that show how he is performing academically, and I will share some information that will highlight his social-emotional and behavioral performance.

I am inviting you to a meeting on March 7, 2023 at 10:00 a.m. at the school. Please call or email me if you are able to attend the meeting or to give me some suggested dates/times that will work with your schedule.

I look forward to meeting with you and working collaboratively to ensure Paul's success in school.

Sincerely,
Charlie Stevens
CStevens@ABCSchool.org
593.224.1298

Purpose: Thank You Note to a Teacher

*Send the request for an evaluation to the director of special education, building principal, or superintendent. It varies from district to district and state to state.

January 18, 2023

Dear Ms. Jones,

Thank you for meeting with me on January 17, 2023.

We discussed Ben's difficulties with reading comprehension and his difficulties with multiplication and division in word problems. Thank you for sharing his MAP scores from September and again how he is currently performing.

I am glad to know his decoding skills are on grade level and that the general education interventions appear to be helping to close the gap.

You reported that Ben is also receiving general education interventions in math. While I appreciate all efforts the school has put forth to address Ben's math issues, I disagree they are making a significant impact, as I witness Ben's meltdowns on a nightly basis.

I did not feel you heard my concerns regarding trying new strategies and reducing the amount of math homework he is being given.

I am not comfortable waiting until the end of February to meet again, as I know that we all do not want to see Ben's math frustrations continue to affect his self-esteem. Therefore, I am requesting a comprehensive evaluation to determine if Ben requires special education services.* Thank you.

Sincerely,
Mary Smith
Mary@MarySmith.com
204.123.4567

Purpose: Thank You Note to Parents

January 9, 2023

Dear Mr. and Mrs. Morris,

I want to thank you for meeting with me on January 6, 2023 via Zoom. As you could see after reviewing Jenny's test scores and seeing writing and math samples, when her performance is closely monitored she is able to perform on grade level.

As I shared with you, my goal is to provide Jenny with strategies, including checklists and templates, to help her complete assignments independently. I like your idea of creating more open lines of communication between home and school in order to ensure Jenny is completing homework and turning it in. Your request for a Friday check-in email with a list of all uncompleted assignments will give Jenny the weekend to catch up.

It was exciting to learn that Jenny taught herself to play the guitar during COVID. This reinforces that she can sustain focus when interested in the topic. Since she is able to complete homework assignments with minimal support from you, it appears the breakdown is being able to get work that is completed at home or in a study hall back to school.

I know working together as partners will help Jenny be more successful. I look forward to our next meeting, on February 16 at 3:30 p.m. At that time, we will review current strategies and discuss if there are additional ones that need to be implemented. Thank you.

Sincerely,
Linda Potter
Linda.Potter.21@whiteville.edu
348.775.3284

Purpose: Requesting an Evaluation to Determine Special Education Eligibility

Hand-deliver letter to the director of special services, building principal, or superintendent.

November 4, 2022

Dear Dr. McBride,

We are writing this letter after having met several times with Sally's classroom teacher, Mr. Harvey White. He shared that there is a general education intervention plan in place (RTI/INRS).

We do not feel that this support is enough. It appears that we have a difference of opinion as to how to best address Sally's educational needs. We have major concerns regarding her ability to organize her thoughts and ideas and assignments. We also are concerned about her lack of attentiveness throughout the school day. We do not believe the general education interventions that Mr. White reported as being in place are working.

Therefore, at this time, we are formally requesting a comprehensive evaluation, which we understand will be discussed at an IEP meeting. We would like the meeting to be convened as soon as possible. We will make attending that meeting our top priority.

We look forward to receiving a date and time for the meeting within the next week. Thank you.

Sincerely,
John and Gertrude Greene
John.Greene@gmail.com
716.987.0987

Purpose: Requesting an Independent Evaluation

Send this letter as a follow-up to an IEP meeting where the school-based team discussed the results of the evaluation and parents do not agree with the results. The letter should be sent to the director of special services or the administrator of the IEP meeting.

March 1, 2023

Dear Mrs. Johnson,

We are requesting an independent assessment at public expense for our son, Dillion Andrews (birthdate January 12, 2012), because we do not agree with the results of the assessment conducted by the Green Elementary School team.

We are requesting a comprehensive independent assessment, which we understand is our right to do if we disagree with the results of the district's testing and recommendations. We also believe the district did not adequately assess Dillion, which is why we are requesting further assessments in all academic areas and in core speech and language competencies that appear to be affecting Dillion's communication, organizational, emotional, and behavioral issues and are preventing him from successfully accessing the curriculum.

We understand that a response to our request must be provided in writing by the school district within 15 days and that the testing examiner must be mutually agreed upon.

We appreciate your help in identifying how to best provide Dillion with the support and services he needs to be able to successfully participate in all aspects of his academic day.

If you have any questions regarding our request, please contact us by phone or email. Thank you.

Sincerely,
Marcia and Lawrence Andrews
LAndrews@gmail.com
522.776.4123

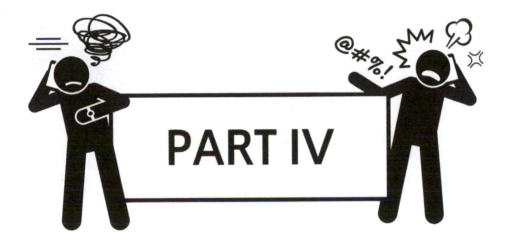

PART IV

STRATEGIES FOR RESOLVING CONFLICTS

Hiring an Educational Consultant

CONSULTANT VERSUS ADVOCATE: WHAT IS THE DIFFERENCE?

When parents and educators hear the words "educational consultant," they think it is synonymous with the term "educational advocate." In many legal systems, the word "advocate" is another term for professional lawyers. An educational advocate acts on behalf of the parents, much like an attorney. The family tells the advocate what they want (for their child), and the advocate works to help them get the program or services, instead of helping the family identify what their child needs.

Bud, P. S., & Jacobson, T. L.
Navigating Special Education: The Power of Building
Positive Parent—Educator Partnerships (pp. 183-194).
© 2023 SLACK Incorporated.

Transparency and Advocacy

Mr. and Mrs. Bishop wanted the local school district to find their 17.5-year-old son, James, eligible for special education. To date, James had always attended private school. He began struggling with anxiety and depression in his junior year of high school. Due to a few violent outbursts, he was expelled from his private school. His parents enrolled him in a wilderness program out of the country. They hired a special education attorney, Mrs. Showalter, who advised them to send James to a therapeutic boarding school for his senior year in high school.

Since James was no longer attending a private school, Mr. and Mrs. Bishop requested their local district to pay for James's therapeutic boarding school. The district, in turn, convened an Individualized Education Plan (IEP) meeting. The family brought their attorney to the meeting to act as their advocate. Mrs. Showalter's role was to convince the school district to support and pay for James to attend a private therapeutic boarding school at the district's expense.

Although Mrs. Showalter clearly understood the special education process and the law, she did not explain it to her clients, James's parents. She also knew it would take the district approximately 60 days to complete an assessment. James would turn 18 around the time the team would convene an eligibility IEP meeting. Sadly, she did not discuss any of this with his parents, including that when he turned 18 all rights would be turned over to him.

The day before the IEP meeting, Mr. Popper, the school administrator, called the family to confirm James would be at the meeting. Mrs. Bishop informed him that James was attending a wilderness program out of the country and was unavailable even by phone. Mr. Popper explained that James needed to agree with any decision the team made, since at 18 the educational rights would now be his.

Mrs. Bishop said she was unaware of the law and thought she could make academic decisions regarding James's placement and program until he graduated from high school. This is the difference between an advocate and a consultant. The advocate, who in this case was a lawyer, appeared to have misled the family. She took their case and agreed to help them get what they wanted because she considered Mr. and Mrs. Bishop to be her client rather than James. She did not even discuss with James what he wanted or help him decide what was in his best interest.

What parents want is not necessarily what is best for the student. It may be a program or service that another child has, and they now want their child to receive the same thing—whether their child needs it or not. Or they may be looking for a way to provide their child with support and believe special education is the answer. In our experience, many advocates take the parents at their word and agree to help the family get them what they want, even if it is not necessarily in the child's best interest. They often spend little or no time reviewing the student's record, which, in our opinion, is the best way to determine what the child requires to be successful. In fact, many advocates or attorneys don't even meet with the child. This is what happened in the story *Transparency and Advocacy*. Was special education the best way to address James's anger management issues? Or would the best plan have been to provide him counseling and have him finish high school in his home school district as a general education student?

The role of a consultant is to help the family successfully navigate the red tape of special education. They are skilled at teaching parents how to listen, learn, and evaluate what is being proposed. This ensures the child gets the program, services, or placement they need to be successful. In addition, consultants can be helpful when it comes to reaching reasonable and appropriate compromises. In the end, a consultant's responsibility is to advise, but parents should always make the final decision. They know their child the best! Therefore, we recommend parents never totally relinquish being their child's advocate.

Getting Cara What She Needs

Cara's parents, Mr. and Mrs. Stevens, were looking for a private school program for their daughter. They wanted the district to pay for her outplacement because they believed the public school was not able to appropriately address her academic and social needs. Cara was struggling to complete her assignments and learn new material. She appeared to be overwhelmed and was isolating herself from her peers. Mrs. Stevens took it upon herself to break down all of Cara's homework assignments. In addition, she would sit next to her while she completed all homework to ensure she remained focused.

continued on next page

To help the family determine the most appropriate program for Cara, Mr. and Mrs. Stevens hired an experienced consultant, Ms. Blackstone. The Stevenses wanted help in determining which private special education program would be able to meet Cara's needs. After reviewing Cara's educational records, Ms. Blackstone suggested several private schools for the parents to visit. The Stevenses visited each school and met with the school director to learn about the school's philosophy, student population, and the credentials of the teaching staff.

After visiting all programs within a 30-mile radius of their home, Mr. and Mrs. Stevens and Ms. Blackstone discussed the benefits and drawbacks of each program. The pros for the private schools were that they were small intimate programs that could individualize Cara's instruction. However, the cons were the programs all appeared to have a watered-down curriculum. It seemed that most students in each of the private schools had significantly more academic challenges than Cara. This led the parents to conclude that none of the special education schools would be able to provide Cara with the type of program the parents believed would appropriately address her needs in the Least Restrictive Environment (LRE).

Ms. Blackstone said the next step was for Mr. and Mrs. Stevens to request an IEP meeting and honestly discuss their concerns. After presenting how they felt Cara's needs could best be addressed, the team agreed that her current IEP was too generic. Mr. and Mrs. Stevens and her teachers discussed ways to revise the goals and objectives and add some modifications to Cara's overall program. The parents presented concrete evidence to support their suggestions.

Together parents and educators determined that pre-teaching key concepts for each unit in science, social studies, and English would be the best way to prepare Cara for the large group lesson. Mr. and Mrs. Stevens then requested the revised goals and objectives be written using the S.M.A.R.T. goal format to help the teachers monitor progress. As the conversations progressed, Cara's parents and teachers developed a shared vision as to how to best address Cara's teaching and learning.

After the new IEP was implemented, Cara started to thrive academically. She appeared to be happier at school and was more social. Through deep conversations and collaboration, Cara's needs were being met in her inclusive classroom. The family was thrilled that she did not have to attend a private special education program.

continued on next page

Mr. and Mrs. Stevens were grateful that Ms. Blackstone understood the role of a consultant was to advocate for the child. It was with her help, together with Cara's teachers, that they were able to have a meaningful conversation. Everyone listened, talked, and found ways to revise the IEP. They realized that the problem hadn't been public school vs. private school but rather making sure Cara's IEP was individualized and addressed her specific learning challenges. It is through conversation and collaboration that teams are able to develop appropriate programs for students in the LRE.

Consultants are professionals who provide expert advice within a particular area. Educational consultants (also called educational specialists) are highly experienced in the field of education and can effectively balance the parents' wants with the student's needs. They act as a coach, teaching parents how to navigate the special education process, interpret data, and use data-driven language to describe what they believe their child needs. Consultants understand the value of a home–school partnership and can facilitate parent–educator conversations about programs and services. They know how to work with the IEP team to develop clearly written S.M.A.R.T. goals and how to identify and evaluate the appropriateness of programs, placements, and services.

An educational consultant can help a family understand what their child needs and empower them to actively participate on the IEP team. This is exactly what happened in *Getting Cara What She Needs*. Ms. Blackstone reviewed the file, met with Cara, and discussed the pros and cons of the outplacement options with her parents. She then encouraged the family to partner with their school district and discuss how to best meet Cara's needs.

Consultants meet with parents and their child and review the child's educational records. Then they advise families on how to navigate the special education process and get their child what they need. Many times, consultants work with the family behind the scenes; other times, they attend IEP meetings and facilitate the conversation. Based on their educational experience and knowledge, they help parents understand the district's perspective and identify reasonable expectations, which helps parents *bridge the gap* from general education to special education.

We want to remind parents that if they bring an educational consultant, advocate, or lawyer to an IEP meeting, it can change the tone of the meeting. That is why we suggest that initially parents have their consultant coach them by working behind the scenes. However, in the name of transparency, if a consultant is going to attend an IEP meeting, we suggest parents alert the district. It is only when a family brings a lawyer to an IEP meeting that the district has their board attorney also attend the meeting.

Hiring a Consultant

No one gets a license to become a parent, nor are you required to take parenting courses. Raising a child can be difficult and presents many challenges—now add a disability to the mix and parents are faced with even more challenges. Unless a parent has a background in special education, they likely lack the knowledge needed to fully participate in the development of their child's IEP. They often find the special education process and the educational jargon confusing and overwhelming. Furthermore, parents tend to get emotional when discussing their child, which impacts their ability to listen and may lead to significant communication breakdowns.

Once parents are given their Procedural Safeguards, which explain their rights, it is crucial for them to be active, informed, and involved participants in their child's IEP development. Since all aspects of the process and documents can be intimidating, we strongly recommend parents contact their school district, ask questions, or ask for clarification. We suggest they speak to either the case manager or an administrator to review the process and answer any questions. This is the best way to avoid problems and is a great step in building a parent–school partnership. Sadly, many parents are reluctant to admit they do not understand or are too embarrassed to ask for help. However, asking questions is the only way to become informed about the special education process, procedures, and vocabulary.

Lack of knowledge is the greatest disadvantage parents have, especially if they have to negotiate to reach a consensus. If parents are reluctant to speak up and ask for help or have tried and been unsuccessful, then we recommend they hire an educational consultant. The consultant will be able to offer guidance, support, and objectivity. Parents may not always agree with their consultant, whose impartiality is vital to the process. Consultants have knowledge that parents may not have and can make the journey smoother.

If parents want to hire a qualified educational consultant, we suggest they turn to their pediatrician, social media special education groups, friends, or state or local parent advocacy groups for a referral. The cost of hiring a private consultant differs from state to state and their fees vary widely—from less than $100 an hour to more than $400 an hour. Some charge on an hourly basis; others have flat fee options. (In most cases, educational consultants are less costly than a lawyer.) Their services usually include meeting with the family and student, reviewing the educational records, and helping the family navigate the special education process. Many consultants work with families behind the scenes, although some attend IEP meetings and facilitate conversations. In all cases, consultants share their educational expertise as it relates to what the child needs. They see the child as their client.

A consultant's goal is to ensure the child gets what they need academically, emotionally, socially, and behaviorally. If the consultant believes the school district is not acting in the student's best interest, they can leverage their experience while not allowing the situation to turn adversarial. Consultants know how to work with the team to create reasonable solutions in the best interest of the student because they see the child as their client, even though the parents are paying for the services.

A strong home–school partnership is the best way to ensure the student gets what they need. However, some parents do not have a good working relationship with their child's teachers and need an impartial person to help facilitate the conversation. The consultant takes on that role and brings objectively to the table, helping the parents distinguish between what is, what was, and what could be. They are also able to advise the family on when and how to compromise.

Some families work with a consultant for many years because of ongoing concerns and unresolved issues. Sometimes consultants work behind the scenes, providing guidance and coaching. Other times, they attend meetings and are active participants in creating special education plans and facilitating the conversations. Consultants develop a broad understanding of the student's program and challenges. They often act as a mediator between the parents and the school district, proving to be helpful negotiators.

The tone of a meeting changes, and unfortunately may become adversarial, when parents invite a consultant to the meeting. We believe in transparency and suggest parents inform their district when they are bringing a consultant to the IEP meeting. We encourage parents to explain to the IEP team that the consultant is there to help facilitate the conversation, help them (parents) understand the IEP process, and interpret what is happening at the meeting. We have found a consultant may actually help to reduce tensions and misunderstandings, diffuse problems, and avoid communication breakdowns, which could lead to the family filing for due process.

Some school districts hire consultants to work with school administrators and legal counsel, with the parents' consent. Other times, they help families through the mediation process. If the case goes to court, the consultant may work with the family's special education attorney to testify as an expert witness.

One Size Doesn't Fit All!

It was late spring, and the IEP team was meeting to determine if Jason needed an extended school year program (ESY). It seemed that each year Mr. and Mrs. Bluegrass, Jason's parents, battled with the district because they believed without a customized ESY Jason would significantly regress and recoupment in the fall would take several months.

Mr. and Mrs. Bluegrass listened respectfully as Dr. Kirk, the director of special education services, reviewed Jason's needs with the IEP team. Everyone, including the parents, agreed that Jason qualified for ESY. Dr. Kirk then went on to describe the ESY program being offered by the district—4 weeks of academic support during the summer recess.

To Mr. and Mrs. Bluegrass's surprise, Dr. Kirk was not offering any customization to the ESY recommendation. Mr. Bluegrass respectfully disagreed by explaining that Jason required academic, speech, and occupational therapy over the summer, not just 4 weeks of academic support. The summer break was 2 months long, which is why Jason's parents felt they were being reasonable in requesting a 6-week individualized program.

Dr. Kirk explained to the parents that this was the program the district offered to all students who qualify for ESY. Mr. and Mrs. Bluegrass politely explained to the team that their son's multiple disabilities required constant support in academics, speech, and occupational therapy to avoid significant regression. They added that there is usually regression between a Friday to Monday break, so without a customized ESY program his recoupment would take a significant amount of time in the fall.

Before leaving the meeting, Mr. and Mrs. Bluegrass requested that Dr. Kirk record in the minutes that they "disagreed with the recommendations." They were frustrated and realized this year they would need help in getting Jason the ESY support he required. They hired Mrs. Winston, an educational consultant, who reviewed all the data. She agreed that it clearly showed a Friday to Monday break resulted in slight regression, and a week-long school vacation took Jason 2 weeks to recoup.

continued on next page

The parents brought Mrs. Winston to their next IEP meeting. Acting as Jason's voice, she shared the parents' data that documented his regression and the time it took to recoup. She also facilitated a conversation between parents and educators to ensure everyone's perspective was heard and understood. The parents and the school-based team collaboratively designed an ESY program to address Jason's needs.

This meant Mr. and Mrs. Bluegrass accepted the district's 4-week academic support recommendation, even though from their perspective it seemed to be a "one-size-fits-all" program. Dr. Kirk modified the rest of Jason's ESY services by creating a customized camp-type program with integrated therapies. Through open and honest conversations, parents and educators were able to collaborate and cooperate to provide Jason with what he needed to avoid significant regression during the summer break.

There are many districts that offer a "one-size-fits-all" ESY program. Yet often from the perspective of the parents, what is being offered isn't enough to avoid significant regression. In Jason's case, without getting the integrated therapies, he would still have significant regression. The intent of ESY is to ensure the student maintains learned skills, avoids significant regression in all areas, not just academic, and doesn't take a longer-than-expected time to relearn skills. ESY services, like all other services, should be individualized to address the student's specific needs.

Students Can Be Their Own Best Advocate

Meetings with consultants can take place via phone, video, or in-person. In addition to meeting with the parents, it is important for them to also meet with the student, whether they are in preschool or high school. Reading a file and only speaking to the parents does not provide a total picture. We recommend consultants observe the student in their academic setting or have a one-on-one meeting with them outside of the school. They can play a game, have the student read to them, or merely have a conversation. An experienced consultant, through an "informal assessment" or conversation, is skilled at gathering valuable information. We have found students often have incredible insight into what will help them be successful.

If You Ran the World

Terry was in eighth grade when he began falling behind in school. Until then, he seemed to be able to compensate for his poor organizational skills. Lately, his parents, Dr. and Mrs. Forest, felt Terry's teachers were not addressing his academic needs, and they were not sure what to do.

Dr. and Mrs. Forest hired an educational consultant to help them determine what Terry needed to be successful in school in hopes that they could resolve his falling grades before it was too late.

Mr. Dakota, their consultant, reviewed Terry's file and discussed concerns and intervention strategies with his parents. Then he asked to speak to Terry and get his perspective. Mrs. Forest warned Mr. Dakota that Terry would not share his thoughts and feelings about the situation with him.

At first, Terry was reluctant to openly discuss his frustrations. When the consultant asked, "If you ran the world, and you could have absolutely anything you wanted to help you in school, what would it be?" Terry sat in silence for a few moments, then said, "My own laptop computer." Dr. Forest said, "You have a computer at home."

Terry explained that if he had a laptop, he could create a folder for each subject and have his notes, homework, and assignments with him always. He went on to say that he was frustrated and often embarrassed that he forgot his homework and was always losing his notes. "I'm a great typist, and I know this would help me stay organized."

Mr. Dakota told Terry, "The best chance you have of getting your own laptop is by telling this same story at the IEP meeting. It will only be powerful and convincing if **you** tell the team what you need with the same passion and conviction you used when speaking to me." He suggested Terry ask for a trial period of 6 weeks.

Terry was worried his teachers wouldn't agree with the accommodation he was requesting. He thought they would argue with him. Although nervous, after some coaching he agreed to speak up at the meeting. Terry confidently explained why having his own laptop would help him stay organized and focused. The teachers were so impressed with his self-advocacy skills that they agreed to trial a laptop for 6 weeks.

continued on next page

Terry's grades improved. When the IEP team reconvened to review the data, they unanimously agreed to provide him with a laptop for the coming school year. Sometimes the best suggestions come from the student. However, it took insight and coaching from the consultant for Terry to have the confidence to voice his opinion. In addition, it opened his eyes to the importance of attending his own IEP meetings and speaking up. A little out-of-the-box thinking may be all it takes to provide a student with an appropriate program or accommodation.

WHAT DOES WORKING WITH A CONSULTANT LOOK LIKE?

Usually, a consultant will ask to review the child's educational file prior to the first meeting with the family. The file consists of all documents, including testing, reports, report cards, and data. They may share their analysis with the family orally or provide them with a written summary of their findings. Asking for a written summary will provide the family with vital documentation.

Initial Meeting With the Consultant

- Parents share their concerns, hopes, and wants for their child.
- Consultant provides advice regarding how parents can get their child what they need.
- Consultant outlines how parents can actively participate in the process.
- Consultant may script letters to request a meeting or summarize a meeting.
- Consultant often meets the child and uses informal tools to assess (books, games, observations).
- Consultant asks the child to share their concerns and wants related to school.

How Consultants Help Parents Get Their Child What They Need

Responsibilities of a Consultant

- Presents an overview of the entire process, including law and policies.
- Coaches on how to actively participate in the meeting, ensuring parents have a voice.
- Outlines specifics as they relate to the child.
- Explains what to expect at the upcoming meeting.
- Builds a relationship with the family and develops an understanding of the parents' concerns, perspective, hopes, and dreams as well as the child's perspective.
- Follows up each meeting with a summary—including new concerns and expectations.
- Walks the family through the process, step by step.
- Creates scenarios of what might be asked and the district's responses.
- Provides guidance related to data collection and organization of files.
- Helps family create three to five memorable sentences to present at an IEP meeting and coaches them on how to present them.

Parents should practice reading the statement with confidence and commitment. Read slowly and enunciate your words so you are understood. Practice giving the statement to your partner or a friend, but avoid memorizing what you want to say because it makes it sound less authentic. Practice looking in a mirror or video tape yourself. Make sure to use positive body language, eye contact, and lean in. Getting emotional and even crying is okay as it helps to build trust and empathy. It is important to sound authentic and transparent. Speak with passion.

Consultant's Role During a Meeting

- Facilitates presentation of parental concern, perspective, and hopes and dreams.
- Provides support to parents in the presentation of documents and data.
- Keeps the IEP team focused on getting the child what they need.
- Works with the team to reach compromises or build consensus.
- If disagreements are unresolved, summarizes the areas of disagreement.

15

Conflict Leads to Creative Solutions

AGREEMENT DOES NOT ALWAYS HAPPEN

It is unrealistic for parents or educators to think everyone is going to always agree, whether at work, a social gathering, or an Individualized Education Plan (IEP) meeting. The good news is that conflict can open doors and lead to creative solutions. This is more likely to occur when everyone's voice is deemed important and everyone can actively participate in the conversation. When diverse viewpoints are presented and discussed, multiple solutions emerge that the team may not have been previously considered.

Bud, P. S., & Jacobson, T. L.
*Navigating Special Education: The Power of Building
Positive Parent–Educator Partnerships* (pp. 195-198).
© 2023 SLACK Incorporated.

Most of us have experienced opposition or conflict during a meeting or conversation, whether at work, at home, or at an IEP meeting. While we cannot prevent conflicts or discourage disagreements, we can stress the importance of learning how to manage them. Being prepared for each meeting is a good first step. We recommend this begins by being able to back up all ideas, suggestions, or solutions with evidence and then bringing the information to the meeting. When this happens, parents and educators will be ready to show they've done their homework so that the conversation can begin.

Negativity does not resolve any conflict and can actually cause progress to backslide. An effective approach is to use active listening strategies to stop disagreements from creating barriers that block progress. We suggest asking each person to make one comment to add to the conversation. Their statements can be suggestions that support or oppose what is being said. However, in all cases, they should build on the conversation by saying "Yes, and ..." rather than "Yes, but ..."

VOICING YOUR OPINION

Agreeing is easy. However, agreeing in silence does not lead to a feeling of partnership. If you agree with what is being said, it is important to let the team know. Letting everyone know you like, support, or agree with an idea or suggestion will help move the conversation along. Simple ways to agree are saying, "I think what you said is a good idea" and "I think you are right, and I would like to add ..." Adding to what was said, even when agreeing, is important.

Disagreeing is much harder. When someone shares an idea and another person disagrees, it can easily change the tone of the meeting. It could even set the stage for conflict or at least one person feeling rejected, dismissed, or irrelevant to the conversation. This could even cloud how others hear the ideas or suggestions being made, especially if an idea was not clearly outlined in the first place. We realize that while most people believe they have clearly explained their thinking, this is not always the case. A good way to clarify a team member's idea is to paraphrase or summarize what they said. This will ensure you understand their perspective. We suggest whether you are an educator or a parent, if you disagree, ask for clarification. This can help move the conversation in a positive direction.

Many people raise their voices when they disagree. When this happens, most people stop listening. We realize that raising your voice is a way of stressing the importance of what you have to say. However, we suggest everyone tries to speak using a modulated tone. Did you realize that the louder you speak, the more agitated others become? The idea is to not raise your voice but rather to use data to support and/or prove your argument. Facts can turn a conversation around. It takes the conversation from being subjective to being objective.

When someone opposes another's idea, they often shut down as listeners and the conversation regresses in a number of ways (pointing out flaws and errors in the argument, making personal attacks against the person, etc.). However, these statements only exacerbate the differences. When disagreeing, we suggest you begin by highlighting what you believe is the other person's perspective, and then you can respectfully disagree. Remember not to use "Yes, but …," as it will only exacerbate the situation.

Instead say we suggest you begin by saying, "I hear what you are saying, and these are the reasons why I disagree …" It is important not to list more than three points. People find it difficult to hold onto more than three concepts at any one time. Conflicts can be averted when you avoid negating what has been said. Instead, add new viewpoints to the conversation based on research, facts, or even data-driven opinions.

People usually deal with opposition in one of three ways:
1. They resist it, becoming combative.
2. They avoid it, ignoring what the other person says.
3. They give in to an opposing idea.

A fourth, and more effective way, is *to listen to what is being said and be open to compromise* (University of Minnesota, 2013). Opposition is then a positive force for the improvement of your ideas and will result in the student getting what they need to be successful.

THINGS TO CONSIDER WHEN ADDRESSING OPPOSITIONAL BEHAVIORS

*   What is the other person really saying? And why?
*   What are the strengths and weaknesses of their idea or position?
*   How is the other person invested in what they are saying?
*   How do you really feel? How do you think the other person really feels?
*   Is the conflict personal?
*   How can we work together and reach a compromise?

*A flight attendant during the safety speech says,
"If you're traveling with a small child, please remember to
secure your air mask before assisting anyone else."*

Apply this philosophy when interacting with the IEP team. If you are angry or unprepared, then you are not in the right mindset to help the child. The first step is to take control of your own emotions, which to us means everyone comes to an IEP meeting having an emotionally positive headspace. This mindset can help you remain calm and interact professionally. If conflict arises, always consider the underlying cause. Is it a philosophical difference? Is it a power struggle? In either case, leave your emotions at the door. Be open to compromise, which means collaborating on a solution. Then together, working as partners, the IEP team can make decisions and recommendations regarding what is best for the child.

16

Facilitated IEP Meetings, Mediation, and Due Process

IF THINGS DO NOT GO MY WAY, WHAT DO I DO?

In the best possible scenario, parents and educators work together and build a constructive parent–educator partnership. They are open to compromising to ensure the student gets the most appropriate services. However, there are times when communication breaks down. Trust is broken. Partnerships are not cemented or may even be severed.

Bud, P. S., & Jacobson, T. L.
Navigating Special Education: The Power of Building Positive Parent–Educator Partnerships (pp. 199-202).
© 2023 SLACK Incorporated.

When parents and the local school district cannot agree on how to provide the child with an appropriate program, their differences may need to be addressed legally. This is costly, time consuming, and may not result in what is best for the child. However, sometimes the problem is actually connected to parental and student rights violations, such as failing to conduct an evaluation or follow the recommendations outlined in the Individualized Education Plan (IEP). On the other hand, the problem may be related to specific parts or all of the IEP that are not being delivered with efficacy. Another reason parents exercise their due process rights is they do not believe the proposed program appropriately addresses their child's needs. Whatever the reason, we suggest beginning with the least litigious option. All options are outlined in the parents' Procedural Safeguards document. They include a facilitated IEP meeting, mediation, or a due process hearing.

We recommend that parents try a less formal process before filing for due process. It can be both financially and emotionally less costly. Using the 5-C Model of Communication can help the team work collaboratively to reach consensus. When parents believe there are significant compliance or program issues that have not been addressed, with no end in sight, they may decide to file a complaint or seek due process. The details of how to file at each level of the process may vary slightly between states.

It is important for parents to understand if they request a due process hearing, they must hire an attorney who specializes in educational matters. Attorneys are costly; they usually charge by the hour. We encourage everyone to try to reach a compromise before hiring an attorney and/or filing due process. We believe it would be a win-win for all.

FACILITATED INDIVIDUALIZED EDUCATION PLANNING MEETING

When parents feel their child's needs are not being met and the district is not listening to their concerns, a good first step would be to request a Facilitated IEP meeting (FIEP). It may help rectify differences, restore trust, and rebuild partnerships. The FIEP is a newly emerging process that appears to be very effective because it adds a neutral party to the team. The neutral party leads the meeting, allowing emotions and personalities to be taken out of the picture so the needs of the child are addressed.

An FIEP meeting is a productive way to avoid due process, address parental problems, and resolve concerns that are not being met through the traditional IEP process. This type of meeting is used as an alternative to the dispute resolution process and is a voluntary process that helps teams restructure the IEP in order to effectively address parent concerns and solve problems. It is different from mediation, which is used to address broader issues and is held outside of the IEP meeting framework.

For more information on the FIEP process, refer to Tracy Gershwin Mueller and Anna Moriarty Vick's article *Rebuilding the Family–Professional Partnership Through Facilitated Individualized Education Program Meetings: A Conflict Prevention and Resolution Practice* (2019).

Mediation

According to the Committee on Education and the Workforce, U.S. House of Representatives, mediation is described as "… an attempt to bring a peaceful settlement or compromise between parties." This is accomplished "through the objective intervention of a neutral party" (J. Dispute, Resolution 187, 2016). When parents and school districts find themselves at an impasse in conflict, they may choose to turn to mediation and rely upon an objective neutral party (professional mediator) to resolve differences.

Many times, the first step that parents choose when they have a dispute with their school district is mediation. This process is faster and cheaper than going to a due process hearing. State Boards of Education pay for the mediator, and parents are not required to hire a special education attorney. Ultimately, mediators act neutrally to discuss and resolve problems, issues, concerns, and complaints amicably without the need to file for due process. Parents may choose to bring a consultant to the mediation, who can help them understand the educational jargon and the mediation process.

Both parents and the school district must agree to try to mediate their differences. As with the FIEP, mediation is a voluntary process. Unlike a due process hearing, mediation usually takes only a few hours. The recommendations are nonbinding because the mediator is not a judge but rather a state-hired professional.

Mediation is only effective if the parents and the school administration go into the process in good faith because they want to reach a solution and are willing to compromise. Both sides usually present data and documentation, but witnesses are not called to testify. Each side has a chance to present their case in front of the mediator. The mediator's role is to suggest next steps and to assist in generating a solution. They often meet with both sides alone as a way to help them reach some type of agreement.

DUE PROCESS HEARING

If an agreement cannot be reached through FIEP or mediation, or if parents are not willing to participate in either of the processes, the only option is for parents to request a due process hearing. This is a formal process used to address special education issues, and the decisions are legally binding. Since due process is considered a legal proceeding, both the parents and the district are required to hire attorneys with a hearing officer acting as a judge. The parents and the school district present written evidence about the disputes and have witnesses testify. Then the hearing officer reviews all evidence and testimony in order to make a decision. If either side does not agree with the outcome of the hearing, they can file an appeal to the state and later to the federal court. If all appeals fail, the decision is binding.

Going through due process is costly and stress-inducing for all involved. We believe in many cases the person most affected is the student. That is why we recommend that whenever possible parents should try to find solutions through FIEP meetings or mediation before exercising their due process rights. The student is impacted because their teacher is going to be away from the classroom spending time preparing documents and data and testifying at the hearing. The student's education will be in the hands of a substitute teacher, which is not in the child's best interest. If the district prevails, the parents have spent a lot of money and emotional energy in their legal endeavors with no changes made to their child's program or services.

It is important for parents to understand that once they exercise their due process rights, the "stay put" provision goes into effect. This provision states that while due process proceedings are pending, the student remains in their current educational placement under 20 U.S.C. § 1415 (j). In other words, if the parents file a due process petition within the requisite time period, the district must maintain the last agreed-upon program until the dispute is resolved. If the parents do not take any action within the time period allotted, the program will automatically go into effect regardless of whether or not the parents consented to the IEP.

Note: This does not apply to initial IEPs, which require parental consent to be implemented.

17

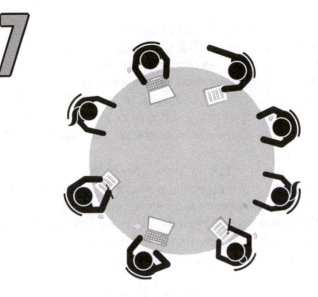

Negotiation and Compromise

THE END GAME

We do not believe that one's willingness to compromise is a sign of weakness. Instead, we believe it sends a strong message that you care about something or someone beyond yourself.

Throughout this book, we have stressed the importance of having a shared vision and building a positive partnership. Since a student's success is in the hands of their parents, educators, and administrators, we urge them to listen and embrace the perspectives of others. Then, through open and honest conversations, we encourage everyone to negotiate, compromise, and reach consensus.

Bud, P. S., & Jacobson, T. L.
*Navigating Special Education: The Power of Building
Positive Parent–Educator Partnerships* (pp. 203-205).
© 2023 SLACK Incorporated.

Embracing our 5-C Model of Communication can lead to building positive partnerships. To paraphrase Alan Greenspan, *unless you are willing to compromise, you cannot work together as partners.* When everyone understands the power of collaboration and the importance of creating a shared vision and mission, the Individualized Education Plan (IEP) team is in a position to co-create the most appropriate IEP. An openness to compromise often means the team is able to develop an educational plan that is *far better* than what was originally proposed.

Negotiating is considered to be a deliberate process. We think of it as the discussions that lead to reaching a compromise. It begins with everyone gathering evidence and data to support their viewpoint. Using data can take the emotion out of the conversation. When the discussion is objective, the team is more likely to reach an amicable compromise. We know that sometimes team members feel they have made too big of a sacrifice, resulting in consensus that may be short lived.

We suggest always negotiating in "good faith," by coming to the meeting with data to support your position. Too often when negotiating, people revert to the use of the "broken record technique," which means they try to wear others down by repeating their point over and over, using a modulated tone. It is their belief they will win because the message they are repeating becomes the prominent point in conversation.

We do not recommend using this tactic and do not think it will get the long-term result that is needed to build a positive parent–educator partnership. Instead, we recommend using data as the best way to support your position. However, we also encourage everyone to listen and be open to hearing the other person's perspective. In the end, it is about being open to finding a way to compromise, which is a two-sided process. Compromise doesn't mean that one person gives in. Through conversation, collaboration, and cooperation, both parents and educators will be able to form a shared vision that results in a partnership. Then, together, they can work as allies. The end game will be the creation of the *best IEP* to address the student's needs.

> *First and foremost: Any compromise should focus on what the student requires to succeed. It is not about what parents want or what the district has to offer, it is about what the student needs!*

NEGOTIATION TECHNIQUES

- *Remain flexible.* Accept revisions and be firm on major issues.
- *Remain friendly.* Monitor your tone and volume, smile while speaking and listening.
- *Separate the people from the problem.* Avoid dealing in personalities.
- *Negotiate as a team.* All members present or stop the meeting.
- *Stay focused.* Stick to the issue on the table.
- *End the meeting.* When progress stops, reconvening provides a fresh start.
- *Negotiation goal.* Free Appropriate Public Education (FAPE) in the Least Restrictive Environment (LRE).
- *Inappropriate tactics.* Claiming "lack of funding" or "what other children get."

When an Agreement Is Reached

- *District:* Sends a written summary that outlines the agreement.
- *Parents:* Send a follow-up letter summarizing the agreement from their perspective.
- *Negotiation conclusion:* A statement that clearly states the course of action, agreements, disagreements, and a timeline to address any disagreements.

Epilogue

After meeting on LinkedIn, it only took a phone conversation and an in-person meeting for us to realize we had a shared vision. We both wanted all stakeholders to be involved in the Individualized Education Plan (IEP) process by building positive partnerships. We knew that meant writing a book to share our vision and hopefully bring about change.

After several deep conversations, we discovered our core values were built around what we have called the 5-C Model of Communication: conversation, collaboration, cooperation, compromise, and consensus. We see these skills as the foundational tools all IEP team members need to learn, use, and embrace. To us, listening and the 5-C Model of Communication comprise the core

Bud, P. S., & Jacobson, T. L.
Navigating Special Education: The Power of Building Positive Parent–Educator Partnerships (pp. 207-209).
© 2023 SLACK Incorporated.

attributes of effective communication. We see them as the crucial components of any discussion, especially when parents, educators, and administrators sit around a conference table to discuss what students need and how to meet their needs appropriately.

We had a clear mission; logistics presented the challenge. Living almost 100 miles apart and being in different stages of our life (Peggy's family was grown and Tamara had young children), we still knew we had a shared vision and had to get our message out there. Our dream was to write a book that would make a difference in the lives of parents and educators as they navigate their landscape of practice.

Our skills and beliefs complemented each other. One of us (Peggy) saw everything through the lens of communication, and the other (Tamara) through the lens of special education. We had both worked in public education as educators and administrators. We had seen districts and parents spend thousands of dollars hiring lawyers who were often unsuccessful in facilitating mutually agreeable conversations. In addition, the discussions often turned adversarial, leaving parents frustrated that their voices weren't heard, and educators thought they were the experts. It also meant that reaching an agreement would be a costly process.

Over our professional careers, we have attended hundreds of IEP meetings. School districts and families have hired us as consultants. Yet, we have consistently observed that parents and educators do not partner to ensure the child's success. We knew intellectually, and emotionally the only way for students to get what they needed was for all members of the child's IEP team to develop positive partnerships. There weren't any books devoted to getting this message out there, so we knew it was up to us to share our vision and transform the world of special education teams.

We believe our book provides all stakeholders (parents, administrators, educators, undergraduate students, and graduate students) with the tools and strategies needed to communicate effectively and bring special education into the 21st century. From a personal perspective, the more time we spent talking, listening, and writing, the more our relationship has grown into a true partnership.

We both were committed to the idea of writing this book. When COVID-19 hit the world, we saw it as our opportunity. We could work via Zoom and use Google Docs to write and edit our book without leaving home. The 100 miles between us no longer mattered. Being given the gift of more time at home allowed us to turn our shared vision into this timely and important book, *Navigating Special Education: The Power of Building Positive Parent–Educator Partnerships.*

In the 10 years from conception to completion, the landscape of education and communication has changed vastly. Yet, the value of partnerships, which is our shared vision, is as important today as it was 10 years ago. It is our hope that after reading *Navigating Special Education,* parents, educators, and administrators will have the skills and strategies needed to build strong partnerships and be vital members of a child's IEP team. In addition, we believe all stakeholders will gain a deeper understanding of effective communication's role in the IEP process, the power of data collection, and the importance of negotiation. We also believe that everyone will develop deeper insights into the intent of special education law.

Our book provides a road map to best practices through its focus on the foundational skills and strategies needed for all things related to the IEP process. The case studies we share are based on our experiences and hopefully encourage stakeholders to make personal connections. The educational theories and approaches, such as active listening, conflict resolution, positive teamwork, and developing S.M.A.R.T. goals, provide the tools to communicate across all platforms successfully. We hope our forward-thinking, best-practice ideas will help districts and parents work more collaboratively.

In conclusion, it is crucial for parents, educators, and administrators to remember the importance of always putting what the student needs ahead of what they want or the district offers. Forging a positive relationship and becoming vital partners includes listening to the other person's perspective and putting yourself in their shoes. Changing the context and culture of the IEP team through the 5-C Model of Communication will form strong parent–educator partnerships. Our dream is that this book will bring about a mindset change regarding the IEP process.

CONCLUDING PARENT–EDUCATOR SELF-REFLECTION QUESTIONNAIRE

Purpose: We hope you now have identified your specific role in the special education community. As you answer the questions below, have your attitudes and perceptions toward the special education process changed? Are you more open to working with the team as positive partners? Do you think you will have an opportunity to implement the 5-C Model of Communication when participating on an IEP team? Do you think your mindset has changed?

What is your attitude regarding the IEP process?
☐ Comfortable ☐ Intimidated ☐ Other

What is your knowledge regarding the IEP process?
☐ Excellent ☐ Fair ☐ Poor

Why do you believe the student requires special education services?
☐ Academic ☐ Social ☐ Behavioral/
☐ Speech ☐ All Emotional

What are your perceptions regarding how others view special education teachers?
☐ Positive ☐ Negative ☐ No Opinion

What are your perceptions regarding how others view parents of children with disabilities?
☐ Positive ☐ Negative ☐ No Opinion

What are your perceptions regarding how others view a child with disabilities?
☐ Positive ☐ Negative ☐ No Opinion

What are your perceptions regarding students leaving the classroom for support?
☐ Positive ☐ Negative ☐ No Opinion

Do you use criteria/data to discuss concerns about the student in the IEP meeting?
☐ Yes ☐ No

What are your perceptions regarding how others measure or label a student?
☐ Respectfully ☐ Intelligently ☐ Uneducatedly

How do you view the special education services in your district?
☐ Positive ☐ Negative ☐ No Opinion

References

American Psychological Association. (2017). *Individuals with Disabilities Education Act (IDEA).* American Psychological Association. https://www.apa.org/advocacy/education/idea

Americans with Disabilities Act of 1990, Pub. L. No. 101-336, 104 Stat. 328. (1990).

Angel, D. W. (2016, December 28). *The four types of conversations: Debate, dialogue, discourse, and diatribe.* https://medium.com/@DavidWAngel/the-four-types-of-conversations-debate-dialogue-discourse-and-diatribe-898d19eccc0a

Banks, J. A., & Banks, C. A. M. (2012). *Multicultural education. Issues and perspectives.* Wiley.

Bardsley, M. E. (2002). Building successful partnerships: A guide for developing parent and family involvement programs. *Childhood Education, 78,* 3. https://link.gale.com/apps/doc/A83661383/AONE?u=nysl_oweb&sid=sitemap&xid=0788c809

Battle v. Commonwealth of Virginia, 406 S.E.2d 195 (Court of Appeals of Virginia).

Bureau of Special Education. (2021). *Procedural standards.* New Jersey Department of Children and Families, Office of Education. https://www.nj.gov/dcf/policy_manuals/OOE-I-A-1-26.pdf

Bureau of Special Education. (2021). *Procedural Safeguards Notice Required Under IDEA Part B.* Connecticut State Department of Education, 1-41. https://portal.ct.gov/-/media/SDE/Special-Education/Prosaf.pdf

Cassel, S. (2019). How to choose a co-teaching model. *Edutopia.* https://www.edutopia.org/article/how-choose-co-teaching-model

Chameroy, M. (n.d.). [District name] public schools notice of planning and placement team meeting. https://portal.ct.gov/-/media/SDE/Special-Education/ED623.pdf

Cohen, D. H. (2015). *Observing and recording the behavior of young children.* Teachers College Press.

Cook, D. L. (1968). *The impact of the Hawthorne effect in experimental designs in educational research.* U.S. Department of Health, Education, and Welfare.

Cook, D. L., & King, J. (1968). A Study of the Hawthorne Effect in educational research. *Research in the Teaching of English, 2*(2), 93-98. http://www.jstor.org/stable/40170508

Dale, E. (1947). *Audio-visual methods in teaching.* The Dryden Press.

Davila, R. R. (1990). Office of Special Education and Rehabilitative Services policy letter 17. *Education for the Handicapped Law Review,* 419.

De Jong, B. A., Dirks, K. T., & Gillespie, N. (2016). Trust and team performance: A meta-analysis of main effects, moderators, and covariates. *Journal of Applied Psychology, 101,* 1134-1150. https://doi.org/10.1037/apl0000110

Dewey, J. (1916). *Democracy and education: An introduction to the philosophy of education.* Macmillan.

Education for All Handicapped Children Act of 1975, Pub. L. 94-142. Elementary and Secondary Education Act of 1965. Pub. L. 89-10.

Esteves, K. J., & Rao, S. (2008). The evolution of special education: Retracing legal milestones in American history. *Principal,* 1-3. https://www.naesp.org/sites/default/files/resources/1/Principal/2008/N-Oweb2.pdf

FBA Sample 1. (2015). Northern Lights Special Education Cooperative.

Framework for Revising School District Codes of Student Conduct. (2014). The School Superintendent Association & the Children's Defense Fund. https://www.aasa.org/uploadedFiles/Childrens_Programs/Code%20of%20Conduct_9.16.14.pdf

Freedom of Information Act of 1967, Pub. L. 89-487. (2000).

Fuchs, D., & Fuchs, L. S. (2009). Responsiveness to intervention: Multilevel assessment and instruction as early intervention and disability identification. *The Reading Teacher, 63*(3), 250-252. http://www.jstor.org/stable/25615816

Fuchs D., Mock, D., Morgan, P. L., & Young, C. L. (2003). Responsiveness-to-intervention: Definitions, evidence, and implications for the learning disabilities construct. *Learning Disabilities Research & Practice, 18,* 157-171.

Garvey, J. (2022). What is an out-of-district placement? *May Institute.* https://www.mayinstitute.org/news/acl/asd-and-dd-child-focused/what-is-an-out-of-district-placement/

Glaser, J. E. (2016). *Conversational intelligence: How great leaders build trust and get extraordinary results.* Routledge.

Gouëdard, P., Ponti B., & Vienneti, R. (2020). Education responses to COVID-19: Implementing a way forward. *OECD, 224,* 1-44. https://doi.org/10.1787/8e95f977-en

Harmon, S., Street, M., Bateman, D., & Yell, M. L. (2020). Developing Present Levels of Academic Achievement and Functional Performance Statements for IEPs. *TEACHING Exceptional Children, 52*(5), 320-332. https://doi.org/10.1177/0040059920914260

Holmes v. Sobol, 690 F. Supp. 154 (United States District Court, W.D. New York 1988). https://law.justia.com/cases/federal/district-courts/FSupp/690/154/2359021/

Individuals with Disabilities Education Act. https://sites.ed.gov/idea/

Individuals with Disabilities Education Act of 2004, Pub. L. 101-476. (2004).

J. Dispute, Resolution 187, 114 Cong. (2016).

Kober, N. (2020). *History and evolution of public education in the US. Center on Education Policy,* 1-8. https://files.eric.ed.gov/fulltext/ED606970.pdf

Least Restrictive Environment—Documents. (n.d.). CT.Gov—Connecticut's official state website. Retrieved January 24, 2023, from https://portal.ct.gov/SDE/Special-Education/Least-Restrictive-Environment/Documents

Lewis, W. A., & O'Neill, H. H. (2021). *Where's the office?: Moving today's leaders from what is to what can be.* AuthorHouse.

Loftus, E. F. (2016). Illusions of memory. *Skeptical Inquirer, 40,* 22-23.

Mehrabian, A. (1971). *Silent messages.* Wadsworth Co.

Mesa (AZ) Public Schools (1989). Office of Civil Rights letter of finding, 16. *Education for the Handicapped Law Review,* 316.

Morin, A. (2021). The difference between push-in and pull-out services. *Understood.* https://www.understood.org/en/articles/the-difference-between-push-in-and-pull-out-services

Mueller, C. (2019). *Beyond stigma: Disability identity in school contexts.* Doctoral dissertation, University of Washington.

Mueller, T. G., & Vick, A. M. (2019). Rebuilding the family-professional partnership through facilitated Individualized Education Program meetings: A conflict prevention and resolution practice. *Journal of Educational and Psychological Consultation, 29*(2), 99-127. https://doi.org/10.1080/10474412.2018.1470934

Murphy, M., & Beam, H. (2021, February 19). 4 tips for a successful self-contained classroom. *Edutopia.* https://www.edutopia.org/article/4-tips-successful-self-contained-classroom

National Parent Teacher Association. (2000). *Building successful partnerships: A guide for developing parent and family involvement programs* (pp. 11-12). National PTA, National Education Service.

National Parent Teacher Association. (2009). *PTA national standards for family-school partnerships: An implementation guide.* https://www.pta.org/docs/default-source/files/runyourpta/national-standards/national_standards_implementation_guide.pdf

Northern Lights Special Education Cooperative. (n.d.). *Emotional or behavioral disorders.* https://www.nlsec.org/resources/EBD

Office of P-12 Education: Office of Special Education. (2013). *Continuum of special education services for school-age students with disabilities.* University of the State of New York, State Education Department. https://www.p12.nysed.gov/specialed/publications/policy/continuum-schoolage-revNov13.pdf

Office of the Student Advocate. (n.d.). *Knowing the difference: 504 Plan or IEP.* https://sboe.dc.gov/sites/default/files/dc/sites/sboe/multimedia_content/Understanding%20the%20Differences%20Between%20504s%20and%20IEPs.pdf

Pennsylvania Training and Technical Assistance Network. (2015). https://www.pattan.net/Forms/INVITATION-TO-PARTICIPATE-IN-THE-IEP-TEAM-MEET-3

Professional Learning Board. (n.d.). What is the difference between the "pull-out" and "push-in" model in special education? https://k12teacherstaffdevelopment.com/tlb/what-is-the-difference-between-the-pull-out-and-push-in-model-in-special-education/

Rehabilitation Act of 1973, Pub. L. 93-112. (1973).

Reusch v. Fountain, 872 F. Supp. 1421 (U.S. District Court of Maryland 1994). https://www.wrightslaw.com/law/caselaw/case_esy_reusch_fountain.htm

Schrag, J. A. (1989). Office of Special Education Programs policy letter. *Education for the Handicapped Law Review, 213*, 255.

South Pasadena Council PTA Special Needs Committee. (2014). *Functional Behavior Assessment.* http://www.spp4snc.com/wp-content/uploads/2014/12/Sample-FBA-2.8.16.pdf

Stacey G. v. Pasadena Independent School District, 695 F.2d 949 (United States Court of Appeals, Fifth Circuit 1982). https://law.justia.com/cases/federal/district-courts/FSupp/547/61/1479050/

University of Minnesota. (2013). *Communication in the real world: Conflict and interpersonal communica-tion.* https://open.lib.umn.edu/communication/chapter/6-2-conflict-and-interpersonal-communication/

U.S. Department of Education. (n.d.). *FAQs on photos and videos under FERPA. Protecting student privacy.* https://studentprivacy.ed.gov/faq/faqs-photos-and-videos-under-ferpa

U.S. Department of Education. (2000). *A guide to the Individualized Education Program.* https://www2.ed.gov/parents/needs/speced/iepguide/index.html

U.S. Department of Education. (2020). *Protecting students with disabilities: Frequently asked questions About Section 504 and the education of children with disabilities.* Office of Civil Rights. https://www2.ed.gov/about/offices/list/ocr/504faq.html

U.S. Department of Education. (2022). *About IDEA. Individuals with Disabilities Education Act.* https://sites.ed.gov/idea/about-idea/

Wee, S. (2013). Development and initial validation of the Willingness to Compromise Scale. *Journal of Ca-reer Assessment, 21*(4), 487-501. https://doi.org/10.1177/1069072712475281

Wrightslaw. (2019). *Procedural Safeguards in IDEA protect the rights of children with disabilities and their parents.* https://www.wrightslaw.com/info/safgd.index.htm

Yell, M. L., & Bateman, D. (2020). Defining educational benefit: An update on the U.S. Supreme Court's ruling in Endrew F. v. Douglas County School District (2017). *TEACHING Exceptional Children, 52*(5), 283-290. https://doi.org/10.1177/0040059920914259

Yell, M. L., Collins, J., Kumpiene, G., & Bateman, D. (2020). The Individualized Education Program: Procedural and substantive requirements. *TEACHING Exceptional Children, 52*(5), 304-318. https://doi.org/10.1177/0040059920906592

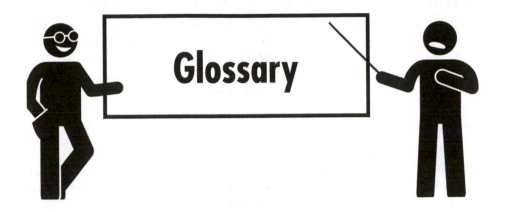

Glossary

SUMMARY OF THE SPECIAL EDUCATION PROCESS

What is special education? Providing specially designed instruction to meet a student's unique needs so they can access the general curriculum of their school district.

Who is on the IEP team? Team members include general education and special education teacher, administrator or supervisor, a pupil services personnel (psychologist, social worker, or counselor), related services teacher (if indicated, i.e., speech pathologist or occupational therapist), and parents. It is important to keep in mind that parents are equal members of the team and have an equal voice.

Bud, P. S., & Jacobson, T. L.
Navigating Special Education: The Power of Building
Positive Parent–Educator Partnerships (pp. 215-224).
© 2023 SLACK Incorporated.

Key Steps in the Process

Eligibility: The student's identified disability must adversely affect their educational performance, and as a result requires specially designed instruction to address their unique educational needs. The program is developed and driven by the goals and objectives. To be eligible for special education, a child must have a disability and must need special education services and related services. If a child has a disability but does not need special education services, the child is not eligible for special education under IDEA, but may be eligible for protections under Section 504 of the Rehabilitation Act.

Evaluation and Re-Evaluation: Evaluations are the objective tools used to determine the student's specific learning strengths and needs and eligibility. Students must be re-evaluated at least every 3 years (triennial review) to determine continued special education qualification.

Identification: Federal law IDEA (2004) identifies the following categories: (1) Autism Spectrum Disorder, (2) Deaf-Blindness, (3) Developmental Delay (3- to 5-year-olds only), (4) Emotional Disturbance, (5) Hearing Impairment (deaf or hard of hearing), (6) Intellectual Disability, (7) Multiple Disabilities, (8) Orthopedic Impairment, (9) Other Health Impairment (includes attention-deficit/hyperactivity disorder [ADD/ADHD]), (10) Specific Learning Disability, (11) Speech or Language Impairment, (12) Traumatic Brain Injury, and (13) Vision Impairment.

Implementation of the IEP: Special education teachers and related service professionals are required to deliver, with efficacy, the program exactly as outlined in the IEP.

Individualized Education Plan (IEP): A written plan that is developed by the team, including the parents, describing the student's special education needs and the program, goals, services, and service providers required to implement the program. It must be reviewed and revised at least yearly.

Pre-Referral: Before a student is referred to an IEP team, alternative procedures and programs in general education must be explored and, where appropriate, implemented into the classroom instruction.

Referral: A written request is made for an evaluation of a student, who parents or educators suspect of having a disability and may require special education and/or related services.

SPECIAL EDUCATION TERMS

Listed here are commonly used abbreviations, terms, and definitions to assist educators and parents in their conversation about special education.

504 Plan: A plan developed to ensure that a student with a disability, identified under the law and attending a public elementary or secondary educational institution, receives accommodations to ensure their academic success and to provide them with access to the learning environment.

Accommodations: These are changes made to how a student learns, not what the student learns. For example, a visually impaired student may need to receive instruction in Braille. A student with ADD/ADHD may have to have information broken down into smaller chunks. A dyslexic student may need to have material presented auditorily.

Department of Labor (DOL): While the U.S. DOL Office of Disability Employment Policy (ODEP) does not enforce the Americans with Disabilities Act, it does offer publications and other technical assistance on the basic requirements of the law, including covered employers' obligation to provide reasonable accommodations to qualified job applicants and employees with disabilities.

Family Educational Rights and Privacy Act (FERPA) (20 U.S.C. § 1232g: 34 CFR Part 99): A federal law that protects the privacy of a student's education records. Parents or eligible students have the right to request that the school corrects records that they believe to be inaccurate or misleading. The law applies to all schools that receive federal funding from the U.S. Department of Education. FERPA gives parents certain rights with respect to their children's education records. These rights transfer to the student when they reach the age of 18 or attend a school beyond the high school. Students to whom the rights have transferred are referred to as "eligible students."

Highlights of FERPA:
- Parents have the right to inspect and review the student's education records maintained by the school district. Schools are not required to provide copies of records unless there are reasons such as great distance. However, parents may request in writing the district provides copies of all records, and the district may charge the family for said copies.
- Parents have the right to request that a school district correct records that they believe to be inaccurate or misleading. If the district does not amend the record, the parent or eligible student then has the right to a formal hearing. After the hearing, if the school still refuses not to amend the student's record, the parent or eligible student has the right

to place a statement with the file setting forth their view about the contested information.

- Schools require written permission from the parent or eligible student before releasing any information from a student's education record. However, FERPA allows schools to disclose those records without consent to the following parties or under the following conditions (34 CFR § 99.31):
    - ◆ School officials with legitimate educational interest
    - ◆ Schools to which a student is transferring
    - ◆ Specified officials for audit or evaluation purposes
    - ◆ Appropriate parties in connection with financial aid to a student
    - ◆ Organizations conducting certain studies for or on behalf of the school
    - ◆ Accrediting organizations
    - ◆ Compliance related to judicial order or lawfully issued subpoena
    - ◆ Appropriate officials in cases of health and safety emergencies
    - ◆ State and local authorities, within a juvenile justice system, pursuant to specific state law

Free Appropriate Education Program (FAPE): FAPE is guaranteed under IDEA and emphasizes that students may require special education and related services in order to access the general education curriculum.

Individualized Education Plan (IEP): An IEP is an individualized plan or program developed by a team, which includes the parents, and outlines the type of instruction, specialized and related services, and supports a student requires to access the general education curriculum.

Individuals with Disabilities Education Act (IDEA): A federal law that ensures all children, including those with disabilities, receive a Free Appropriate Public Education in the Least Restrictive Environment.

Least Restrictive Environment (LRE): LRE was first introduced as part of the original special education law in 1975. LRE refers to the setting where a child with a disability receives their education, either alongside their general education peers or with peers that have a similar diagnosis. The purpose of LRE is to make sure that with extensive accommodations and modifications the student is able to remain with neurotypical peers (i.e., students without disabilities) to the maximum extent appropriate.

Modification: A modification changes what a student is taught or expected to learn. For example, a student could be assigned shorter or easier reading assignments or homework that is different from the rest of the class.

Present Level of Academic Achievement and Functional Performance (PLAAFP): This is a section of the IEP. In this section, the student's present level of performance in the following areas is reported: language arts, math, science and social studies, communication, behavior, and social-emotional and general health, including fine and gross motor skills. If there are no concerns in a specific section, then it is marked "n/a." The data recorded include test scores, grades, and anecdotal information describing the areas of strength and concern and how identified concerns are impacting the student's ability to successfully access the curriculum. All areas of concern must be addressed with goals and objectives in the IEP.

Special Education: Special education means that a student with an identified disability requires specially designed instruction in order to be able to fully access the general education curriculum. Both special education services and programs are provided to the student at no cost to the parents.

Stay Put: If parents disagree with their school district's placement, programming, or service recommendations, the services are in a "Stay Put" mode while the dispute is being resolved. The services being delivered are those that were in place prior to the dispute. The parents should *not* sign the IEP if they disagree with the placement or programming or services offered.

THERAPISTS

Applied Behavioral Analyst (ABA): ABA is a type of therapist that uses positive reinforcement to increase attention and to target specific behaviors. This type of therapy targets communication as well as social and learning skills and is usually delivered across multiple-hour sessions to students with developmental disorders.

Board-Certified Behavior Analyst (BCBA): A BCBA therapist is trained in applied behavioral analysis therapy and is qualified to train and supervise others. Many ABA therapists are not board-certified but know how to use the techniques of positive reinforcement to increase attention and to address specific targeted behaviors.

Occupational Therapist (OT): Occupational therapy is a health care service that focuses on fine motor skills and sensory integration difficulties that affect the student's ability to perform activities of daily living, such as eating, dressing, and handwriting. The occupational therapist is licensed by the Board of Health and may or may not be employed by the school district. They assess fine motor capabilities and identify areas of weakness that are interfering with the student's ability to access their school day. The occupational therapist also designs intervention plans, writes goals and objectives related to fine motor weaknesses, and provides therapeutic services.

Physical Therapist (PT): Physical therapy is a health care service that focuses on the gross motor skills that affect the student's ability to access activities of daily living such as going up and down stairs, using playground equipment, and navigating the school. The physical therapist is licensed by the Board of Health and may or may not be employed by the school district. Physical therapy services in the public school require a medical diagnosis. The doctor must state why the service is required and identify the student's specific needs, which are written into the IEP and carried out by the physical therapist .

Speech-Language Pathologist (SLP): Speech-language services address all areas of communication. The SLP is responsible for assessing students, developing IEP goals, and providing direct speech-language services. To work in a public school, the SLP must be certified by the state Board of Education, and in many states also licensed by the state Board of Health. Many SLPs are also licensed by the American Speech and Hearing Association (ASHA).

PLACEMENTS AND PROGRAMS

Academic Supplemental Support: Some students are eligible for Academic Supplemental Support, which is a service provided to a student who is performing 1 to 2 years behind in math and/or reading. The service is a general education intervention and often uses multisensory teaching techniques, manipulatives and visualization, and verbalization strategies.

Child Study Team: A school-based team that evaluates and designs appropriate programs for students who are experiencing learning, health, and/or behavioral difficulties. It consists of professionals (school psychologists, school social workers, learning disabilities teachers or consultants, and speech-language specialists) who are responsible for determining if a student should be referred for special education services or requires classroom accommodations or modifications.

Elementary and Secondary Education Act of 1965 (ESEA): The ESEA provides funding for professional development, instructional materials, and resources that support educational programs. The U.S. Department of Education distributed funding through this Act to public school districts that had a high percentage of low-income families. The intent of the Act was to give all children an opportunity to get an equitable and high-quality education.

Extended School Day (ESD): This is additional instruction provided to the student beyond their typical school day, which is required for the student to make meaningful progress toward their IEP goals. Recommendation for this service is an IEP decision.

Extended School Year (ESY): ESY services are provided to students with disabilities beyond the scope of the school year usually due to recoupment concerns. Determining the need for ESY is an IEP team decision and should be based on the individual needs of the student. These services are usually provided for 4 to 5 weeks in the summer.

No Child Left Behind (NCLB): Title I and NCLB were born out of ESEA and signed into effect by George W. Bush. These acts were trendy because they held individual schools and school districts accountable. NCLB stated if a child was more than 1 year behind in reading or math, interventions must be put in place. It ensured that a child could not just be pushed through the system. However, under Barack Obama, NCLB was replaced by Every Student Succeeds Act (ESSA), which became law in December 2015. The new act received some criticism because it relied too much on standardized testing and schools faced harsh penalties when all students weren't on track to reach proficiency on state tests. Some of the components of NCLB remained in place, such as states are still required to report progress of traditionally underserved students; this includes students with disabilities. ESSA is over 1000 pages long, and holding schools accountable shifted from the federal government to the states. However, the federal government still provides a broad framework and requires each state to set and evaluate goals. States are required to create plans for improving struggling schools in underserved communities that teach underperforming students. The act also outlined the testing protocol, which stated that third and eighth graders and high school students with IEPs and 504 Plans should be tested in reading and math.

Related Services: Related services are services that are required to assist a student with a disability to benefit from special education. These services may include speech-language therapy, audiological support, an interpreter, occupational therapy, physical therapy, behavioral therapy, psychological support or counseling, social work support, or ABA therapy. Special transportation accommodations or services are also considered to be a related service.

Self-Contained Classroom: A classroom setting where students with academic, social-emotional, and/or behavioral disabilities spend the majority of the day with other students with disabilities and go into the general education classroom for therapies, lunch, and specials. Multi-discipline teachers come into the room to address academic, behavioral, and social-emotional needs of a small group of students. Students on the autistic spectrum who require one-to-one ABA or other types of specialized teaching may also be in some type of self-contained classroom. In this educational model, special education teachers are considered to be the student's primary teacher. They are responsible for breaking down all assignments and working with the students one-on-one for the academic portion of the class.

Special Education Assessment Tools

Academic Assessment: The process of using evidence to understand and improve student learning in academic programs. These assessments provide teachers with diagnostic information about gaps in student learning that can be used to tailor programing and curricular improvement.

Functional Behavioral Assessment (FBA): An assessment used to evaluate and understand what is causing specific behavioral challenges by using methods such as observation and data collection. This approach takes into consideration that children act in certain ways for different reasons. The assessment provides recommendations to ensure the student is given personalized education and approached with the appropriate teaching methods.

Independent Educational Evaluation (IEE): When a student receives an IEE, the evaluation is conducted by a highly qualified person who is *not* employed by the student's home school district. Therefore, the evaluation is considered to be objective and can be helpful when there is a breakdown in trust between parents and the school district. Under IDEA, parents have the right to request an IEE, which their home school district is obligated to pay for, if they disagree with the results of the district's evaluation or if the district did not find a specific disability yet a previous outside evaluation contained a specific diagnosis.

Psychological Assessment: A structured series of interviews of the student as well as parents and/or teachers, observations, standardized tests, and questionnaires designed to evaluate strengths and weaknesses, learning style, cognitive ability, and social-emotional functioning.

Relevant Cases

These laws are the guidelines to everything parents do during the special education process. The sources and links in our References have a lot more in-depth information and should also be perused in order to understand the law thoroughly. An educational consultant or expert can also help you interpret and understand the nuances of these protections.

Americans with Disabilities Act (ADA)—Definition, Examples, Cases: According to ADA, which is where Section 504 appears, the term "disability" refers to a major life activity related to caring for oneself and performing all task that we take for granted: walking, talking, sleeping, eating, learning, etc. The ADA prohibits discrimination and guarantees that people with disabilities and other marginalized groups are able to participate equally in all life activities. It should be noted that school is considered to be a major life activity, which is why children who require accommodations in order to access the curriculum have a 504 Plan.

The ADA considers the term "disability" to be a legal term rather than a medical one. Medically a person has a disability if they have an impairment that prevents them from performing physically or mentally at maximum level. This means that the ADA's definition of disability is different from how the term "disability" is defined under other laws, such Social Security Disability. In 2008, additional amendments were added to the ADA. The ADA Amendments Act of 2008 (ADAAA) overturned the previous law, making it a complicated process to prove someone has a disability that qualifies them to be covered by the ADA.

Parent Training and Information Programs: There are state-run programs across the United States that provide information on state and federal laws regarding the rights of individuals with disabilities. These programs are designed to inform or make people aware of their rights, to provide legal definitions, or to explain laws/regulations. However, they do not provide legal representation or legal advice; their purpose is merely to educate.

Title II of ADA (State and Local Government) and Importance: Title II of the ADA prohibits discrimination against qualified individuals with disabilities in all programs, activities, and services of public entities. It applies to all state and local governments, their departments and agencies, and any other instrumentalities or special purpose districts of state or local governments. It clarifies the requirements of section 504 of the Rehabilitation Act of 1973. It has been amended for public transportation systems that receive federal financial assistance and extends coverage to all public entities that provide public transportation, whether or not they receive federal financial assistance. It establishes detailed standards for the operation of public transit systems, including commuter and intercity rail (e.g., Amtrak).

This act outlines the administrative processes to be followed, including requirements for self-evaluation and planning; requirements for making reasonable modifications to policies, practices, and procedures where necessary to avoid discrimination; architectural barriers to be identified; and the need for effective communication with people with hearing, vision, and speech disabilities. This title is regulated and enforced by the U.S. Department of Justice.

Title III of ADA (Public Accommodation): Title III prohibits private places of public accommodation, such as privately owned, leased, or operated facilities like hotels, restaurants, retail merchants, doctor's offices, golf courses, private schools, day care centers, health clubs, sports stadiums, and movie theaters from discriminating against individuals with disabilities. It establishes the minimum standards for accessibility for alterations and new construction of facilities. It also requires public accommodations to remove barriers in existing buildings where it is easy to do so without much difficulty or expense. This title directs businesses to make "reasonable modifications" to their usual ways of doing things when serving people with disabilities. It also requires that they take steps necessary to communicate effectively with customers with vision, hearing, and speech disabilities. This title is regulated and enforced by the U.S. Department of Justice.

Title IV of ADA (Telecommunications): Title IV is regulated by the Federal Communication Commission (FCC) and requires telephone and internet companies to provide a nationwide system of interstate and intrastate telecommunications relay services that allows individuals with hearing and speech disabilities to communicate over the telephone. It also requires all federally funded public service announcements to use closed captions.

Title V of ADA (Miscellaneous Provisions): The most important aspect of Title V of ADA is that it has regulations about retaliation or coercion connected to a person who is exercising their civil rights. This section also explains the connection between ADA and already-existing laws and the rights related to insurance issues.

SUMMARY

We believe all meetings must be built on open and honest conversations and all participants must feel they are valued and welcome members of the Individualized Education Plan (IEP) team. Only when everyone's voice is heard will there be trust and transparency. Developing an appropriate IEP happens when teachers and parents share their perspective regarding the student's strengths and areas of concern and back it up with evidence. Working together, creating a shared vision, effectively communicating using the 5-C Model of Communication, and using data to drive all recommendations and decisions leads to building positive partnerships. It is also the best way to ensure the child is most successful academically, social-emotionally, and behaviorally.

Bud, P. S., & Jacobson, T. L.
Navigating Special Education: The Power of Building
Positive Parent–Educator Partnerships (pp. 225-265).
© 2023 SLACK Incorporated.

In this Appendix, we have provided exemplars, templates, and data collection sheets that parents and educators can use as they prepare for participating in IEP meetings.

Review of Key Points Presented in
Navigating Special Education

◆ Parents and educators must work together as partners to ensure student success.

◆ Collaboration creates the most appropriate programs and leads to the student making meaningful progress from year to year.

◆ Partnerships are built around trust and transparency.

◆ Every team member brings relevant and important information to the team.

◆ Effective decision-making should be a data-driven process.

◆ Keep all documents.

◆ Written correspondence is important; send requests, concerns, and thank you notes in writing.

PARENTS AS RESEARCHERS

It is important for parents to feel they have a voice in the IEP process. They have valuable information to share, but often do not realize it. They may be unsure of what to share with the team. Below are some questions that can act as a springboard for parents when preparing to share information with educators.

- Describe how you see your child performing at home.
- Describe your child's strengths and weaknesses.
- Share something your child does at home that demonstrates their strength.
- Tell your fears regarding your child's ability to learn or be successful in school.
- Tell what you believe are the barriers to your child's learning.
- Describe the hopes and dreams you have for your child.
- Describe how you think your child learns best.
- Tell some of your child's favorite activities outside of the school day.
- Explain how you think the district should incorporate your child's personality into the IEP.
- What do you believe your child needs to better serve their academic, social-emotional, or behavioral needs?

Data are powerful and hard to argue with. Therefore, whenever sharing your perspective with the team, it is important to back up any statement, concern, or request with data or evidence. Examples of data that parents can bring to the IEP meeting include, but are not limited to, photos, recordings, videos, and work samples. There are many other data collection tools presented within this Appendix that can be used by parents and educators so that their concerns are presented objectively rather than subjectively.

EXEMPLARS

- Exemplar 1: Invitation to an Individualized Education Planning Meeting
- Exemplar 2: Individualized Education Planning Meeting Agenda
- Exemplar 3: Least Restrictive Environment Checklist
- Exemplar 4: Procedural Safeguards Notice

Exemplar 1: Invitation to an Individualized Education Planning Meeting

School District

Date: _____

Parents'/Guardians' Names: _____

Address:_____

Child's Name:_____ Date of Birth:_____

Date of Meeting:_____ Time:_____ Location:_____

Purpose of IEP Meeting (check all that apply):
- ☐ Referral to special education
- ☐ Plan an initial evaluation
- ☐ Conduct an annual review
- ☐ Review evaluation results
- ☐ Plan re-evaluation
- ☐ Develop, review, revise IEP
- ☐ Extended school year
- ☐ Consider transition needs/services
- ☐ Review re-evaluation results/determine continued eligibility
- ☐ Conduct a manifestation determination
- ☐ Other (such as parent request):_____

Individuals Invited to IEP Meeting:

Administrator: _____

General Education Teacher: _____

Special Education Teacher: _____

Student: _____

Psychologist/Counselor/Social Worker: _____

Other Relevant Staff:_____

Outside Agency (if applicable): _____

☐ Procedural Safeguards enclosed.

If you need to reschedule, please contact _____

Sincerely,
[administrator's name and title]

Exemplar 2: Individualized Education Planning Meeting Agenda

Student's Name: _____

Date of Meeting: _____

Purpose of the Meeting: _____

Each IEP team member should be given a copy of the agenda at the beginning of the meeting. Sometimes they are posted on a white board/smart board in the conference room.

1. Welcome from the administrator/introductions
   a. Review purpose of the meeting
   b. Ask all members to sign in

2. Parent statement

3. School team reports
   a. Present level of performance in all areas
   b. Review testing (if applicable)

4. Brainstorm/discuss
   a. Purpose of meeting
   b. Shared vision
   c. Proposed goals and objectives
   d. Program recommendations

5. Review agreed-upon changes

6. Review disagreements
   a. Discussion related to disagreement
   b. Work collaboratively to reach consensus

7. Conclusion
   a. Review actions
   b. Next meeting date/purpose

Exemplar 3: Least Restrictive Environment Checklist

Student's Name: _____

Date of Birth: _____

School: _____   IEP Meeting Date: _____

Complete this form at the meeting *after* all other aspects of the student's IEP have been fully addressed.

LEAST RESTRICTIVE ENVIRONMENT SCREEN	
1. Student's classes are all in general education environment.	☐ Yes ☐ No
2. Student has opportunity to participate in all nonacademic and extracurricular services/activities.	☐ Yes ☐ No
3. Student is attending school they would attend if neurotypical.	☐ Yes ☐ No
If any "No" box was checked, complete the rest of the form.	
1. Placement on student's IEP.	☐ Yes ☐ No
2. Student will be with nondisabled students to the maximum extent appropriate.	☐ Yes ☐ No
3. Student will participate in nonacademic and extracurricular activities with nondisabled students to the maximum extent appropriate.	☐ Yes ☐ No
4. The use of supplemental aids and services were considered along with general education placement.	☐ Yes ☐ No
5. Even with supplemental aids and services, student's disability prevents them from satisfactory achievement in a general education classroom.	☐ Yes ☐ No
6. Placement selected is within the continuum of alternative placements.	☐ Yes ☐ No
7. Harmful effect placement would have on the student considered.	☐ Yes ☐ No
8. Harmful effect placement would have on quality of services considered.	☐ Yes ☐ No

9. Harmful effect placement would have on education of other children considered.	☐ Yes	☐ No
10. Placement provided is as close as possible to the student's home.	☐ Yes	☐ No
11. Student is receiving their education in an alternative setting.	☐ Yes	☐ No
12. If in a hospital, do they have to be there during the school day?	☐ Yes	☐ No
13. If in a residential facility, do they have to be there during the school day?	☐ Yes	☐ No
14. If in a detention facility, do they have to be there during the school day?	☐ Yes	☐ No
15. If placed in a private facility by parents, is the student receiving their education at the facility?	☐ Yes	☐ No
Comments:		

IEP Chairperson's Name and Title: _____

IEP Chairperson's Signature: _____

Exemplar 4: Procedural Safeguards Notice

(a) General. A copy of the procedural safeguards available to the parents of a child with a disability must be given to the parents only one time a school year, except that a copy also must be given to the parents—
  (1) Upon initial referral or parent request for evaluation;
  (2) Upon receipt of the first State complaint under §§300.151 through 300.153 and upon receipt of the first due process complaint under §300.507 in a school year;
  (3) In accordance with the discipline procedures in §300.530(h); and
  (4) Upon request by a parent.
(b) Internet Web site. A public agency may place a current copy of the procedural safeguards notice on its Internet Web site if a Web site exists.
(c) Contents. The procedural safeguards notice must include a full explanation of all of the procedural safeguards available under §300.148, §§300.151 through 300.153, §300.300, §§300.502 through 300.503, §§300.505 through 300.518, §§300.530 through 300.536 and §§300.610 through 300.625 relating to—
  (1) Independent educational evaluations;
  (2) Prior written notice;
  (3) Parental consent;
  (4) Access to education records;
  (5) Opportunity to present and resolve complaints through the due process complaint and State complaint procedures, including—
     (i)   The time period in which to file a complaint;
     (ii) The opportunity for the agency to resolve the complaint; and
     (iii) The difference between the due process complaint and the State complaint procedures, including the jurisdiction of each procedure, what issues may be raised, filing and decisional timelines, and relevant procedures;
  (6) The availability of mediation;
  (7) The child's placement during the pendency of any due process complaint;
  (8) Procedures for students who are subject to placement in an interim alternative educational setting;
  (9) Requirements for unilateral placement by parents of children in private schools at public expense;
  (10) Hearings on due process complaints, including requirements for disclosure of evaluation results and recommendations;

(11) State-level appeals (if applicable in the State);

(12) Civil actions, including the time period in which to file those actions; and

(13) Attorneys' fees.

(d) Notice in understandable language. The notice required under paragraph (a) of this section must meet the requirements of §300.503(c).

Reproduced from the Individuals with Disabilities Education Act. Sec. 300.504. *Procedural safeguards notice.* https://sites.ed.gov/idea/regs/b/e/300.504.

For Procedural Safeguards for a specific state, visit the state's Board of Education website.

WRITTEN CORRESPONDENCE BETWEEN HOME AND SCHOOL

Best Practice

The purpose of written correspondence between home and school is to make requests or share concerns. Having a paper trail helps avoid communication breakdowns and helps to have the request answered.

General Information

- Date all letters.
- Clearly state the purpose of the correspondence.
- Sign all letters with your name, phone number, and email address.
- Customize all notes so they target your specific concerns.
- Correspondence should be addressed to only one person (e.g., teacher to parent, parent to teacher, parent to administrator).
- When an email or hand-delivered letter is not answered in 1 to 2 days of receipt, it is appropriate to resend the email (letter) with a copy to an administrator.
- If there is still no response, it is permissible to write directly to the administrator and copy the teacher.
- Only send group emails if the message is positive (i.e., "good news" or saying thank you).

LETTER TEMPLATES

The templates use the pronouns "we" and "our." Please adjust the letters to reflect your personal pronoun usage.

Requesting a Meeting

- Letter 1: Requesting a Meeting With the Classroom Teacher
- Letter 2: Requesting a Meeting With an Administrator/Case Manager
- Letter 3: Requesting a Follow-Up Meeting With the Classroom Teacher
- Letter 4: Requesting a Meeting With the Special Education Director
- Letter 5: Teacher Requesting a Second Meeting With Parents
- Letter 6: Requesting an Individualized Education Planning Meeting

Requesting an Evaluation

- Letter 7: Requesting a Comprehensive Evaluation to Determine Eligibility
- Letter 8: Requesting a Comprehensive Evaluation
- Letter 9: Requesting a Re-Evaluation
- Letter 10: Requesting an Independent Evaluation

Requesting Due Process

- Letter 11: Requesting a Complaint Investigation
- Letter 12: Requesting a Due Process Hearing

Thank You Notes

- Letter 13: Thank You Note to Teacher Following Initial Meeting
- Letter 14: Thank You Note
- Letter 15: Thank You Note to Parents
- Letter 16: Thank You, But There Are Still Concerns
- Letter 17: Thank You Note to Teacher/Administrator

REQUESTING A MEETING

Letter 1: Requesting a Meeting With the Classroom Teacher

It is always best to begin the process by speaking to your child's teacher.

[date]

Dear [classroom teacher's name],

We believe parents are a vital part of their child's educational team and that home–school communication is very important.

We are writing this note to request a meeting with you to discuss our concerns about [child's name]'s [academic, social-emotional, and/or behavioral performance] as soon as possible.

Please send us a date, time, and location for this meeting to occur within the next week. We will arrange our schedules to accommodate yours.

Thank you.

Sincerely,
[name and outgoing signature]

Letter 2: Requesting a Meeting With an Administrator/Case Manager

Send if concerns discussed with the classroom teacher are not getting addressed.

[date]

Dear [name],

We are writing this letter after having met with [child's name]'s classroom teacher, [teacher's name], to discuss our concerns. [State the concerns.]

We have reviewed our child's abilities and disabilities with the teacher. We continue to have concerns and want to discuss next steps with you.

We are trying to build a partnership with the school and develop a shared vision about our child's education. Unfortunately, we did not agree with the teacher on [identify specific issues/concerns] related to our child's [academic, social-emotional, and/or behavioral needs].

In addition to meeting with you, we are requesting a comprehensive evaluation to determine if our child is eligible for special education.

We would like to meet with you as soon as possible to discuss how best to move forward and to get our child the support they need.

Please send us a date, time, and location for the upcoming meeting. We will arrange our schedules to accommodate yours.

Thank you.

Sincerely,
[name and outgoing signature]

Letter 3: Requesting a Follow-Up Meeting With the Classroom Teacher

[date]

Dear [classroom teacher's name],

We would like to meet with you to discuss [child's name]'s present level of performance as we feel the gap we discussed during our last meeting is continuing to widen and our concerns are growing.

Although we met on [date] and had agreed to [state what agreed to at last meeting], the concerns we discussed are [still present/getting more significant]. Therefore, we are requesting a follow-up meeting with you as soon as possible.

Please send us a date, time, and location for this meeting, which we would like to occur within the next week. We will arrange our schedules to accommodate yours.

Thank you.

Sincerely,
[name and outgoing signature]

Letter 4: Requesting a Meeting With the Special Education Director

Use this for a complaint of current services or program.

[date]

Dear [special education director's name],

We are writing to you on behalf of [child's name, birthdate], who attends [school name] and is in [grade].

We have significant concerns about [child's name]'s [state concerns accurately and concisely.] We have already discussed these issues with [teacher's name, subject area].

We have proposed the following suggestions/strategies as a way to resolve the situation: [list your top three suggestions].

We have not been able to reach an agreement with the teacher regarding next steps. We would like your help in reaching a compromise and/or consensus, which is why we are requesting a meeting with you (and the teacher) as soon as possible.

We look forward to hearing from you with a date, time, and location for a meeting. We will arrange our schedules so we can attend the meeting.

If you have any questions, please call [phone number] or email us [email].

Sincerely,
[name and outgoing signature]

Letter 5: Teacher Requesting a Second Meeting With Parents

This is NOT for an IEP meeting and an administrator will NOT attend the meeting.

[date]

Dear [parents' or guardians' names],

I believe parents are a vital part of their child's educational team. I know we have met in the past to discuss [state concerns].

At this time, I believe we need to meet again in order to take a proactive approach and build a comprehensive partnership through the triangulation of home, school, and therapeutic services.

Working collaboratively is the best way to ensure [child's name] is able to make [academic, social-emotional, and/or behavioral] progress. (If applicable: Your child's behavior has become increasingly disruptive and is now affecting their ability to grow and learn. It is also starting to have a negative impact on the other students.)

I am inviting you to a meeting on [date/time/location].

Please call or email me if you are unable to attend the meeting with some suggested dates/times that will work with your schedule.

I look forward to meeting with you and working collaboratively on [child's name]'s behalf.

Thank you.

Sincerely,
[name, email, and school phone number]

CC: [superintendent and building principal]

Letter 6: Requesting an Individualized Education Planning Meeting

[date]

Dear [name],

As parents, we understand we can request an IEP meeting at any time. Therefore, we are requesting a meeting in order to [develop, review, revise, and/or discuss the program/placement] for [child's name, birthdate].

(If there are specific concerns add: Our concerns are [list no more than three bullet points to concisely describe your concerns].)

Thank you for your prompt attention to this matter. If you have questions, we can be reached at [phone number] or [email].

Please send us the date, time, and location of the meeting, and we will arrange our schedules to accommodate the meeting.

Sincerely,
[name and outgoing signature]

REQUESTING AN EVALUATION

General Directions

Evaluation letters should be hand delivered to the director of special education for your district or sent via U.S. Postal Service. In either case, parents should request a delivery receipt of the letter.

Meeting with evaluator(s) prior to testing in order to share information and historical background is highly recommended.

Additional Recommendations

Even though you have requested an evaluation, it must be discussed and agreed upon at an IEP meeting.

When sending a written request for an evaluation, if there is no response after 3 to 5 days of the district's receipt of the letter, parents should contact the department of special services. Continue calling until a meeting has been scheduled to discuss the request.

Letter 7: Requesting a Comprehensive Evaluation to Determine Eligibility

[date]

Dear [director of special services' name],

We are writing this letter after having met with [child's name]'s classroom teacher and the educational team to discuss our child's [academic, social-emotional, and/or behavioral] concerns.

At this point, we continue to have significant concerns regarding our child's [academic, social-emotional, and/or behavioral] progress.

We would like to formally request a comprehensive evaluation of our child at an IEP meeting and then to discuss the results at a follow-up IEP meeting.

We hope to receive your response within the next week indicating a date, time, and location. We would like to have testing begin as soon as possible.

Thank you for your time.

Sincerely,
[name and outgoing signature]

CC: [superintendent and building principal]

Letter 8: Requesting a Comprehensive Evaluation

[date]

Dear [name],

We are requesting a comprehensive evaluation for [name, birthdate, grade, and teacher].

The purpose of this assessment is to determine if our child satisfies eligibility for special education as stipulated in the Individuals with Disabilities Education Act.

We have concerns that [child's name] is not reaching appropriate milestones due to their ongoing struggles [academically, social-emotionally, and/or behaviorally].

We understand that the evaluation is to be in all areas of suspected disability, and that the school district is to provide this evaluation at no charge.

(If deemed appropriate add: [child's name] has been medically diagnosed with [diagnosis] or [child's name] is awaiting a medical evaluation for [diagnosis].)

We have attached documentation from [include all provider letters/reports] to support our request and have highlighted their key recommendations.

We plan to be involved in any meetings related to the evaluation, identification of disability, provision of services, placement, or other decisions regarding our child.

We would appreciate meeting with each evaluator prior to testing our child to share information and historical background. We also request copies of the written reports prior to the team meeting where the results will be shared.

We understand the district must have our written permission for these tests to be administered. We will be happy to provide that upon receipt of the proper forms.

We appreciate your help on behalf of [child's name]. If you have any questions, please call us at [phone number] or email us at [email].

Sincerely,
[name and outgoing signature]

CC: [names and titles of anyone who will receive copies]

Letter 9: Requesting a Re-Evaluation

This letter can be sent to a case manager or building administrator.

[date]

Dear [name],

We are requesting [child's name and birthdate] be re-evaluated. We understand that a special education student is evaluated at least once every 3 years.

[child's name] was last evaluated on [date]. We are requesting this re-evaluation because [explain reasons for re-evaluation request]. We hope the testing can be completed as soon as possible.

We appreciate your help and will be expecting to hear from you soon. If we need to sign any paperwork or attend an IEP meeting, please let us know.

Sincerely,
[name and outgoing signature]

Letter 10: Requesting an Independent Evaluation

Parents can send this letter to the director of special services or the administrator of the IEP meeting if they do not agree with the decision after the IEP team discusses the results of the evaluation.

[date]

Dear [name],

We are requesting an independent assessment at public expense for our child [child's name, birthdate], because we do not agree with the results of the assessment conducted by [name of school or district].

We are requesting a comprehensive independent assessment, which we understand is our right if we disagree with the results of the district's testing and recommendations. We also believe [state why requesting evaluation and what requesting].

We understand that a response to our request must be provided in writing by the school district within 15 days and that the testing examiner must be mutually agreed upon.

We appreciate your help in identifying how to best provide [child's name] with the support and services they need to be able to successfully participate in all aspects of their academic day.

If you have any questions regarding our request, please contact us by phone [phone number] or email [email].

Thank you.

Sincerely,
[name and outgoing signature]

REQUESTING DUE PROCESS

Letter 11: Requesting a Complaint Investigation

Mandatory Letter to Inform of Request for Complaint Investigation

Drop off at superintendent's and director of special services' offices.

[date]

Dear [director of special services' name],

We are informing you that we have submitted a form requesting a complaint investigation. You will find a copy of it appended to this letter.

Sincerely,
[name and outgoing signature]

[append copy of due process request form, which can be downloaded from your state website]

Letter 12: Requesting a Due Process Hearing
Drop off at superintendent's and director of special services' offices.

[date]

Dear [director of special services' name],

We are informing you that we have submitted a form requesting due process. You will find a copy of it appended to this letter.

Sincerely,
[name and outgoing signature]

[append copy of due process request form, which can be downloaded from your state website]

THANK YOU NOTES

Letter 13: Thank You Note to Teacher Following Initial Meeting

[date]

Dear [classroom teacher's name],

Thank you for meeting with us on [date].

We appreciate your sharing the test results and evaluations with us regarding [child's name]. We felt our voices were heard and that you validated our concerns. You explained your community of practice to us and intervention strategies that are already in place.

You clearly laid out the next steps and welcomed us as partners in our child's education.

We are looking forward to our next meeting in 5 weeks.

Sincerely,
[name and outgoing signature]

Letter 14: Thank You Note

Can be sent by a teacher, administrator, or parent.

[date]

Dear [name],

Thank you for meeting with us on [date], discussing [list concerns], and listening to our suggestions about [child's name].

During our conversation we agreed to the following [list no more than three bullet points] and/or we also disagreed regarding [list no more than three bullet points].

We look forward to [continuing to work/working collaboratively] to find a way to address [child's name]'s [identify specific academic, social-emotional, and/or behavioral needs].

If we do not hear from you within the next week, we assume you agree with the summary of our meeting.

We agreed to meet in 4 weeks to continue this conversation.

Thank you very much.

Sincerely,
[name and outgoing signature]

Letter 15: Thank You Note to Parents

From teacher, administrator, or other staff member.

[date]

Dear [parents' or guardians' names],

I want to thank you for meeting with me on [date].

I hope it was helpful reviewing [child's name]'s [list tests and documents shared with parents].

As I shared with you during our meeting, I am using [list strategies, supports, or services being provided] to address [child's name]'s [academic, social-emotional, and/or behavioral] needs.

Thank you for sharing with me your concerns [state what parents shared and include specific strategies or next steps discussed].

I know working together as partners will help [child's name] be more successful. I look forward to our next meeting, on [date and time]. At that time, we will review [whatever was agreed upon] and discuss how to continue to move forward.

Thank you.

Sincerely,

[name, email, and school phone number]

Letter 16: Thank You, But There Are Still Concerns

[date]

Dear [name],

Thank you for meeting with us on [date].

(For letter to teacher only: We appreciate you sharing the test results and evaluations with us regarding [child's name]. You explained your community of practice to us and intervention strategies that are already in place.)

While we had a good conversation, at this point we were not able to reach consensus regarding how best to meet our child's needs. We are hoping that we can formulate a shared vision going forward.

At this time, we are requesting the district conduct a comprehensive evaluation in all areas: academic, social-emotional, and behavioral.

We look forward to receiving the date of our next meeting.

Sincerely,
[name and outgoing signature]

Letter 17: Thank You Note to Teacher/Administrator

[date]

Dear [name],

Thank you for meeting with us on [date].

We had a good conversation and felt our educational concerns for our child were met. We are on our way to formulating a shared vision moving forward in order to help our child be successful at school.

We appreciate your time and look forward to forming a long-lasting partnership with you and the school district through positive communication, collaboration, cooperation, and compromise.

Sincerely,
[name and outgoing signature]

DOCUMENTS TO KEEP

Here are directions on how to keep all of the paperwork related to the child's special education services organized and easily accessible.

Keep all paperwork in a binder with tabs labeled as outlined following:

- Papers in each section should be filed in chronological order, beginning with most recent information.
- Create two binders.
  - Binder 1 contains paperwork for the last 3 years, with the current year's papers on the top of each section.
  - Binder 2 is either another binder or a file box with all of the child's educational files from the moment they were recommended for special education.
- Teachers should also keep binders on each student for the current year so they have data that demonstrate progress or concerns that can be used to drive the conversation when meeting with parents.

List of Documents to Keep and Why

- *Response to Intervention (RTI) is required in some states.* The data collected should also be filed in this section.
- *504 or IEP packets.* Legal document identifying the responsibility of the school district regarding goals and objectives, modifications and accommodations, programs, and support services.
- *Invitations linked to each planning and placement team (PPT) or 504 meeting.* Confirms due process rights were not violated.
- *Report cards, teacher reports.* Identifies present level of performance; identifies/documents progress or lack of progress.
- *District and state testing.* Initial evaluation for special education. Re-evaluation must be done at least once every 3 years, called triennial review, and conducted by the district to assess all areas addressed in the IEP. Results of this assessment should be provided to parents in writing and filed in this section of the binder. (They are another data point to document strengths and areas of concern.)
- *Outside testing and outside reports.* Include information from all outside providers.
- *Correspondence between home and school.* Notes, emails, texts, etc.
- *Phone logs.* Keep a record of all phone calls between school and home. Records should include date, who you spoke to, and summary of conversation.

- *General education strategies and data.* Documentation of adjustments made to general education program, i.e., modifications and accommodations (data to document effectiveness). RTI required in some states—data driven.
- *Yearly work samples highlighting strengths and weaknesses.* Tests, writing samples, math papers, titles of books child reads, projects, all data sheets.
- *Your personal notes from conferences/meetings with school personnel.*
- *Medical information linked to school success/difficulties.*
- *Any other information.*

DATA COLLECTION TOOLS

Student Portfolio

We recommend parents and teachers create a portfolio that represents the student's performance during the school year. In addition, we suggest parents keep a 3-year portfolio as a way to measure and document their child's long-term growth and, in some cases, to highlight that there has been regression. Information collected for both the home and school portfolios can be used by the IEP team as part of the annual review process. This information is also helpful in identifying if the student's performance varies from home to school.

Creating yearly portfolios for all students is not standard practice across all school districts, or even within a town. If teachers maintain student portfolios, district policies vary regarding the type of information collected and what is done with the child's portfolio at the end of the school year. Some districts recommend that each student's portfolio is passed along to the next year's teachers; other districts send the portfolios home at the end of the year. We suggest if/when parents get a portfolio from their child's teacher, they review the material and save any relevant documents.

> *Remember!*
> Copy and file all correspondence;
> it is considered to be part of the student's educational record.

Short-Term Portfolios Collected to Document Student Performance

Portfolio Related to School Work

When putting together a portfolio to document school performance, we suggest the following information is included: report cards; pre-tests; tests; quizzes; most recent school standardized test results; most recent state standardized test results; reading, writing, and math samples; reading, writing, and math assignments; and social studies and science work/assignments. In addition, it is important to collect schoolwork over a short period of time (approximately 3 weeks) in the area(s) of concern. (See the following checklist to help organize portfolio information.) The use of a short-term portfolio of schoolwork can help teachers and/or the IEP team understand the student's present level of performance.

Homework Portfolio

If parents have specific concerns that they want to discuss with the IEP team and/or the classroom teacher, we recommend they keep a collection of 3 weeks of homework in the area(s) of concern. Information that should be collected includes homework samples such as a written assignments, copy of a page from a book being read, and math homework. (See the following checklist to help organize portfolio information.)

Portfolio Checklist:
Schoolwork Samples From the Area(s) of Concern

We suggest that all materials be numbered and dated.

Student's Name: _____   Age: _____   Grade: _____

DOCUMENT	SUBJECT	DATE	DESCRIPTION/COMMENTS

In addition to keeping schoolwork and homework, it may be helpful to also maintain an anecdotal checklist that is paired with the portfolio information being collected.

Anecdotal Evidence and Behavioral Checklist (Check Yes or No)

Student's Name: _____   Age: _____   Grade: _____

DATE	TIME	LOCATION	CONCERN	INTERVENTION TRIED	WORKED?
					☐ Yes ☐ No
					☐ Yes ☐ No
					☐ Yes ☐ No
					☐ Yes ☐ No
					☐ Yes ☐ No
					☐ Yes ☐ No
					☐ Yes ☐ No
					☐ Yes ☐ No
					☐ Yes ☐ No
					☐ Yes ☐ No
					☐ Yes ☐ No
					☐ Yes ☐ No

Checklists are used to document concerns that can then be shared at an IEP meeting.

Checklist 1: Frequency of Behavior—Physical

Child's Name: _____   Age/Grade: _____

Siblings: ☐ Yes   ☐ No

Check all behaviors that apply.

PHYSICAL BEHAVIOR	OCCURRENCE			DESCRIPTION AND PARTIES INVOLVED
	HOURLY	DAILY	WEEKLY	
Hitting				
Spitting				
Kicking				
Constant rocking				
Head banging				
Screaming				
Temper tantrums				
Excessive crying				

Checklist 2: Frequency of Behavior—Emotional

Child's Name: _____   Age/Grade: _____
Siblings: ☐ Yes   ☐ No

Check all behaviors that apply.

EMOTIONAL BEHAVIOR	OCCURRENCE			DESCRIPTION AND PARTIES INVOLVED
	HOURLY	DAILY	WEEKLY	
Lying, cheating, stealing				
Anxiety, depression				
Self-harm (cutting)				
Experimental or excessive drug use				
Eating disorder				
Class/school attendance and difficulty getting up				
Focus/hyperfocus				
Distractibility/ difficulty sitting				
Bullying/fighting				
Procrastination				
Long-term academic regression				
Short-term academic regression				
Poor personal hygiene				
Difficulty sleeping				

Checklist 3: Location of Behavior—Physical

Child's Name: _____   Age/Grade: _____

Siblings: ☐ Yes   ☐ No

Check all behaviors that apply.

PHYSICAL BEHAVIOR	LOCATION			DESCRIPTION AND PARTIES INVOLVED
	SCHOOL	HOME	OTHER	
Hitting				
Spitting				
Kicking				
Constant rocking				
Head banging				
Screaming				
Temper tantrums				
Excessive crying				

Checklist 4: Location of Behavior—Emotional

Child's Name: _____   Age/Grade: _____
Siblings: ☐ Yes   ☐ No

Check all behaviors that apply.

EMOTIONAL BEHAVIOR	LOCATION			DESCRIPTION AND PARTIES INVOLVED
	SCHOOL	HOME	OTHER	
Lying, cheating, stealing				
Anxiety, depression				
Self-harm (cutting)				
Experimental or excessive drug use				
Eating disorder				
Class/school attendance and difficulty getting up				
Focus/hyperfocus				
Distractibility/ difficulty sitting				
Bullying/fighting				
Procrastination				
Long-term academic regression				
Short-term academic regression				
Poor personal hygiene				
Difficulty sleeping				

Checklist 5: When the Behavior Occurs—Physical

Child's Name: _____   Age/Grade: _____
Siblings: ☐ Yes   ☐ No

Check all behaviors that apply.

PHYSICAL BEHAVIOR	WHEN				DESCRIPTION AND PARTIES INVOLVED
	MORNING	AFTER-NOON	EVENING	WEEKEND	
Hitting					
Spitting					
Kicking					
Constant rocking					
Head banging					
Screaming					
Temper tantrums					
Excessive crying					

Checklist 6: When the Behavior Occurs—Emotional

Child's Name: _____   Age/Grade: _____

Siblings: ☐ Yes   ☐ No

Check all behaviors that apply.

EMOTIONAL BEHAVIOR	WHEN				DESCRIPTION AND PARTIES INVOLVED
	MORNING	AFTER-NOON	EVENING	WEEKEND	
Lying, cheating, stealing					
Anxiety, depression					
Self-harm (cutting)					
Experimental or excessive drug use					
Eating disorder					
Class/school attendance and difficulty getting up					
Focus/ hyperfocus					
Distractibility/ difficulty sitting					
Bullying/fighting					
Procrastination					
Long-term academic regression					
Short-term academic regression					
Poor personal hygiene					
Difficulty sleeping					

Phone Log

We suggest that both parents and educators keep phone logs. It is the best way to document all conversations related to the student. Depending on the frequency of phone calls, phone logs can be kept on a weekly or monthly basis.

Conversations Related to (Child's Name): _____

Month or Week of: _____

DATE	TIME	SPOKE TO	SUMMARY OF CONVERSATION

Index

active listening, 51–58
  listening vs. agreeing, 55–56
  listening vs. hearing, 51–55
  strategies, 56–58
    answering, 58
    asking for clarification, 57
    open-ended vs. yes-no
      questions, 58
    paraphrasing, 56
    perspective-taking, 57
    S.T.O.P. (stop, take a breath,
      observe, proceed), 57–58
    summarizing, 57
    W.A.I.T. (talking vs. listening), 58
advocate vs. consultant vs., distinguished,
  183–193
agenda, value of, 131
alphabet soup of education, 83–87
analysis of plan, 103–148
answering questions, 58

behavioral concerns, data collection tools
  for, 164–166
board attorney, responsibilities of, 97

calmness, importance of, 75
case manager, role/responsibilities, 97
checklists, 257–265
  anecdotal evidence and behavioral
    checklists, 258
  frequency of behavior
    emotional, 260
    physical, 259

location of behavior
  emotional, 262
  physical, 261
phone log, 265
portfolio checklist, 257
timing of behavior
  emotional, 264
  physical, 263
clarification, requesting, 57
classroom teacher, role/responsibilities,
  97
cognitive-communication disorders/
  deficits, 128
communication in special education,
  3–12
  eligibility, 5
  evaluation and re-evaluation, 4
  identification of disability, 5
  Individualized Education Plan, 5
    implementation of, 6
    team, 9–12
  pre-referral, 4
  referral, 4
compliance with Individualized
  Education Plan, 136–141
compromise, 203–206
conflict resolution, 181–205
  oppositional behaviors, addressing,
    197–198
  voicing opinion, 196–197
correspondence, written, 169–180
  correspondence, as legal documents,
    171–172
  electronic protocols, 173

purpose, 170–172
requesting meeting, 172
sample letters, 174–180
    requesting independent
        evaluation, 179
    requesting meeting with
        parents, 175
    requesting meeting with
        teacher, 174
    requesting plan evaluation
        to determine special
        education eligibility, 178
    thank you note to parents, 177
    thank you note to teacher, 176
texting, 170–171

data collection, 151–167
    baseline data, 153
    collected on all students, 152
    cumulative files, 156–157
    data collected on all students, 152
    disciplinary records, 159–160
    formal assessments, 155–156
    importance of, 151–155
    importance of data, 151–155
    Individualized Education Plan
        progress reports, 161
    informal assessments, 156
    methodologies/tools, 162–167
        for behavioral concerns, 164–
            166
        Functional Behavioral
            Assessment, 166–167
        logs, 162
        phone logs, 167
        recordings, 162–164
        student portfolios, 164
    parents' cumulative file, 157–158
        comprehensive IEP or 504
            packets, 157
        correspondence between home/
            school, 158
        district and state testing, 158
        documents to keep, 157
        formal assessments, 158
        independent evaluations, 158

        invitations to IEP or 504
            meetings, 157
        phone logs, 158
        report cards, 157
    progress monitoring, 152–153
    response to intervention, 152
    types of data collection supporting
        decision-making, 155–161
    when to collect, 153–155
    yearly academic portfolio, 158–159
data collection tools
    checklists, 257–265
        anecdotal evidence and
            behavioral checklists, 258
        frequency of behavior—
            emotional, 260
        frequency of behavior—
            physical, 259
        location of behavior—
            emotional, 262
        location of behavior—
            physical, 261
        phone log, 265
        portfolio checklist, 257
        when behavior occurs—
            emotional, 264
        when behavior occurs—
            physical, 263
    student portfolio, 255–256
        to document student
            performance, 256
        homework portfolio, 256
        portfolio related to school work,
            256
decision-making, types of data collection
    supporting, 155–161
    cumulative files, 156–157
    formal assessments, 155–156
    informal assessments, 156
    parents' cumulative file, 157–158
disability, identification of, 5
disagreements, 67–76
    how to disagree, 71–72
    "I" statements, 74
    listening strategies, 72–76
    perspective-taking, 74
    recapping, 75

remaining calm, 75
summarizing, 75
what to do, 67–71
"Yes, and ...," 72–73
disciplinary records, 159–160
draft Individualized Education Plan, 134–135
due process
    hearing regarding, 202
    requesting, 247–248

educational consultant, 183–194
    consultant vs. advocate, distinguished, 183–193
    hiring consultant, 188–191
    parents, providing help to, 194
        consultant's role during meeting, 194
        responsibilities of consultant, 194
    student as advocate, 191–193
    working with consultant, 193
        initial meeting with consultant, 193
electronic protocols, 173
eligibility, determination, sample letter requesting plan evaluation, 178
eligibility issues, 5
email, 170–171
end game, 203–204
evaluation, 4
exemplars, 227–233
    Individualized Education Planning meeting agenda, 229
    invitation to Individualized Education Planning meeting, 228
    Least Restrictive Environment checklist, 230–231
    Procedural Safeguards, 232–233

Facilitated Individualized Education Planning meeting, 200–201
fair access, 117–142
    agenda, value of, 131
    cognitive-communication disorders/ deficits, 128

compliance with Individualized Education Plan, 136–141
creating best Individualized Education Plan, 131–132
draft Individualized Education Plan, 134–135
importance of Individualized Education Plan, 117–118
Individualized Education Plan, 118–124
    frequency of meetings, 119
    meetings, 122–123
    Procedural Safeguards, 119–122
    stockholders in attendance, 118–119
meetings, factors triggering request for, 123
motor dysfunction disorder, 128–129
outside evaluations, 129–131
reading Individualized Education Plan, importance of, 132–134
revision of Individualized Education Plan, 135–136
special education eligibility, determining, 124–127
5-C model of communication, 13–32
    categories of conversations, 31–32
    collaboration, 14–16
    communication attributes, 29–31
    compromise, 20–21
    consensus, 22–23
    conversation, 14–15
    cooperation, 6–9
        shared vision, 6–9
    meetings
        agenda, 24
        effective communication, 24–25
        greeted by plan administrator, 23–24
        introductions, 24
        introductory meeting, 23
        process, 27–29
        terminology, 27–29
        trajectory of, 23–29
        trust, 25–27

504 Plans vs. Individualized Education
    Plans, 107–116
    Americans with Disabilities Act,
        111–112
    Individualized Education Plan,
        109–110
    Individualized Education Plan vs.
        504 Plan, 112–116
    Individuals with Disabilities
        Education Act, 108
    similarities/differences, 112–116
    summary of special education law,
        108–109
Functional Behavioral Assessment, for
    data collection, 166–167

hearing, regarding due process, 202
hiring educational consultant, 183–194
    consultant vs. advocate,
        distinguished, 183–193
    parents, help for student, 194
    responsibilities of consultant, 194
    role during meeting, 194
    student as advocate, 191–193
    working with consultant, 193
        initial meeting with consultant,
            193

"I" statements, 74
identification of disability, 5
Individualized Education Plan
    access to, 117–142
    active listening vs, passive listening,
        51–58
    compromise, 203–206
    correspondence, written, 169–180
    data collection, 151–167
    disagreements, handling, 67–76
    due process, 199–202
    educational consultant, hiring,
        183–194
    eligibility, 5
    equitable access, 111–142
    evaluation, 4
    5-C model of communication, 13–32
        attributes of communication,
            29–31

collaboration, 14–16
compromise, 20–2
consensus, 22–23
conversation categories, 31–32
conversations, 14–15
cooperation, 16–19
meetings
    agenda, 24
    effective communication,
        24–25
    introductions, 24
    introductory, 23
    plan administrator
        greeting, 23–24
    process, 27–29
    terminology, 27–29
    trajectory of, 23–29
    trust, 25–27
shared vision, 16–19
504 Plan, contrasted, 107–116
504 Plans, similarities/differences,
    112–116
identification of disability, 5
implementation of, 6
importance of, 117–118
mediation, 199–202
meetings
    frequency of, 119
    mediated, 199–202
    setting tone, 59–66
negotiation, 203–206
partnerships, 77–94
pre-referral, 4
Procedural Safeguards, 119–122
program models, 41–49
    accommodations, examples of,
        45
    co-teaching model, 42
    consultation model, 43
        examples of consultation
            services, 43
    inclusive education model, 41
    modifications, 44–45
        examples of, 44–45
    out-of-district placement, 43–44
    pull-out vs. push-in model,
        41–42

resource room, 42–43
self-contained classroom, 42
transition planning, 45–49
re-evaluation, 4
referral, 4
sections, 33–50
S.M.A.R.T. goals, 143–144
solutions, from conflict, 195–198
stockholders in attendance, 118–119
team, 9–12
teamwork, 95–102
trust, building, 77–94
written correspondence, 169–180
Individualized Education Plan progress
reports, 161
Individualized Education Plan sections,
33–50
extended school day, 40
extended school year, 40
individual health/transportation
plan, 39
key sections, 33–38
academic achievement, 34–38
conversation starters, 36–37
delivery of service, 37
goals, 37
objectives, 37
parent–student input, 35
types of amount of services, 38
meetings, minutes of, 49
paraprofessional support, 38–39
responsibilities, 39
roles, 39
program models, 4–49
accommodations, 45
co-teaching model, 42
consultation model, 43
inclusive education model, 41
modifications, 44–45
out-of-district placement, 43–44
pull-out vs. push-in model,
41–42
resource room, 42–43
self-contained classroom, 42
transition planning, 45–49

Individualized Education Plans vs. 504
Plans, 107–116
Individualized Education Plan,
109–110
Individualized Education Plan vs.
504 Plan, 112–116
Individuals with Disabilities
Education Act, 108
Section 504 of Americans with
Disabilities Act, 111–112
504 Plan, 111–112
similarities/differences, 112–116
summary of special education law,
108–109
intended/unintended messages, 87–90

key sections, functional performance,
present level of, 34–38

legal documents, correspondence as,
171–172
letter templates, 234–253
library education teacher, role/
responsibilities, 98
listening, active vs. passive, 51–58
active listening strategies, 56–58
answering, 58
open-ended vs. yes-no
questions, 58
paraphrasing, 56
perspective-taking, 57
requesting clarification, 57
S.T.O.P. (stop, take a breath,
observe, proceed), 57–58
summarizing, 57
W.A.I.T. (talking vs. listening), 58
listening vs. agreeing, 55–56
listening vs. hearing, 51–55
listening strategies, 72–76
logs
for data collection, 162
phone, 167

mediation, 201
meeting with parents, requesting, sample
letter, 175

meeting with teacher, requesting, sample
    letter, 174
meetings
    agenda, 24
    consultant's role during, 194
    effective communication, 24–25
    factors triggering request for, 123
    greeted by plan administrator, 23–24
    introductions, 24
    introductory meeting, 23
    process, 27–29
    requesting, 172
    setting tone, 59–66
        success of meeting, 65–66
        tone of meeting, 61–63
        value of individuals, 60–61
    summary, 49
    terminology, 27–29
    trajectory of, 23–29
    trust, 25–27
messages, intended/unintended, 87–90
methodologies/tools for data collection,
    162–167
    data collection tools for behavioral
        concerns, 164–166
    Functional Behavioral Assessment,
        166–167
    logs, 162
    phone logs, 167
    recordings, 162–164
    student portfolios, 164
minutes of meetings, 49
models, 41–49. See also program models
motor dysfunction disorder, 128–129
music teachers, role/responsibilities, 98

negotiation, 203–206
    techniques, 205
nurse, school, role/responsibilities, 98

occupational therapist, role/
    responsibilities, 98
open-ended questions, 58
    yes-no questions, contrasted, 58
opinion, voicing, 196–197

oppositional behaviors, addressing,
    197–198
out-of-district placement, 43–44
outside evaluations, 129–131

parental disagreements, 81–83
parents
    as researchers, 226–227
    role/responsibilities on team, 99
parents as researchers, 226–227
parents/districts, partnerships, 80
participation strategies for meetings, 66
partnerships, 77–94
    parents/districts, 80
    power of, 77–80
pathologist, speech-language, role/
    responsibilities, 98
perspective-taking, 74, 90–94
phone log, 265
    for data collection, 167
physical therapist, role/responsibilities,
    98
pre-referral, 4
preparation for meeting, 63–64
program models, Individualized
    Education Plan, 41–49
    accommodations, examples of, 45
    co-teaching model, 42
    consultation model, 43
        examples of consultation
            services, 43
    inclusive education model, 41
    modifications, 44–45
        examples of, 44–45
    out-of-district placement, 43–44
    pull-out vs. push-in model, 41–42
    resource room, 42–43
    self-contained classroom, 42
    transition planning, 45–49
psychologist, school, role/responsibilities,
    97
pull-out vs. push-in model, 41–42

questions
    answering, 58
    open-ended vs. yes-no, 58

reading Individualized Education Plan, importance of, 132–134
recapping, 75
recordings, for data collection, 162–164
referral, 4
requesting independent evaluation, sample letter, 179
requesting meeting with parents, sample letter, 175
requesting meeting with teacher, sample letter, 174
requesting plan evaluation to determine special education eligibility, sample letter, 178
researchers, parents as, 226–227
resolution of conflict, 181–205
    oppositional behaviors, addressing, 197–198
    voicing opinion, 196–197
resource room, 42–43
revision of Individualized Education Plan, 135–136

sample letters, 174–180
school administrator/director of special education/special services, role/responsibilities, 97
school day, extended, 40
school nurse, role/responsibilities, 98
school psychologist, role/responsibilities, 97
sections of Individualized Education Plan, 33–50
    extended school day, 40
    extended school year, 40
    individual health/transportation plan, 39
    key sections, 33–38
        academic achievement, present level of, 34–38
        conversation starters, 36–37
        delivery of service, 37
        goals, 37
        objectives, 37
        parent–student input, 35
        types of amount of services, 38
    meetings, minutes of, 49

paraprofessional support, 38–39
    responsibilities, 39
    roles, 39
program models, 41–49
    accommodations, examples of, 45
    co-teaching model, 42
    consultation model, 43
        examples, 43
    inclusive education model, 41
    modifications, 44–45
        examples, 44–45
    out-of-district placement, 43–44
    pull-out vs. push-in model, 41–42
    resource room, 42–43
    self-contained classroom, 42
    transition planning, 45–49
self-contained classroom, 42
S.M.A.R.T. goals, 143–144
    defining, 145
    examples
        format 1, 146
        format 2, 146–148
    progress reporting, 145
social worker, role/responsibilities, 98
special education, communication in, 3–12
    disability, identification of, 5
    eligibility, 5
    evaluation, 4
    Individualized Education Plan, 5
        implementation of, 6
    pre-referral, 4
    re-evaluation, 4
    referral, 4
special education eligibility, determining, 124–127
special education teacher, role/responsibilities, 97
special teachers (art, music, library education), role/responsibilities, 98
speech-language pathologist, role/responsibilities, 98
student portfolios, for data collection, 164
summarizing, 57

talking vs. listening, 58
team, for individualized education
    program, 9–12
team members, role/responsibilities of,
    97–99
teamwork, 95–101
    parental involvement, 95–96
    role/responsibilities of team
        members, 97–99
        board attorney, 97
        case manager, 97
        classroom teacher, 97
        occupational therapist, 98
        parents, 99
        physical therapist, 98
        school administrator/director of
            special education or special
            services, 97
        school nurse, 98
        school psychologist, 97
        social worker, 98
        special education teacher, 97
        special teachers (art, music,
            library education), 98
        speech-language pathologist, 98
        students, 99
    Willingness to Compromise Scale,
        99–101
texting, 170–171
thank you notes
    to parents, sample letter, 177
    to teacher, sample letter, 176
tone of meeting, setting, 59–66
    participation strategies, 66
    preparation, 63–64
    success of meeting, 65–66
    tone of meeting, 61–63
    value of individuals, 60–61
tools for data collection, 255–265
transition planning, 45–49
types of data collection supporting
    decision-making, 155–161
    cumulative files, 156–157
    formal assessments, 155–156
    informal assessments, 156

parents' cumulative file, 157–158
    comprehensive IEP or 504
        packets, 157
    correspondence between home
        and school, 158
    district and state testing, 158
    documents to keep, 157
    formal assessments, 158
    independent evaluations, 158
    invitations to IEP or 504
        meetings, 157
    phone logs, 158
    report cards, 157

voicing opinion, 196–197

Willingness to Compromise Scale,
    99–101
written correspondence, 169–180
    correspondence, as legal documents,
        171–172
    electronic protocols, 173
    email, 170–171
    between home/school, 234
    purpose, 170–172
    requesting meeting, 172
    sample letters, 174–180
        requesting evaluation to
            determine special
            education eligibility, 178
        requesting independent
            evaluation, 179
        requesting meeting with
            parents, 175
        requesting meeting with
            teacher, 174
        thank you note to parents, 177
        thank you note to teacher, 176
    texting, 170–171
written correspondence between home/
    school, 234

yearly academic portfolio, 158–159
yes-no questions, 58
    open-ended questions, contrasted,
        58

CPSIA information can be obtained
at www.ICGtesting.com
Printed in the USA
LVHW051338100223
738952LV00003B/3

9 781638 220909